American Issues

A SOURCEBOOK FOR SPEECH TOPICS

AMERICAN ISSUES
A Sourcebook for Speech Topics

Edwin Black
WASHINGTON UNIVERSITY
AND
Harry P. Kerr
HARVARD UNIVERSITY

Harcourt, Brace & World, Inc. *New York · Burlingame*

Library of Congress Catalog Card Number: 61-13138

Printed in the United States of America

[a. 4. 61]

ACKNOWLEDGMENTS

The editors wish to thank the following for their permission to reprint copyrighted material in this book:

Mrs. Bernard DeVoto: The selection by Bernard DeVoto, "Why Professors Are Suspicious of Business." Copyright 1951 by Bernard DeVoto. Reprinted by permission of Mrs. Bernard DeVoto.

McIntosh and Otis, Inc.: The selection by John Steinbeck, "Atque Vale." Copyright © 1960 by John Steinbeck. Appeared originally in *Saturday Review*. Reprinted by permission of McIntosh and Otis, Inc.

Farrar, Straus and Cudahy, Inc.: The selection by John Jay Chapman, "Coatesville." From *The Selected Writings of John Jay Chapman,* ed. by Jacques Barzun. Copyright © 1957 by Farrar, Straus and Cudahy, Inc.

The Macmillan Company: The selection by John E. Burchard, "The Engineer—A New Perspective." From *Brainpower Quest,* ed. by Andrew A. Freeman. Copyright © 1957 by The Cooper Union for the Advancement of Science and Art. Used by permission of The Macmillan Company.

John Fischer: The selection by John Fischer, "The Harm Good People Do." © 1956 by Harper & Brothers. Reprinted by Permission of the Author.

John Fischer: The selection by John Fischer, "Television and Its Critics." © 1959 by Harper & Brothers. Reprinted from *Harper's* Magazine by Permission of the Author.

Preface

This collection is offered in the hope that it will stimulate students to address themselves to subjects of significance. The reader will find six different issues herein, treated in rhetorical discourses by rational and responsible speakers and writers. From the ferment of these controversies, the reader can acquire ideas for the composition of his own discourses. Further, he can see how different people, representing differing points of view, approach the same subjects, and how well or ill their rhetorical techniques serve them.

Courses in public speaking, like those in English composition, seek to train the student in the lucid, reasonable, and graceful expression of his ideas. This objective presupposes that the student has ideas to express, ideas that deserve the labor of the speaker and the attention of his audience. Unfortunately, this presupposition is not always correct. Too frequently, speakers and writers dissipate the techniques of exposition, analysis, or persuasion on trivial subjects, subjects which cannot evoke the fullest resources of the student or enable him to express his mastery of rhetorical techniques through the medium of a worthy subject matter. The result is likely to be futility for the speaker and boredom for the audience. Only by addressing himself to issues of wide importance can the speaker hope to enlist his own highest talents and the intelligent concern of his audience. The subjects discussed in this collection constitute such issues.

Two criteria have guided the editors in this selection of rhetorical discourses. First, we have attempted to provide discourses which are strong and clear expressions of significant points of view. Some of them are good enough to serve as models of rhetorical accomplishment; others are instructive failures; all, we believe, are stimulating. Our second criterion has been that each discourse must deal with a "live" issue, one that has bearing on current public discussion in the United States.

In making our selections we have required only that the discourses be rhetorical in nature. Beyond that requirement we have made no distinction between speaking and writing, believing that the means of explaining, analyzing, and arguing about ideas do not differ between the spoken word and the written text. Both speakers and writers of rhetorical discourses must accommodate their ideas to audiences and must give force to their material in similar ways. Neither the techniques of rhetorical performance nor the techniques of rhetorical criticism are restricted to oral delivery. Hence, our only standards have been quality and relevance.

A number of technical concerns—of organization, of adaptation, of style, and of evidence—are exemplified in this collection. The section introductions and headnotes will direct the reader's attention to some of these concerns as they are illustrated in specific discourses. Further, we have accompanied each section with a critical note which, we hope, will encourage the reader to apply his own appraisals to these rhetorical performances and, in this way, gain a judicious insight into his own compositions. The questions at the end of the sections are designed to stimulate the reader to further reflection on the issues themselves; the answers to these questions will, we feel, constitute additional topics for discourse. The "Suggestions for Further Reading" are short, selective bibliographies to which the reader can turn for yet more discussion of the particular issue.

In some cases, the editors have made minor deletions, especially of material which did not serve the objectives of this collection. Such deletions are indicated by ellipses (three spaced periods). We have, of course, tried to avoid distorting the ideas of any contributor or criticizing any deficiencies which the editors' pen may have produced. We are most grateful to our contributors, their publishers, and their estates for permission to reprint their work here.

If the reader finds himself angered, startled, or dismayed by any of the selections in this book, then he has the beginnings of a speech of his own. It will almost assuredly be a speech on a consequential subject and, if the reader's reaction is sufficiently strong, it will be a composition informed by a vital concern for the subject. In such an event, this collection will have accomplished its purpose.

E. B.
H. P. K.

March 1961

Contents

3. Civil Rights

4. Education

5. Censorship

6. Communications Media

1. The Temper of American Society

Introduction

When, during the 1960 presidential campaign, there was extensive public discussion of our "national purpose," a long-simmering interest of social critics finally reached the level of popular dispute. The direction in which our country is moving, the kind of country it is becoming—subjects which heretofore have had attention only from a relatively small group of thinkers —have become political inquiries of high interest.

Some of our critics find us a society with extremes of private opulence and public squalor. While we busy ourselves, they claim, with a proliferation of washing machines, sports cars, and fur-lined beer can openers, our cities decay, our countryside is made ugly with billboards, and our lives are vulgarized.

Other critics insist that private expenditures of our national wealth are preferable to public expenditures of it; that the private citizen can usually decide more wisely than government the style of his own life; and moreover, even if he cannot, that he has the right to his errors.

Thus, the issue has been drawn: on one side, the advertisers, as the articulate spokesmen of the business community, defending private choices in the expenditure of wealth; on the other side, the commentators who demand a reappraisal of our national goals.

It has been many years since President Calvin Coolidge said, "The business of America is business." The world has revolved many times since then. And now, once again, men ask themselves, What is the business of America?

ADOLF A. BERLE, JR.

The Irrepressible Issues of the Sixties

Delivered to the Opening General Session of the fifteenth National Conference on Higher Education, sponsored by the Association for Higher Education, Chicago, March 6, 1960.

Berle, professor of law at Columbia University, has published several studies in economics and law. He has served in various capacities in the State Department and is currently an advisor to President Kennedy on South American affairs.

Educators and teachers are today facing a severe trial. They are no longer accorded the protection of an ivory tower. Results are expected from them. If, in the next few years, the United States encounters trouble or disaster, at home or abroad, educators are likely to be held partly, perhaps even primarily, responsible.

Quite plainly, we are approaching the end of an era. In the savage, implacable world drawing nearer to America every hour, new demands are made on our human resources. The added freight alone of a population which will increase by one hundred millions or so in the next generation, would give strain enough. We shall also be under bitter attack from other civilizations. Briefly, we have a single choice: renaissance or regression. The first means triumph, and the attainment of a splendid, new plateau. The other means defeat, with unknown consequences. A perilous share of the burden in making the choice and achieving the renaissance rests on the institutions of higher education.

College presidents and classroom professors are not used to being treated like politicians. Insensibly almost, they have moved from staff headquarters to the firing line. They are likely to occupy that position for a good while. So we had best get used to it, understand what is wanted of us, take inventory of our own resources, and prepare to meet some very precise demands.

My belief is that the United States will have reverses, possibly serious ones, in the next few years. In part these will be ascribed to the failures of the government. Secondarily, it will be charged, that the universities of the country, as its intellectual general staff, failed to prepare the country to take the necessary preventive measures. But at the same time, universities will be expected to supply the ideas, the analysis, the measures and even the men to meet any current emergency in almost any field.

Specifically, I think:

First. Within the next two or three years there will be an economic recession. I cannot forecast its proportion. It could come as soon as late summer 1960. It seems certain before, say, mid-1963.

Second. In foreign affairs there will be turbulence. This could come any time. The Summit Conference this spring will not be a love-feast. It may well prove the most dangerous crisis since World War II. As one result the United States will be compelled either to lead or to follow in a reconstruction of the world economic system, or at any rate of a big regional economic system.

Third. Either separately or in connection with both these events, there will be an American moral crisis. Included in it will be a demand that Americans generally stop their self-indulgence, develop a far higher degree of personal conscientiousness, accept great engagements toward common effort looking towards a better civilization both here and in other parts of the earth. There will be insistence on a new era of intense personal responsibility, resting on every man, woman and child, in every expression of life.

It is not possible to suggest the particular incidents which will spark any of these crises. Conditions are such that any of a number of things might happen, triggering an explosion in national life or international affairs. A tiny local incident illustrates. We have just rediscovered the old institution of private bribery now known as "payola." This has already crystallized a general question: How honest—or how crooked—is our system of mass communication? Have our advertising media become a moral menace? Where and why did the motivations go wrong? Is there a connection between cheating in school, misreporting on income tax returns and corruption in commercial and public life? Inevitably it will be asked, where have parents, teachers, professors, schools and colleges been all this time? None of this is fanciful, and you all know it. The Association of Higher Education is meeting some of these questions now.

A second, more striking evil may shortly come up. This is the notion, now tolerated in some quarters, of commercially "planned" or "designed" obsolescence. This means manufacturing machines, appliances, cars or other products so designed that after a limited length of time they will go to pieces, wear out, become obsolete, or otherwise unusable. Obsolescence can be hastened by other methods, for example, marketing propaganda, or failure to provide maintenance service. The purpose, of course, is to force consumers to buy the product oftener than necessary, each time, of course, at a profit to the manufacturer. At best the result is organized waste. At worst it falls uncomfortably close to sabotage or cheating. The resulting moral reproach easily becomes applied to innocent as well as guilty corporations and business organizations whose operations are the country's supply line. The results could be profound. The profit motive is a useful economic incentive toward getting things done. But if this sort of thing can be included in the commercial value system, the danger is obvious. The question will arise, where were the men trained who accepted this perversion of values?

Simultaneously, there has recently been a sudden discovery that a number of countries are doing a better job of education than seems to be true here. In some cases, other systems produced better quality of top brains in research and administration. In other cases, greater quantity in technical training was achieved.

At the top of the scale, it is apparent we are not training enough scientists. In technical fields, we are not training enough engineers. Despite severe limitation of medical education and the high standing accorded it, the number of students seeking to enter medical schools is beginning to drop off, although we need more doctors. It so happens that in these, and other fields, students have to be willing to do hard, disciplined and exact work. Somehow they have been diverted. Education and training, or at least its rewards, it was thought, could be effortlessly acquired, without the grueling labor involved in mastering any subject, or the dedication needed to push out into new ground. We are discovering that America is entering a period of great national stress and of unlimited international rivalry, without adequate resources of trained and responsible men at all levels. That discovery has already led to an uproar, directed at educational institutions all the way from top to bottom. It has not died down.

Each successive realization that the quality of American life and American intellectual effort must be far tougher, far better disciplined and far more productive will bring more criticism of our educational system, from parents to graduate faculties. The only question is how long it must last before something really gets done. At the moment, we are still listening to the old siren songs. Possibly we can find a cheap and easy way out by television teaching. Perhaps shifting administrative patterns will be enough. Possibly raising teachers' salaries all along the line will change the picture. Maybe personal purpose can be instilled by mass media, and paid for by complaisant advertisers. And so forth. Everyone knows the list of panaceas, from capsule textbooks (sold at a profit) to high-minded basketball teams, or adult education in painless installments. Devices run all the way from true-false examinations marked by clerks to centralized psychological testing.

I am not attacking any of these things as such. Probably some can learn something by television. Perhaps true-false testing can contribute something to evaluation of a student's character and work. I like sports, though I regret that only a tiny fraction of students get a chance to engage in them. But none of this can possibly do much toward development of individual character, dedicated to putting something into our civilization, and not merely toward getting the most out of it. Nor will it replace the limitless influence of parents and teachers who devote their efforts to the personal development of their children and students. Machines and mechanics do not make values. Honor and truth are not products of aptitude adjustment. Purpose cannot be inspired by IBM machines. Love and devotion are not synthetic forms of address: they are lambent flames. The aggregate of all the results will be the nation that is America, entrusted in its youth to teachers and scholars, whom we must serve. But of this comes national purpose, and international success or failure in the greatest era history has yet recorded. What this shall be, and how produced, is the crucial problem in every walk of life.

The issues we have to meet in the next few years all arise, I think, out of this central problem. Let us confront it, squarely, without fear and without favor. It splits into several divisions. The first is far and away the greatest and deepest for it is essentially philosophical. The second is social, and fixes the direction of current politics. The third raises problems of technique and organization—the level at which most of us have to work.

In the first and deepest issue, universities and American intellectuals have, I am clear, been running away from the greatest and most constant of all human issues. This is, quite simply, whether life has an enduring significance, or whether it is an anarchy of chance, meaning nothing. Properly, this should have been the concern of the Departments of Philosophy in our universities. Yet so far as I recall, the last great study of eternal values in the United States was published by Hugo Muensterberg of Harvard—who died in 1916. Nor have historians and social scientists filled the gap, though some of them have tackled fragments of it. England's Toynbee has had the courage to make the attempt to make a philosophy of history, whether one agrees with it or not. Sociologists describe—and commonly let it go at that. Economists set out the result of human wants. None of these have dealt with the primary question of values.

As a student of the American business and financial machine, I know that without an accepted system of values as a base the economic system simply cannot be sound. We can play as our statisticians must do, that production of plastic balloons is no less "productivity" than building cathedrals or developing first-rate housing. But we all know better. We can, and our figures do, classify the ten billions a year Americans spend on liquors as of equal value to the ten billions they spend on education. But we know that the comparison is discreditable. We know that taxes paid for necessary work, from roads to schools, are a way of buying something infinitely important, and we know the same amount of money spent privately on luxuries or diversion takes lesser rank of importance. Yet we are content to let go, without challenge, the idea that taxes are a form of robbery—while inflated installment charges collected by finance companies for anything from mink coats to summer vacations on pay-later plans can be considered sound bargains. The best brains in the country, which I still think are represented in our universities, must be saying with bluntness what things are first and first rate, and what are secondary and second rate, and what are discreditable, and due to be discarded. Bluntly, universities everywhere ought to concern themselves with a moral order. In academic lingo this is called a value system.

The second group of issues necessarily relates to politics and social organization. Obviously, these cannot be met unless there is consensus on values.

Here I think the unsung American public at this moment is far ahead of its politicians, even ahead of the public expressions of its teachers and college presidents.

Most Americans realize that the greatest values come not from personal pleasure or profit, but from contributions made to the community, the country, and the progress of humanity. They know quite well that education comes ahead of transient luxuries. They know that the running gear of business is justified not by its profit, but because it meets human needs. Profit is essential, but secondary. They know there is more to a job than the paycheck, essential as the paycheck is, but that a paycheck without a real job is a form of poorhouse. So they want a system providing stable employment. They also want the jobs to mean active participation in civilization and in life. They want an economics that does not accept slums as a necessary condition of housing. They want business that does not organize waste at consumers' expense, and they understand quite well that "planned obsolescence" is either cheating or waste, or both. In other words, they want an organization of affairs that realizes instead of violates their value system.

All this adds up to two things. It means that the United States must produce more. Also, that she must plan or guide her economy.

I know the gust of abuse that comes from saying this. Classical economists talk about the road to serfdom—but they don't live in New York's Harlem or in Chicago's Cicero. Chambers of Commerce mouth old clichés about free enterprise. But they do not induce their members to make ice chests that will last, or prevent mass medium advertising from peddling class-symbols instead of well-made products, or show us how slums will be cleared. Social advice from these quarters will be more impressive when they are doing the job better.

Planning a democratic economy at bottom is a straightforward matter. It means providing a place where certain decisions can be made. The decisions settle what activities are most important, what are less important, what are non-essential, and what can be let go. This is the economic expression of the value system we have been talking about. High on this list comes health, education, scientific research. Close behind, transportation and communications, staple commodities like food, basic materials like steel, copper, oil. Then, adequate housing, heavy consumers goods, and then the soft goods. I am not trying to make a list: make your own. The community will decide what it wants, under the guidance of the best thinking available to it.

Many of these needs are adequately met. Many are not. The job of the planner is to steer enough of the goods and services produced in this country towards meeting the list in order of their importance.

Are we doing this now? We have, for example, quite recently committed many tens of billions of government money to building roads. This helps motor cars and motor travel. Did we need this more than we needed a program of education and health—which we are told we cannot afford? On the private side we commit more than twelve billions to buying motor cars. Should not an equivalent sum be steered into slum clearance? If we want both slum clearance and twelve billions worth of motor cars, should we not increase our productivity and put some of it where there is real need?

This places new burdens on our economists, and our social scientists. It puts new obligations on businessmen. A good beginning would be abandonment of the style racket in cars and household appliances which organize waste rather than provide honest service. Politicians will have to meet the issue in the coming campaign. Elected officials will have to deal with it when in office.

The issue of guiding the economy so that it will increasingly realize an honorable, effective and civilized value system is dimly understood by everyone. It awaits the solid academic and political work that will make it real.

One touch of economic emergency will explode all this into a set of immediate, fighting political issues. Then, politics becomes rough and personal. The system comes under fire—but the attacks are leveled against the men in positions of power, and responsibility and influence, for sins of commission and of omission, often unjustly; at this stage personal scapegoats are sought and found. So it was in 1930, and so it can easily be again.

I hold it the task of the universities, guardians of our intellectual dynamo, to give definition, form and intellectual leadership in developing the new social concepts and the new measures we obviously need.

The last level—providing technique and personnel—is in some ways as profound as the philosophical problem. Through our school system every effective American must pass. From it are supplied, at every level, from top to bottom, the men and women whose individual efforts and whose combined opinion give direction to American national purpose. Out of the school system come the men who think and study and write, who push the world into new fields, intellectual and spiritual. From it also come the captains, the lieutenants, the engineers, the maintenance crews and the operating crews. They supply the men who must plan and direct the compaigns and conduct the continuous operations of life, civilian and, if necessary, military; and the men whose devotion and responsibility carry out the design to success. As international affairs become more complex, they are likely to have to pilot America towards the emerging stages of regional organization, and in the farther future, perhaps, towards a higher degree of world organization. Their combined resources of character and of capacity, from the children coming out of grammar school to the Doctors of Philosophy attacking great problems in social or physical science, will determine what happens.

The educational system, in conjunction with their parents, will determine what they are.

We are fortunate in having a country and a system technically and physically able to produce material goods enough for everyone, beyond the dreams of our grandfathers. Do we also have spiritual and intellectual resources capable of mobilizing this enormous heritage? We are at long last learning that this cannot and will not be decently done by Madison Avenue, or smart sales campaigns, or political quackery. Clearly appeals to not-so-enlightened self-interest, excesses based on opinion polls do not assist. We know that the rat race for status-symbols is a pathetic humbug propagated by hucksters for personal gain. From our education we are entitled to have a product of graduates who know this, and who cannot be fooled into false values by the monkey-business of public relations counsel.

All this means a value system. It means teachers who teach according to that system. It means a public life carried on in that system. It requires men who would rather not be in office than get office by false promises, or by promising to support measures they believe are unsound, or who, once in office, want merely to coast from election to election. It means judging statements with fearless honesty. It means social engineers at all levels, from the village council to Washington, who act with the integrity of trustees for their community. It means lawyers (by trade I am a lawyer) who use their technique to secure justice and honorable arrangements, instead of peddling influence.

HARRY D. GIDEONSE

Plato and Eisenhower's America

Delivered at the Scholastic Achievement Convocation, Syracuse University, April 18, 1960. The audience consisted mainly of students and faculty members.

Gideonse is president of Brooklyn College in New York City. A former professor of economics, he has authored several works in economics and educational philosophy.

Robert M. Hutchins, my former chief at the University of Chicago, used to say that it was a college president's principal duty in life to "afflict the comfortable." This might well serve as my text for these remarks to an honors assembly. And let me say at once that my choice of the topic "Plato and Eisenhower's America" does not indicate any intention to direct these remarks specifically or exclusively to one partisan group rather than another —the qualities in America that I shall discuss are shared by Americans irrespective of political identification. It would be as easy to cite Democratic as well as Republican examples. In fact, I could find my best single representative source in a statement from a recent television program in which Carl Sandburg, who had just returned from a visit to the Soviet Union, was asked for a one-sentence summary of his principal concern about America. The old poet—who is something of an actor as well—looked very wise for a moment, and then he said, "Well, the country is just dripping with fat."

We live in a time of historically unparalleled material prosperity, of smug complacency and of deep-rooted anxiety. We live in a time of slogan-thinking—not only among the untutored but amongst the intellectually most privileged. I have a deep-rooted liking for plain speech and a healthy distrust of folks who live verbally beyond their intellectual means. I will speak to you of simple things in plain words.

In intellectual circles it is fashionable to decry the "conformity" of our time—and it is usually suggested that this "conformity" is a special characteristic of America in the present decade, a by-product of McCarthy-ism and of a large scale corporate industrial civilization. Anyone who knows his Tocqueville or John Stuart Mill knows that this is a parochial and a provincial view. The trend towards a discipline of likemindedness came with the earliest phases of a large market economy. It is a deep-seated cultural by-product of our commitment to the attractions of an industrial society. "Conformity" was the great hazard of the new economically oriented society, and it would be easy to document this statement with scores of citations from classical sources, all more than a century old. I do not say this to deny the hazard but rather to restore our perspective. To think of "conformity" as a peculiar characteristic of a Madison Avenue culture is to underestimate the depth of its materialistic roots. It is as silly as the characteristic tendency to praise "non-conformity" as the opposite of "conformity." There is no special virtue in non-conformity for its own sake—I need only to remind you of an especially repulsive type of conformity which can be found in the conventional form of Beatnik non-conformity. Everything depends upon the yardstick of conformity—or of non-conformity. Clearly the opposite of conformity is not non-conformity. The opposite to being a conformist is to "*Be Yourself.*"

To be yourself is first of all a question of integrity and truthfulness about yourself. It is a question of knowing where to find evidence, and how to test it. It is a question of honesty and courage in facing that evidence. These are rare virtues—even amongst scholars and professional intellectuals, and amongst liberals as well as conservatives.

Take, as an example, a quotation from a recent speech of one of America's most conscientious scholarly liberals. I refer to Professor Adolph A. Berle's recent address to the fifteenth National Conference on Higher Education. He was speaking on the subject "The Irrepressible Issues of the Sixties," and he declared that American colleges and universities would play a leading role in determining whether the nation would experience a "renaissance or a regression."

Then he went on to say: "We are fortunate in having a country and a system technically and physically able to produce material goods enough for everyone." The big question, he said, is whether the nation has the spiritual and intellectual resources "capable of mobilizing this enormous heritage."

He said this mobilization "cannot and will not be decently done by Madison Avenue, or smart sales campaigns, or political quackery," and declared: "We know that the rat race for status symbols is a pathetic humbug propagated by hucksters for personal gain. From our education, we are entitled to have a product of graduates who know this, and who cannot be fooled into false values by the monkey business of public relations counsel."

Here we have a choice collection of conformist slogans in what appears to be a non-conformist sermon. It is easy to define sin in others—in this case in "Madison Avenue," in "the monkey business of public relations." It is even easier to cherish illusions about yourself—in this case about our colleges and universities. Ask yourself one leading question. What—honestly now!—is the truth about higher education in relation to "the rat race of status symbols"? Are not the colleges and universities deeply involved in this "rat race"? Do American students typically choose their colleges on the basis of their concern for learning—or do they choose them on the basis of the enhanced social status that is deemed to be attached to their baccalaureate diplomas? If we are—and rightly so—critical of the spiritually empty "rat race for status symbols," would it not be more relevant to look to ourselves rather than to that much-flogged horse on Madison Avenue?

Professor Berle's definition of a sin on "Madison Avenue" that can be easily found on almost any campus in the United States, reminds me of John Cotton's distrust of "man's perverse subtlety in inventing new ways of backsliding." If we are honest with ourselves, is it not true that the American "image" of college education is an image of social status—differentiated social status—and not an image of learning"? Do American students or parents select their colleges of "first choice" because of reasoned convictions about the quality of learning to be pursued in these institutions—or do they choose these colleges because of a reasoned conviction about the social status to be derived from their diplomas? Is this false perspective due to "Madison Avenue," or is it due to weaknesses in our own colleges and universities, and in the goals which we set for ourselves? There are indeed large impersonal forces in any historic period which none of us as individuals can budge or deflect. But do not the value commitments of a scholar require —as Albert Camus has so convincingly insisted throughout his short life— that we face the facts about *ourselves* rather than hide behind comfortable slogans that give a pleasantly non-conformist flavor to essentially conformist ideas?

In American education we live in a period characterized by a weird mixture of anxiety and complacency which is reflected in the battle of the slogans which have become a form of contemporary dogma. After a decade of shrill warnings from all our educational leaders, we developed a sudden panic at the news of "Sputnik and all that," and in a binge of self-criticism we disregarded all the warnings of American teachers, and painted ourselves an idealized picture of Russian education, only to discover that Russia itself has chosen this very moment for a major overhauling of its own educational system. Our mass media have mouthed so many stereotypes about American education that it has become almost impossible to use certain words—such as "adjustment" and "needs," especially "felt needs"—which have become verbal tools of confusion although many of these terms have a definite and constructive meaning.

Education is not just a matter of "running" a school or a college. It is—as Plato and Aristotle already understood and taught—the method by which a state or community insures its own stability and continuity. A country's education can therefore only be understood in relation to the values of its own culture, and education itself is—as Woodrow Wilson insisted throughout his life—"a branch of statesmanship." If Americans never cease to quarrel among themselves about what our education is—or should be—and if our educational opinions swing more widely from hysteria to complacency than American public discussion of any other issue, this may be ascribed to a vague but sure instinct for the vital relationship between the quality of national life, including its capacity for survival, and the quantitative as well as qualitative achievements of our educational programs.

A country's educational system is always an expression of its culture in general. American education has plenty of strengths and weaknesses—and they are the strengths and weaknesses of American culture in general. If our criticism of education gets below the surface level of a heated argument about a school bond issue or "the numbers that should go to college," and if we begin to inquire into the nature of a free society, and into the character of educational programs that would be likely to give us men and women fit for the intellectual and moral responsibilities of such a society, we are at once involved in a discussion of the most basic issues of statesmanship. Such a critical re-thinking of our educational fundamentals will be in the deepest sense of the term a critique of the values of free men, it will lead into problems of motivation and the sources of responsibility, and it will ultimately be concerned with the question whether in the modern world a free society can survive if its public priorities are not anchored in a deep respect for trained intelligence.

Our national weaknesses today are real—in foreign policy we are, as Carl Sandburg said, "dripping with fat" in our concern for consumer spending rather than national needs, and we have neglected our capacity for strength in defense so flagrantly that we would be unable to carry out an airlift in Berlin or to fight a Korean war if the aggressor chose to test our national determination in that manner. These weaknesses are terrifying, but they can be remedied in short order by crash programs if the will and the purpose can be found to impose discipline on ourselves. It is crucial to recognize that our weakness does not arise from the strength of the Russians and their associates. Their relative strength lies in our deficiencies, and these deficiencies are inherent in our own pattern of motivation and values.

Specifically, in the schools and colleges, our weaknesses are only educational in a superficial sense. A country's educational values are derived from the country's value pattern as a whole. American schools cannot be better than America itself. Plato knew this long ago when he said that nothing is *cultivated* in a country except what is *honored* in that country. If we are today deficient in the achievement of intellectual standards of the highest order in mathematics, in science or in foreign languages, in history or in philosophy, let us ask whether *adult* America *honors* such achievement. If it did, our educational institutions would reflect these educational values. If it does not honor such achievement, our schools will continue to buck the tide with indifferent success, and our schools will continue to reflect the values of adult American life. In this basic sense the remedy for our deficiencies in intellectual achievement is not to be sought in education itself—it is rather a problem, and a vital life-determining problem, of American culture as a whole.

Let me remind you briefly of some of the things that have taken place in the past eighteen months. First, we had Sputnik and Lunik, and all the rest of it, and we saw American smug complacency and pride shaken as ten years of speeches by educators and college presidents had not managed to shake it, because, after all, they had been predicting that critical weaknesses were going to develop in American education, talking themselves hoarse, as a matter of fact, in the process, and not registering anywhere significantly with American public opinion.

But then came that mistake in the judgment not of educators or of scientists but of American public officials on the highest possible political level, who had not understood the dramatic implications of using funds in public budgets for one purpose rather than another. The weaknesses of the imagination with which we had contemplated the International Geophysical Year were suddenly revealed in the fact that the Russians beat us to it, not because we didn't have the scientists—because well-trained scientists were available in handsome numbers—but because we did not have the political imagination to see the implications in terms of world public opinion of our decision to use the trained manpower we had in a way which met the needs of the international rivalry in which we found ourselves involved.

Following the vested interests in the military services as well as in industry, we chose to subsidize obsolete forms of armament rather than the emerging new ones, and then we blamed the results of this very sad disappointment on education, and on science, rather than on the poor political judgment that had not known how to use the available economic resources and the available scientific resources. It is crucial to keep our eyes focussed on this basic fact. There was no shortage of scientists or of ideas. The scientists were there. The ideas were there. General James M. Gavin has told the whole sad story in his volume entitled *War and Peace in the Space Age.* There was never a reply to the basic thesis of this book. The storm broke over the heads of the educators rather than over the heads of the political leaders who had not used the ideas and the scientific resources that were available, and that were in fact itching to be used.

How often do we hear as we discuss problems of an educational type—"Now, when I was young . . . ," and then comes a good speech on what one should do about it in terms of a romantically nostalgic picture of a past that never was. We are not dealing with a past that never was. We are dealing with a present that *is*—even if some people are trying very hard not to see it.

In American education we are not dealing with people who *once were* young. We are responsible for the education of boys and girls who are young *now.* And in the total picture of the formative, that is to say, educational, influences that are brought to bear on the young now, and the 40 per cent increase in the number of teen-agers that lies ahead in the next five years, we are dealing with an educational process in which the formative influences are much wider than the school.

We all know it; we are all deeply aware of it. Education is not just what goes on in the school. Much more than in the past, education is what goes on in American culture as a whole—in competitive advertising, competitive advertising in the press and magazines and television and radio, sadistic and violent dramatic sketches for six- and eight-year-old children, all of it pitched on the appropriate intellectual level, all of it financed very well, with the ability to hire the ablest talent in writing, in drama, in music, that is available in the national market, all of it designed to create a materialistic discontent with what is and with what you now have, a design to create a premature obsolescence in the things that you can now consume, to make you reach out for more than you can immediately hope to attain.

It is very naive indeed to assume that this is not a major *educational* formative influence on the young today. And if you add to that all of the other forces that come out of a commercial, competitive society, if you keep in mind that it is quite possible to be an admirer of a market society, a competitive society in terms of the impact it has on productivity, on material standards of living, and at the same time to believe that competitive and market controls may be a very poor test indeed of cultural achievement and of educational standards, you can readily see that you cannot safely rely upon a nostalgic dependence on the achievements of the past. We must deal with the present, and the boys and girls who are enrolled in our schools and colleges today are, if the Lord is merciful and the life expectancy tables retain their validity, going to live well on into the twenty-first century, under conditions of ever-increasing speed of social change and rapidity of social and economic transition, of a type that we now see before us and of which there is only one thing certain: The speed of transition is going to intensify unless we in some way or another once again take control of ourselves through the one educational agency that is subject to social control, that is to say, through the agencies of formal education. There is an eager market for almost any type of criticism today. But there is no enthusiasm for this deeper type of social criticism of our educational pattern.

This is not just a question of money; this is a question of *motivation* in the broadest possible sense of the term. It is a matter of the values by which you intend to live the rest of your life. And it is not just a matter of getting at the boys. Directly—and indirectly—it involves the girls. In American life as it is today—as anyone can tell you who has taught graduate students, and I have done my share of it—when you have sold a boy on a career of commitment to scholarship for the rest of his life, you have merely taken the first steps in a long, continuous struggle with the prevailing values in our society. After you have recruited him, he goes into graduate school and after he has been there for some time he runs into *the* girl, *and* he runs into the girl's parents. They want to know, "Are you a complete and total fool to marry a future college professor? Haven't you heard what that means in terms of the cars you can't buy and the home you can't furnish, and so on?"

This is a broader problem than budget. This is a problem of the culture of America, the basic core of the cultural motivation of the country in which we live. Book VIII of Plato's *Republic* should be required reading for all adult Americans. Unless we cope with its central thesis, and cope with it reasonably soon—I would say within a period which is dramatically short, of about five years—we are likely to find that the loss of that cultural battle will risk the survival of the free society which we all cherish. If there is one thing certain in the world in which we now live, it is that a country is not going to survive unless it builds into its culture—and then into its private and public budgets—a respect for trained intelligence, trained intelligence in *all* of its ramifications.

The most hopeful thing about contemporary America is the increasing recognition of the cultural challenge to our inertia and complacency. Let me read two paragraphs from a remarkable book by Thomas Griffith, one of Mr. Luce's editors, entitled *The Waist-High Culture,* published by Harper's last year.

> . . . It is sometimes said that all we need is leadership, and while it is true that we have lately lacked it, I believe that what men generally mean by that complaint pays too little heed to the immensity of the difficulties we face. Rather, we need a revolution of goals, a change in what we value, what we preserve and what we pursue. It may be that our discontent is what most justifies optimism. It may also be that when the younger generation is accused of lacking ambition what is really meant is that it is no longer inspired by the old standards, and it may be that this is what the "silent generation" is being silent about. (page 271)
>
> Whether today's rustle of discontent will tomorrow become a breeze, I do not know, but I suspect that it would not take gale force to recapture the center of our society. It is not stoutly defended: "Troy in our weakness lives, not in her strength." The center is not well commanded: it is minded by men protecting their own interests but incapable of seeing even them clearly; they are uncertain of purpose and divided in counsel; they are listening at the door, and it is we who are still. *The news about our times is that the center is empty.* (page 273)

This—I repeat—is *not* a question of budgets, except indirectly. It is *not* a question of exclusive preoccupation with the gifted or with specialized scholarship. The Greeks had, as they often did, a word for it. The word *idiot* as we use it today describes, technically, a type of feeble-minded person and, popularly, a person who is very stupid and incapable of intellectual effort, one who has an *idiotic* way of doing things. The Greek word, of course, meant something very different, although it is the word from which we drew ours. The Greeks used the word *idiot* for a man who might have very keen analytical capacity, who might be a scholar, but who had *no interest in the whole of things.* The Greek idiot was an altogether private man. He had no public spirit, as we might express it. He had no awareness of his being part of a larger whole. In that sense, we can say that the American college and university, with all of its specialists who know only one thing and are very little interested in the total impact of all these separate things on the whole of the young personality for which they are responsible, contains—in the original Greek use of the term—a larger percentage of idiots than the population of the country as a whole.

And the whole of public life is full of *idiocy* in the Greek sense of the term, because all of public life is rooted in the assumption that the determining fact of all public policy is its bearing on the pursuit of higher standards of material living. This is taken for granted on the right as well as on the left. Presidential candidates differ in the United States not in their acceptance of this objective, but in methods of achieving that objective. Some Democrats will say that we can achieve it with a little more public action, some Republicans with a little less public action, but they will all agree that the purpose should be the increase of material standards of living. But increasing material standards of living implies more specialization, more division of labor, more conveyor-belt, doing-just-one-thing-all-the-time action, because that's the only way in which analytical man has demonstrated that he can increase material returns per individual involved in production. The crucial weakness of free society does not lie in its economic aspect—it lies rather in the diminished effectiveness of the sources of responsibility upon which we rely for our social discipline and the determination of our priorities in the use of our talent and of our wealth.

We live in a time of danger and a time of great hope. Whatsoever offers us complacency blinds us to the danger and denies us the hope. The most positive thing in America today is the reorientation of its youth. The adult generations talk of the changing goals of America—and a generation bankrupt in leadership looks to the President of the United States for the appointment of a national commission to give us a report on the long-range goals of America. Even a child should know that in a free society the goals come from individual men and women. We are in a stage of our national development in which the conflict between the achievement of the goals of an earlier generation—goals of an individualist type reflected in our concern with the technical control of natural forces—and the rearrangement of our priorities in our individual lives is reflected in a younger generation which in a quiet and determined way is seeking within itself for some principles of order in the chaos of conflicting claims on our national and on our individual energy. An older generation of parents and teachers speaks with concern on a "silent generation," a "generation characterized by apathy and complacency"—because it does not understand that the present student generation does not attach the highest priority to the broad social and economic issues that led students in the twenties and thirties to mass participation in organized causes. The preceding generation does not understand the searching quest for order within themselves that is illustrated by the concern for commitment, the search for a tradition that can be embraced in self-respect and in the light of reason, and—as Camus put it—"without shame."

In fact, the sudden discovery of the undergraduate's interest in Camus is a significant watermark between the generations. The zest for ideas has not disappeared—as some older observers are inclined to say. It has shifted its focus, and the concern—and it is widespread among American undergraduates, as it is amongst German and Scandinavian students—with the intellectual and moral pilgrimage of Albert Camus is a healthy and positive sign of the new light that is appearing on the horizon.

Camus was an essentially lonely figure, rejecting the old commitments on the traditional right and left, deeply involved in and reflecting the disintegration of the old values but, in the darkest depths of his generation's essential nihilism, always committed to a search for the means of *transcending* it. He was preoccupied with the search for that "truth without shame" —in a lonely search for the convictions which could restore the dignity of man for a generation which was quietly determined, as he said, "to remain honorable in the midst of a history which is not honorable." Sartre—Camus' old ideological enemy—was speaking for American students as well when he said at the time of Camus' death in a silly accident that "rarely has the nature of a man's work and the conditions of the historical moment so clearly demanded that a writer go on living."

Americans today are not living up to their potential capacity—and I am not speaking of industrial productivity and the standard measurement of capacity in our conventional use of the term. We must indeed *stretch* ourselves but we must stretch ourselves in our own conception of the range of our intellectual and moral powers. This is nothing new in human or in American history. Every achievement of a human goal simply sets new limits and new horizons for other types of achievements. A period of smug complacency with the achievement of national goals is traditionally a time in which the seeds are sown for a new generation with new aims and new discontents—and the beginning of all growth is a clear view of the truth about ourselves, including a balanced view of the role of reason in understanding the rational as well as the irrational elements in human experience.

William James had a favorite quotation from the Bible that is directly relevant. It is from the Book of Ezekiel. Ezekiel was having his trouble with the Israelites of his time, who were, as the Bible says, "a rebellious house," "impudent children and stiffhearted." They *were not* interested in spiritual warnings. And Ezekiel sought council from his God, and as he prayed he "fell on his face."

And then, it says in the second chapter of the Book of Ezekiel, that the Lord said to Ezekiel, "Son of Man, *stand on thy feet,* and I will speak to thee."

In other words: The truth will be revealed only if you have the courage to seek it—and to face it.

We must stretch ourselves—morally, philosophically, intellectually, and this means education and effort on *all* levels. To this group of Syracuse students who have shown their ability to profit by the highest intellectual opportunities made available by the American university, I add that specialized intellectual effort is only the beginning—the essential beginning. Specialized learning is not the faith men live by. If we are to commit ourselves to the faith of free men—and without such commitment we shall perish—that faith must be nourished by the devoted cultivation of the general philosophical and moral framework from which the specialized learning draws its meaning, and without which it can be a tool to serve totalitarian ends.

We must stretch ourselves—and if we do, we shall find new meaning for our time and for ourselves in our own moral tradition and in the spiritual insights of that tradition.

"Son of Man, *stand on thy feet, and I will speak to thee.*"

JOHN F. KENNEDY

Inaugural Address

The thirty-fifth president of the United States delivered this speech at Washington, D.C., January 20, 1961.

We observe today not a victory of party but a celebration of freedom—symbolizing an end as well as a beginning—signifying renewal as well as change. For I have sworn before you and Almighty God the same solemn oath our forebears prescribed nearly a century and three-quarters ago.

The world is very different now. For man holds in his mortal hands the power to abolish all forms of human poverty and all forms of human life. And yet the same revolutionary beliefs for which our forebears fought are still at issue around the globe—the belief that the rights of man come not from the generosity of the state but from the hand of God.

We dare not forget today that we are the heirs of that first revolution. Let the word go forth from this time and place, to friend and foe alike, that the torch has been passed to a new generation of Americans—born in this century, tempered by war, disciplined by a hard and bitter peace, proud of our ancient heritage—and unwilling to witness or permit the slow undoing of those human rights to which this nation has always been committed, and to which we are committed today at home and around the world.

Let every nation know, whether it wishes us well or ill, that we shall pay any price, bear any burden, meet any hardship, support any friend, oppose any foe to assure the survival and the success of liberty.

This much we pledge—and more.

To those old allies whose cultural and spiritual origins we share, we pledge the loyalty of faithful friends. United, there is little we cannot do in a host of new cooperative ventures. Divided, there is little we can do—for we dare not meet a powerful challenge at odds and split asunder.

To those new states whom we welcome to the ranks of the free, we pledge our word that one form of colonial control shall not have passed away merely to be replaced by a far more iron tyranny. We shall not always expect to find them supporting our view. But we shall always hope to find them strongly supporting their own freedom—and to remember that, in the past, those who foolishly sought power by riding the back of the tiger ended up inside.

To those people in the huts and villages of half the globe struggling to break the bonds of mass misery, we pledge our best efforts to help them help themselves, for whatever period is required—not because the Communists may be doing it, not because we seek their votes, but because it is right. If a free society cannot help the many who are poor, it cannot save the few who are rich.

To our sister republics south of our border, we offer a special pledge—to convert our good words into good deeds—in a new alliance for progress—to assist free men and free governments in casting off the chains of poverty. But this peaceful revolution of hope cannot become the prey of hostile powers. Let all our neighbors know that we shall join with them to oppose aggression or subversion anywhere in the Americas. And let every other power know that this hemisphere intends to remain the master of its own house.

To that world assembly of sovereign states, the United Nations, our last best hope in an age where the instruments of war have far outpaced the instruments of peace, we renew our pledge of support—to prevent it from becoming merely a forum for invective—to strengthen its shield of the new and the weak—and to enlarge the area in which its writ may run.

Finally, to those nations who would make themselves our adversary, we offer not a pledge but a request: that both sides begin anew the quest for peace, before the dark powers of destruction unleashed by science engulf all humanity in planned or accidental self-destruction.

We dare not tempt them with weakness. For only when our arms are sufficient beyond doubt can we be certain beyond doubt that they will never be employed.

But neither can two great and powerful groups of nations take comfort from our present course—both sides overburdened by the cost of modern weapons, both rightly alarmed by the steady spread of the deadly atom, yet both racing to alter that uncertain balance of terror that stays the hand of mankind's final war.

So let us begin anew—remembering on both sides that civility is not a sign of weakness, and sincerity is always subject to proof. Let us never negotiate out of fear. But let us never fear to negotiate.

Let both sides explore what problems unite us instead of belaboring those problems which divide us.

Let both sides, for the first time, formulate serious and precise proposals for the inspection and control of arms—and bring the absolute power to destroy other nations under the absolute control of all nations.

Let both sides seek to invoke the wonders of science instead of its terrors. Together let us explore the stars, conquer the deserts, eradicate disease, tap the ocean depths and encourage the arts and commerce.

Let both sides unite to heed in all corners of the earth the command of Isaiah—to "undo the heavy burdens . . . [and] let the oppressed go free."

And if a beach-head of cooperation may push back the jungle of suspicion, let both sides join in creating a new endeavor, not a new balance of power, but a new world of law, where the strong are just and the weak secure and the peace preserved.

All this will not be finished in the first one hundred days. Nor will it be finished in the first one thousand days, nor in the life of this Administration, nor even perhaps in our lifetime on this planet. But let us begin.

In your hands, my fellow citizens, more than mine, will rest the final success or failure of our course. Since this country was founded, each generation of Americans has been summoned to give testimony to its national loyalty. The graves of young Americans who answered the call to service surround the globe.

Now the trumpet summons us again—not as a call to bear arms, though arms we need—not as a call to battle, though embattled we are—but a call to bear the burden of a long twilight struggle year in and year out," rejoicing in hope, patient in tribulation"—a struggle against the common enemies of man: tyranny, poverty, disease and war itself.

Can we forge against these enemies a grand and global alliance, north and south, east and west, that can assure a more fruitful life for all mankind? Will you join in that historic effort?

In the long history of the world, only a few generations have been granted the role of defending freedom in its hour of maximum danger. I do not shrink from this responsibility—I welcome it. I do not believe that any of us would exchange places with any other people or any other generation. The energy, the faith, the devotion which we bring to this endeavor will light our country and all who serve it—and the glow from that fire can truly light the world.

And so, my fellow Americans: ask not what your country can do for you —ask what you can do for your country.

My fellow citizens of the world: ask not what America will do for you, but what together we can do for the freedom of man.

Finally, whether you are citizens of America or citizens of the world, ask of us here the same high standards of strength and sacrifice which we ask of you. With a good conscience our only sure reward, with history the final judge of our deeds, let us go forth to lead the land we love, asking His blessing and His help, but knowing that here on earth God's work must truly be our own.

DEVEREUX C. JOSEPHS

The Cultural Lag

Delivered at the annual dinner of the Insurance Law Section, New York State Bar Association, New York City, January 27, 1960.

Josephs is chairman of the New York State Temporary Commission on Economic Expansion. Retired as chairman of the board of the New York Life Insurance Company, he is director of numerous corporations.

I am delighted to be with you for dinner tonight for a number of reasons. I have a great respect for lawyers—their crisp minds and orderly process of thinking. (I always hope that by association some of it will rub off on me.) Then, I am glad to accept Harry McCallion's invitation. Now that I am no longer an officer of the New York Life, I cannot *command* his services, but now he is in my debt (or I hope he will think so—you can help my plan along by expressions of enthusiasm and applause) and I intend to cash in on it. Lastly, it gives me a chance to share with you a concern I have about the rosy future that the prophets have pretty generally been projecting. Incidentally, I have tried to disassociate myself from them ever since I read in Samuel Butler's Notebook the dictum: "The lions would not eat Daniel, they would eat most anything but they drew the line at prophets." However, the future is where we will spend the rest of our lives and we had better be aware of it. . . .

If the economists are right (and I believe they are) we have a future which will be worth making every effort to bring about. There is no need, for the purpose of my thesis, to repeat the optimistic economic projections which have been made by the Government, or C.E.D., or others. It is enough to say that our economy is currently increasing at better than 3% per annum. Considering population growth and our dedication to an ever-rising standard of living, it is very likely that we will expand faster than 3%. This will mean more income per capita and an even greater growth in discretionary income, which is the technical term for money in the family budget not dedicated to the necessities of food, housing and clothing.

These projections by the economists are based upon the assumptions that we will choose the right paths to the future—or at least we will not go blindly over a cliff or stumble into a hidden bog. But as the philosophic rover, it is my duty to suggest that we may not long enjoy this attractive picture unless we modify some of our attitudes to keep up with the changes. Change is the order of the day. There are fundamental breakthroughs in our physical and material concepts.

In many of the sciences, what we believed a decade ago is no longer certain. In some of our learning, what was accepted yesterday is doubted today. The application of modern science, the new techniques of manufacture, the new procedures of business are changing our society at a bewildering pace.

The trouble is that man's habits, attitudes and behavior change more slowly than his knowledge, his artifacts and the economy he has created. This is often referred to as the cultural lag. With the explosion of knowledge in recent decades, this lag is growing larger and the bewilderment is growing greater.

The danger lies in the inability of society, habituated to a slower pace, to adjust itself to the richer, fuller, swifter, more intricate growth of the economy.

I think a few illustrations might make my meaning clearer. Here is one. We have become an urban society and are growing steadily more so. Yet we still are bound by many outgrown rural forces. Fifty years ago 37% of our population lived on farms—now it is only about 11%. The 26% have moved to towns and cities. Yet there has been little change, for example, in the legislative process. The upper house in each state legislature is based upon equal county representation. This was a protective device in the early history of the republic. But now the rural minority can veto the legislative changes desired and needed by the overwhelming majority in the urban areas. Those interested in some horrible examples can find them in the first article in the November [1959] issue of *Harper's* magazine.

But one or two may interest you. A rural village in Vermont with 66 inhabitants has the same representation as the city of Burlington. Los Angeles county with 4 million has the same representation as 30,000 in an inland area. The same anomalies exist in New York State, but nationally, our two senators represent 14.8 million against 160 thousand for Nevada.

Let me nail down this anomaly with one more illustration—the Farm Program. Whatever the original purpose of the program, the current situation is disastrous. It is expected to cost the government $6½ billion this fiscal year. It will take constantly more money and material to store crops we have bought and can't eat, can't give away, and can't dump in foreign markets without losing allies, and destroying economies less robust than ours.

I suspect the problem grew out of a disproportionate tenderness for the rural vote. How we get out of the mess I do not know, but it can't be done without some suffering in some quarters. But to suggest that we must continue to accept such a maladjustment, once it is recognized, is to admit that we cannot achieve the bright future that lies ahead.

Now for another illustration of cultural lag—the settlement of employer and employee controversies. Of course most labor differences are settled by bargaining and compromise, and without the involvement of the general public. This is not the place to discuss the rights and wrongs in the steel strike settlement but it serves to make this point. In most disputes in a civilization dominated by law and order, we expect differences to be settled between the contending parties in such a way as not to damage the life or property of the rest of the society. This does not mean necessarily an advocacy of universal remedies such as compulsory arbitration, special labor courts or anti-strike injunctions, but more *ex parte* umpiring will surely be necessary. For I do believe that man can be called civilized only to the extent he has learned how to settle personal disagreements without the use of a stone ax, a sword, a blunderbuss, or the threat of general havoc.

I hope that we have not drifted into continued acceptance of procedures which we know are long since out-dated but which, as a group, we seem unwilling to change.

I could continue with many more illustrations in this same vein but these are enough to make my point. If you still doubt that our group behavior lags behind the intricate society we have constructed, give thought to further examples among such diverse subjects as building codes vs. new materials; Sunday Blue Laws; the annual battle royal of the three services vs. the defense of the country; state educational laws; and the jerry-built federal tax structure with its intricacies and repressions.

We would not tolerate such nonsense in the management of our own affairs and yet as a group, we seem to be willing to suffer the deadening influence of outworn customs, accidental procedures and illogical behavior.

Now is the time for the rover to quit knocking the ball about the field at random and take a shot at a particular object—let us say the legal profession. Here are a few questions which a layman might ask to test the flexibility of your profession's thinking:

> The public is deeply concerned by an overly complex court system and what appear to be inordinate delays in the administration of justice.
>
> Has the legal profession wholeheartedly supported an adequate plan of court-reorganization to replace our present archaic hierarchy of courts? What evidence is there that the profession has made this an important order of business?
>
> Why have lawyers failed to project to the public a better image of their profession?
>
> The overwhelming experience of the public with lawyers (not the law) is excellent, yet an American Bar Association study of public attitudes toward the lawyer indicated just the opposite.
>
> Is there a systematic effort being made to re-focus that image to reflect the great body of conscientious, honest lawyers?
>
> Have you adequately policed your profession to eliminate those who do not conform to the high standards of conduct required of them as officers of the court, so that the public may be properly protected?
>
> With legal problems increasingly impinging on all segments of the public, should proper steps be taken to encourage individuals to consult lawyers earlier and more often?
>
> In this study I spoke of, fear of exorbitant fees was given as one of the main causes of suspicion of lawyers. For example, could Bar Associations promulgate, and adequately publicize, reasonably low flat fee schedules for initial exploratory consultations of short duration?

But all of you can ask these questions with better taste than I can. The point at issue is not the questions or whether they are sensible, but the capacity to make appropriate changes to coincide with our changing society.

Reluctance to adopt change has some advantages in the proper place. It means that our society, our business, or your profession are more stable thereby. We are less apt to suffer the consequences of hasty decisions and rash action. But mere contentment in repeating the past can be insidious. The cultural lag does not bring about immediate destruction like a flood or an industrial disaster. It is more like dry rot. The need for repair and adjustment goes unnoticed until irreparable damage has been done and replacements are too late. Venturesome individuals who chafe under unreasonable repression become discouraged. Thus frustration slows our natural enterprise and cheats us of our expected economic expansion.

This is becoming a more serious matter than many of our citizens realize (another cultural lag). It is not only that we may not in this country achieve the full potential that the forecasters believe possible, but we are in deadly competition with others beyond our borders who are more serious and more disciplined. Nor is our competition only with the Russians. In the United States we no longer have a monopoly of "know how"; other nations are as capable, more eager to achieve, and equally educated for this future.

We have arrived at a time in our national life, in my opinion, when we will have to change some of our attitudes—not hastily, but thoughtfully—and narrow the gap (it can never be closed) between our potential abilities and our customary procedures. Let me illustrate what I have in mind by naming three concepts which I believe we should abandon or materially modify.

The first is the doctrine of laissez-faire. Our traditional belief is that the effect of innovations would be absorbed by our society by slow degrees. The laissez-faire economists of the 18th and 19th centuries, such as Smith, Malthus, Ricardo and Mill, formed their theories on what they believed to be inexorable social forces. I can add Marx to this list. He did not believe conditions could be modified and so he prophesied revolution. These theories are the basis of much of our traditional economic thinking. These men did not consider how political steps could modify or even avoid unfavorable social consequences. Their doctrines of political economy had meaning in a highly stratified society in which privilege was fiercely protected. But the context of their theories has largely disappeared although their doctrines have not.

Let us beware of the credulity of Candide that "All is for the best in this best of all possible worlds."

For my second example, let's look at the word "planning." It was not so long ago that this word was a political liability. A planner was believed to be a little soft—a little pink—and what's more he was probably an egghead.

In this competitive world of science and ideas, it is the intellectual who, in the future, will be our most valuable national asset. We had better not think of him in derisive terms. Fortunately, planning and organizing are beginning to be regarded with less suspicion in government and community operations. Of course we plan our business but we have not yet fully accepted the need to plan our society. Our sprawling noisy cities are more than mute witnesses to this omission. We can do much more in planning community health and juvenile activities in cities where normal outlets for energy are absent. Our educational systems can be better coordinated and so can our various forms of transportation. In fact—and this is a magnificent example of cultural lag—the railroads are operating today under rules and customs imposed when railroading was a profitable monopoly and its infant rivals needed protection and encouragement.

Now my third suggestion is for a modification of our traditional attitude toward government. We have always said to each other that the least government is the best government. This, as we have used the phrase in the past, is just plain nonsense in the middle of the 20th century. There are so many complications arising in our economy that we need more and more umpires. It would be pleasant perhaps for some of us if this were not so, but we have passed the point of return to the simple procedures of our forefathers. There are more and more obligations which are our general responsibility but cannot be the responsibility of one or just a few individuals. Government action seems to be the only practical solution. In my opinion we should admit that the government in one way or another, will have more and more influence upon our affairs: business, societal and educational. It follows, therefore, that we should spend more of our time seeing how we can work with the government instead of against it.

We will need to participate more in government and I say this knowing that your profession participates more (I guess) than all others combined. We will need to join with it in mapping our courses of future action. We had better concede that government, in spite of all its rules and regulations, is unavoidably our partner and not our traditional opponent.

The danger of expanding government lies, of course, in the conflict between group endeavors and individual freedom. Both of these concepts are being modified and we must be sure that in the process we do not lose something of a personal nature that we can never regain. And you of all people can guide us. In my opinion we cannot hold back the rising tide but we can plan to survive on it, maneuver with it, and turn it to our use.

Such is the character of the American that I do not fear the danger of being engulfed. He has a tradition of individual freedom, belief in personal opportunity, and is confident of a vigorous society in which to achieve his ambitions.

The danger is not that our present prosperous condition may change quickly but that too great reliance on tradition may blind us to the advantages of currently unwelcome changes that are for the best in the long run.

There you have my message. I fear the comforts of laissez-faire, the avoidance of planning and lastly, an habitual hostility to all things governmental.

Maeterlink, with a poet's capacity to express an idea with a flourish, wrote some lines a half century ago, with which I would like to close this talk:

> At every crossway in the road that leads to the future, each progressive spirit is opposed by a thousand men self-appointed to guard the past. Let us have no fear lest the fair towers of former days be sufficiently defended. The least that the most timid among us can do is not to add to the immense dead weight which nature drags along.

CHARLES H. BROWER

The Year of the Rat

Delivered before the Advertising Federation of America in Boston, Massachusetts, February 9, 1960.

Brower is president and chairman of the executive committee of Batten, Barton, Durstine & Osborn, Inc., one of the largest advertising agencies in the United States.

Those people who believe in statistics tell us that things really boomed in the latter half of 1959. Car loadings were up. Retail sales were up. Dow-Jones averages were up. But the thing that was *really* up was the production and use of rose-colored glasses. Rose-colored glasses were used in main for gazing happily into the golden haze that came to be known as the Soaring Sixties. Rose-colored glasses are never made in bifocals, for nobody reads the small print in dreams, nor are they interested in handwriting on the wall, or clouds no bigger than a man's hand on the horizon.

There are, however, only two things that we really *know* about the Sixties: First, they will not perform as advertised, for no decade ever has. Try it yourself—pick any decade. Did anyone call it in advance or even come close? Certainly not. The second thing that we know is that we are already in the Sixties today—and they look very much like the same old neighborhood. Nothing has really happened to change things except that we have crossed a line which we ourselves have drawn in the sands of time. It is only 1960 because the Chinese have not yet been able to convince us that it is the year 4658, which they celebrated on January 28 as The Year of the Rat.

We have started out, for instance, by a wave of church desecrations—and by throwing a nice fresh billion dollars to the Insatiable Money Eater. The

Money Eater has eaten up half the value of the American dollar in the past 20 years. Each year in the past four he has eaten another penny.

We are not a nation that is enthusiastic about having its money eaten. So, from time to time, we have taken bold measures against the Money Eater. We have deplored him from the pulpit and caricatured him in the press. We have called upon our economic doctors and made big medicine. But no one can make the animal take the medicine.

It is not hard to see why. Hunting for the causes of inflation in the fields of economics and finance is like hunting for crocodiles in Nome. For all I know, there may be a crocodile in Nome—but it's not the place to look when you find yourself suddenly short of crocodiles.

Economic phenomena do not cause inflation any more than high thermometers cause hot weather. Inflation is a disease of the American backbone and can be cured only by large and frequent doses of courage and unselfishness.

Traditionally the American dollar comes out of every war wearing wound stripes, for war without conquest creates no wealth. There is a bill to be paid—but no one wants to pick up the check, and this is where the real trouble starts.

When any ship—except the Ship of State—beings to founder at sea, certain traditions are observed; certain courtesies prevail. The Captain stays on the bridge, pitting his authority against the tendency to panic. The crew man the pumps and help the women and children into the lifeboats. The strong give up their life jackets to the weak.

But when our country begins to sink into the sea of inflation, a different picture is seen. The Captain stays on the bridge all right, but his orders are unheard in the shouting as the life jackets are wrested from the weak by the strong. The crew man the pumps, but more often than not they pump the sea in instead of out. Gangs of passengers band together with the silly, but desperate, conviction that they can keep their small part of the ship afloat, even though all the rest may sink. Labor seeks to keep its section afloat by ceaseless demands for more take-home and more fringe benefits. The farmer demands that his part of the deck be kept solid under him by price supports. Management has more than once left one part of the ship and set up in another where conditions seemed more favorable. Meanwhile Government, beset by scores of demands backed by the threat of political punishment, grabs everyone it can catch and holds him under a drowning tide of confiscatory taxes.

But it won't work. A bill that is owed cannot be paid by passing it around. It can't be paid by the natural, unorganized victims, the people on fixed incomes, for there are not enough of them. It *can* be paid by hard work, by devoted management—by returning an honest day's work for a full day's pay, by ending government waste, by insisting on a balanced budget, by doing away with all needless jobs in every industry, by starting to reduce our almost 300-billion-dollar debt instead of buying a new roof for it each year. But who wants that?

Inflation thrives on living it up. On getting more and spending more. And, boy, do we love to do that. Inflation makes a $20,000 man out of a $10,000 man. It makes millionaires out of people who never could have been millionaires otherwise. It makes us all poor-boys-who-made-good, because our fathers made so much less than we do. But it also saps and destroys all the good disciplines that made us great. Today, it seems, the only way to be penny-wise is to spend the penny—the only way to be pound-foolish is to save the pound. Smart people no longer pay debts; they incur them. For being in debt is another way of passing the bill to your neighbor. You don't have to borrow *money,* of course. You can borrow trips to Europe. Or anything you like. Name it, and you can have it now and pay later. And by lumping all of your small debts into one impossible total, you can get the finance company to do all your bookkeeping for you.

Even old familiar sayings take on new and sinister meanings. When we were taught that "God helps them that help themselves," it was an admonition to idlers and daydreamers. Nowadays it seems more of a divine go-ahead for the shrewd and the ruthless.

Nobody needs to be told today not to count his chickens before they hatch. Today people do not wait for the eggs to hatch. They *eat* the eggs, then borrow to *buy* chickens.

I have said that inflation is a disease of the American spinal column. What I have not said is that almost all of our troubles come as a result of the same disease. The disease might be called Epidemic Cynical Selfishness —it is the healthy cells of rugged individualism gone wild.

Epidemic Cynical Selfishness. Or, E. C. S. It might be called "ME-FIRST-ITIS," or "MAKE WAY FOR NUMBER ONE," or "WHAT'S IN IT FOR ME?," or "GOOD GUYS FINISH LAST," and it is about as far away from the Golden Rule as it is possible to get. And I do not think you can name a sickness of our modern society that does not go right straight back to that EPIDEMIC CYNICAL SELFISHNESS.

Here are a few: juvenile delinquency, increasing divorce rate, death on the highways, the rising crime rate, church and synagogue desecrations and the evils which have recently beset our own business—rigged quiz shows, payola and TV commercials which are less than truthful.

Every one of those is directly related to our new cult of mass selfishness. And so, for that matter, are a lot of less dire habits—such as always getting away first at the traffic light, such as the Lower Slobovia school of teen-age dress, such as defacing our pleasant land with trash thrown from cars.

Suppose I take just one of the symptoms of our time: the rigged quiz show. We were all properly indignant about this spectacular form of coast-to-coast cheating. But we do not read the message right if we all decide to chop down our antennas, or even if we heap too much blame upon the young and uneasy industry in which it occurred. And it is not for Charles Van Doren that we should mourn. It is for the rich, the poor, the brilliant, the ordinary, the gifted, the unskilled, the taxi drivers and the professors—for all the people who took the fixing quite in stride and never complained until one man felt that he had not been paid enough.

There are plenty of rigged quizzes that are not on TV, you know. Take the one in which Uncle Sam asks us each year how much money we earned last year . . . and then hires 50,000 men to make sure that we do not cheat.

Consider the quiz held every second at the checkout counter of the supermarket. Executives of our large chain stores have decided that one-fourth of us will not steal under any circumstances; one-fourth of us will steal anything, especially if it's nailed down; and the other half of us vary according to the strength of the temptation and the chances of getting away with it.

Consider the quizzes held in our colleges. Twenty and thirty years ago the great hope was the honor system. This system exists in only a handful of colleges today, and in most cheating is an accepted practice—one professor estimating that one in every three students cheats regularly.

This country today is filled with men who always go first class on expense accounts, but who happily adjust to tourist when on their own; with people who would never think of stealing from a wallet they found, but who almost always return a half-empty day to their employers.

Our business today is getting more than its share of the attention of those in the government. Certainly, anyone who attended our midwinter conference last Friday in Washington, or who read his Sunday morning papers, will find little difficulty in understanding that we, as an industry, are looked upon as transgressors. But let no one think that the root of all our country's evil has been belatedly discovered within our midst, or that we have cornered the market on deviousness. No, whatever evil there is in the advertising industry—and I for one am sure that we have even less than our share—is but a sign of our time.

The trouble that Epidemic Cynical Selfishness brings us may be great. For selfishness is not the path of Democracy. Selfishness is the path of Tyranny. In a Dictatorship the strong and selfish subdue the others, and a government based on terror exists—but the very foundation of Democracy is that each must sacrifice something for the good of all.

Just now the Sputniks and Luniks of Tyranny seem to fly better than ours. This is not, I think, because the Russians are greater scientists, or because they captured the better Germans. It is because the launching of such a complicated mechanism requires the utmost teamwork by thousands of people. And thus far the threat of liquidation has been a better incentive to teamwork than the responsibility of the individual. It is the tiny things that fail with us—the average cost of failing components in recent rocket heartbreaks was around $2.60. As they say "Somebody goofed"—someone who didn't realize perhaps how much Democracy depended upon him that day. Indeed, the "goof-off" in this country has become a sort of status symbol—it takes a real he-man to let everyone else down and get away with it.

Now it is a fascinating characteristic of our people that we are greatest when we have a cause. Communities visited by storm and flood do not have time for selfishness or ME-FIRST-ITIS. And all of us were better, tougher, less selfish and finer people when we had a Fascist Empire to get off our backs. Today we seem to have nothing much to do. We are no longer building our house. We are not defending it. We are just living in it. And we are so bored with prosperity and happy-happy happiness that we hardly know what to do.

Of course, there is danger, perhaps the greatest that we have ever faced. But it is not too clear or too present. We don't really believe it. We can't visualize our daughters being carried off by Red invaders, or nuclear bombs actually falling in the streets of our cities. We cannot really believe that Mr. K., whose wife looks so much like somebody's mother, would ever be unkind with his nuclear weapons.

Besides, we can't depend upon disaster to pull us together this time, for if it strikes, we will have nothing left to pull together.

What else brings out greatness in people? Leaders. Yes, even in times of peace real leaders can set a nation aflame with enthusiasm. But in a Democracy we don't want just one big man on horseback—we need a hundred thousand of them, at all levels, in every village, town, school, factory and farm.

Which brings me back just for a moment to the disease analogy again. Medical science often studies healthy tissue to determine what elements fight disease and decay. Haven't we been spending too long a time studying the wrong people? What would happen if, for a while, we turned our microscopes away from studying the selfish, the crafty, the lazy and the morally weak, and focused them instead on the industrious, the honest and the morally strong?

What would happen if we stopped psychoanalyzing and dissecting the chicken-chested kids in leather jackets . . . and started to pay some real attention to the squares who have not yet stabbed a teacher or mugged an elderly woman?

Think of the millions and millions of dollars we have spent trying to find out what makes the delinquent delinquent. Think of the billions of hours the sociologists have spent trying to understand the criminal, to comprehend the urge to alcoholism, to analyze the broken home.

Is there any professor in any college across this land who has written, is now writing, or is even *thinking* of writing, a book on the noncriminal mind?

Has there been a paper delivered in the past twenty years dealing with nonneurotics, nonalcoholics, nondelinquents, nonscrewballs? Has any great foundation offered a grant to promote the study of the simple, corny, honest, God-fearing American? You know the answer as well as I do.

Yet even the breeders of animals know better than this. Nobody tries to develop winning race horses by studying the losers. Nobody even develops prize pigs by studying the runts.

We have taken the good guy for granted so long in this country that we know nothing whatever about him. Is he religious? Sometimes, but quite often not. Was he properly whaled by his parents when young? Again sometimes, but quite often not. Was he a delight to his teachers in school? Not always—often he was the lad who turned their hair gray.

But do we know about the bad guy? You bet we do. We know that he is misunderstood, misguided, misdirected, miserable—and a victim of his environment. We know that we must pity and pamper him, and pay for his rehabilitation. We must at all costs—and the costs are almost beyond measure—be nice to him.

I trust I will not be thought unsympathetic if I say nuts to him—and to our national preoccupation with the overwrought and discontented . . . with the anxiety-ridden student who cannot afford premium gas for his Jaguar . . . with the neurotic personality, the disturbed psyche and the complex complex.

Russia is not panting at our heels today . . . Russia is walking all over our feet. Isn't this a sensible time to get our attention for the time being from the remedial and to the excellent?

Couldn't our grade schools somehow give as much extra time to the development of the gifted, the brilliant and the natural leaders as they give to those who have not yet adjusted to group play?

Must our secondary schools continue to pump our colleges full of the well-off, the show-off and the goof-off . . . along with the talented and the able and the devoted? According to Dr. James Conant, between thirty and forty per cent of our young people go to college today. But no one knows whether or not it is the right thirty or forty per cent. We think that if Mom and Dad were what used to be known as "college material," Junior must be college material, too. Except that Junior may think that Mom and Dad and study are all from Squaresville, which I am told is no place. We have implicit trust in Regents and College Boards, even though we know that most teachers in junior and senior year have learned to predict the questions pretty well.

I, for one, do not ask that we abandon the charitable instincts that mark us as Americans. I do not even suggest that we abandon our role as the feeder and father of the world's hungry and fatherless. I ask only that we look for talent and excellence as avidly as we look for uranium—and that we cherish it and cultivate it as thoughtfully as we do many of our less valuable natural resources.

If there were a suspected Communist in your neighborhood, you would know where to report him. If there were a good left-handed pitcher with a fast drop in your high school, the scouts from both leagues would be after him. But if you ran across a junior Einstein, would you know what to do about him?

It is true that the Ford Foundation is scratching at the surface of this problem. But this is not basically the Ford Foundation's problem. It is your problem. And it is my problem.

I think that our educators, our ministers, our editors, our businessmen, our unions and our organizations like yours should join in a mammoth talent hunt to be sure that we are giving every gifted boy and girl as much attention as we give our better criminals. It could easily start right here. There have, from time to time, been some thrilling manhunts in our country—but there has never been one like this—in which a whole dedicated nation might work together to uncover this treasure of brains which Dr. Conant believes is hiding in unlikely places all over America.

Thus we might in time develop the leadership that a Democracy needs—a leadership that would again give us the right to include that word "United" in the name United States of America—a leadership at all levels that would make it *smart* to be hard-working, honest and unselfish—that would point out the stupidity of inflation, laziness, moral weakness, delinquency, divorce, tax evasion, goofing off and free-loading.

It won't be done in a day, perhaps not in a decade.

Meanwhile, what can you and I do about ourselves?

We can start taking our temperatures today, I think, and see whether or not we are victims of that American disaster disease—Epidemic Cynical Selfishness. Let's let someone beat us at the light . . . let's let the other fellow win one argument . . . let's even let the wife have the last word . . . and see how much it hurts.

Our secret weapon as a nation was given us 1700 years before we *were* a nation by a man who said, "Love thy neighbor as thyself."

Maybe we can't *love* our neighbors right at first, after so many years of loving ourselves. But we might start by treating them as *allies* at least.

When the management man hates the union man, when the city man hates the farmer, when the workingman hates the professor, when the white-collar man hates the blue-collar man, when the rich man hates the poor man and *everybody* hates the government . . . that is when the Kremlin rocks with laughter.

We may never learn to love the jolly folks in the Kremlin—but it doesn't seem fair to us to make them kill themselves with laughter!

You know about that "tide in the affairs of men, which, taken at the flood, leads on to fortune."

There is also a tide in the affairs of nations . . . and this may be it for the United States.

If it is, let us pray that you and I will not be found wanting!

Thank you.

Critical Note on Brower

The key question we must ask of his speech is, Who is Brower's audience?

Brower is an advertising man delivering a speech to fellow advertising men. His immediate audience, then, consists of his colleagues, subordinates, and competitors. However, since Brower is one of the top advertising men in the United States—a man of considerable power and influence in his field of work—he has a more than ordinary responsibility in addressing this immediate audience. He is obliged, by his "success," to appear before this audience as a model speaker and to deliver a speech which will be the realization of what this highly articulate audience holds to be an ideal performance. The hemming and hawing of an ordinary mortal will not do. Great things are expected of the president of Batten, Barton, Durstine, and Osborn.

Moreover, there is an unseen and unacknowledged audience which will "overhear" the speech. That audience is the general American public, seeming, at least to the advertisers, to sit in silent judgment on Brower and his peers.

The methods and aims of advertising have endured considerable public criticism in recent years (see, for examples, the sections on Business and Labor, and Communications Media). Jokes about Madison Avenue have become commonplace, and many a recent second-rate novel has made its hero an advertising man who is torn between saving his soul and satisfying the wicked demands of his occupation. As a consequence of this public criticism, advertising men have sometimes displayed a chronic self-consciousness about their work and a chronic defensiveness in discussing it. Hence, Brower's rhetorical objectives must be to set an impressive example for his fellow advertisers and to present to the unseen public an image of an honest, intelligent, and responsible spokesman for an honest, intelligent, and responsible industry.

Brower's rhetorical technique for dealing with this dual challenge is both simple and ingenious. It is: dwell upon the corruption of American life, showing the evils of advertising to be but symptoms of a deeper corruption, and then endorse courage, thrift, and Christian virtue as The Answers. It is an elegant strategy. It enables Brower to shift the attack on the advertising industry to an attack on "our time." It enables him to ally himself with "the simple, corny, honest, God-fearing American," against selfishness, delinquency, neurosis, and communism. Incidentally, this strategy enables him to oppose such diverse villains as inflation, divorce, tax evasion, laziness, and shoplifting. Clearly, Brower is on the side of the angels against the forces of darkness and of sin. And Brower fights his verbal battle in racy, down-to-earth language, colloquial enough to show that the speaker has no "airs," is tough and blunt, is "one of the boys."

An elegant strategy indeed: but we must return to the question, Who is Brower's audience? What does the speaker assume about his audience when he implies that we should not participate in rigged quiz shows or steal groceries from supermarkets? Or when he brings charging through the speech periodically, "Epidemic Cynical Selfishness"—this train of ominous terms, head, torso, and crocodile tail, which breathes fire and eats victims? Or when he characterizes the moral maxim of Christianity as "our secret weapon as a nation?" Or when he dismisses the neurotic and the psycopathic personality with "nuts to him?" Or when he uses such expressions as "somebody goofed?" Does an intelligent and mature man in a responsible position ordinarily talk in this way? No, not ordinarily. We have only to examine the other speeches in this book to see what an extraordinary level of language Brower's speech contains.

If one were telling a bed-time story to a small child, one might invent so fearsome a monster as "the Insatiable Money Eater," the terrible dragon who is fought by the handsome prince. Obviously Brower could not have assumed an audience of small children. But he could have assumed that his audience was child-like or that it had a childish mentality and a childish view of the world. In fact, when we examine his speech carefully, we can see that Brower must have held an exceedingly low opinion of his audience's intelligence.

Look carefully at the speech. The call for courage and unselfishness is surrounded by wisecracking humor, as if the audience could not seriously contemplate these Spartan virtues. The call for intellectual excellence is justified by our competition with the Soviet Union and our contempt for intellectual mediocrity, as if the audience were incapable of valuing excellence for its own sake, as if the audience, devoid of any generous emotion, required something which it could despise for every object it was asked to admire. The preachment, "Let's let someone beat us at the light . . . let's let the other fellow win one argument . . . let's even let the wife have the last word," assumes an audience with the mentality of hot-rodders and the temperament of spoiled brats.

The speech is permeated with a low and patronizing view of its audience. Almost certainly, no one hearing or reading the speech could identify himself with that audience without being insulted. Our natural defense is to dissociate ourselves from that audience whom we perceive is being addressed. We find ourselves, then, reading the speech not as auditors to whom a man is communicating ideas, but as detached spectators of a shoddy and offensive rhetorical performance. Who would identify himself with Brower's assumed audience of spoiled brats, petty thieves, and hatemongers? The answer is, nobody. And that is the audience for which Brower's speech was designed. Nobody.

Questions

Berle says that "universities everywhere ought to concern themselves with a moral order." How does a university go about doing this? Would a university which concerned itself with "a moral order" end up by indoctrinating its students instead of educating them? Is there a difference between indoctrination and education? Do you agree that "Most Americans . . . know quite well that education comes ahead of transient luxuries" and that "Profit is essential, but secondary"? Do they care whether or not they have "an economics which does not accept slums as a necessary condition of housing?"

Is the "rat race for status symbols" caused or intensified by our civilization, or is it an inevitable expression of human fears and desires? Would it be a good thing if all Americans devoted themselves to the same ends in life? What is a "national purpose?" Does the United States have one? Should it?

Is "respect for trained intelligence" increasing in the United States? How can intellectuals and intellectual effort become more prestigeous in American life? In what respects, if any, should our economic activities be "planned"? Is our country "dripping with fat"? If so, why? If not, why do people say so? Are Americans "bored with prosperity"? What are the symptoms of this boredom? Are all Americans prosperous? What proportion of our population is not? Is their lack of prosperity their own fault? Should government agencies aid them? Why?

Mr. Josephs suspects that disproportionate representation is a major cause of the farm problem. But most farmers seem to be unhappy with federal farm programs enacted with the help of their Congressmen. Is there really a connection between greater representation for farmers than urban dwellers and our huge, expensive crop surpluses? Are there serious differences among the educational laws of the several states? Is so, would it be better to have a uniform federal law? Does the rivalry of the three military services foster inefficiency or discourage excesses? Are there important inequities in federal tax laws?

How many parallels can you find in earlier American society for the "sicknesses of our modern society" cited by Brower. Was there more honest workmanship in the United States during World War II than there is today? Do the groups Brower mentions hate each other? If they all loved one another, would any problems remain?

Is our society deteriorating or are the American people becoming more self-critical? Were the McCarthy witch hunts worse than those at Salem in the 1690's? Does the discouraging record of captured American soldiers in Korea reflect the use of more effective techniques by our enemies or less effective training of our youth? Are the intellectual stresses and strains of modern civilization a greater or lesser burden than the physical hardships of yesteryear?

Suggestions for Further Reading

Chodorov, Frank. "Van Doren, Payola, and the Freudian Ethic," *Human Events*, Dec. 8, 1960, p. 619.

Cogley, John, ed. *Religion in America*. New York: Meridian, 1958.

Cone, Fairfax M. "Advertising is Not a Plot," *Atlantic Monthly*, January 1958.

Griffith, Thomas. *The Waist-High Culture*. New York: Harper, 1959.

Guiding Metropolitan Growth. Committee for Economic Development pamphlet, 1960.

Horton, Paul B., and Gerald R. Leslie. *The Sociology of Social Problems*. 2nd. ed. New York: Appleton-Century-Crofts, 1960.

Lipset, Seymour M. "Religion in America: What Religious Revival?" *Columbia University Forum*, Winter 1959, p. 17.

McDonald, Donald, ed. *Religion and Freedom*. Fund for the Republic pamphlet, 1958.

Miller, William L., and others. *Religion and the Free Society*. Fund for the Republic pamphlet, 1958.

Millis, Walter. *The Constitution and the Common Defense*. Fund for the Republic pamphlet, 1959.

Packard, Vance. "The Growing Power of Admen," *Atlantic Monthly*, September 1957.

"Protestant Voices," *Harper's*, July 1959, p. 74.

Rockefeller, Nelson. "Purpose and Policy," *Foreign Affairs*, April 1960.

Stone, Gregory P. "Halloween and the Mass Child," *American Quarterly*, Fall 1959, p. 372.

Symposium. "Our Country and Our Culture," *Partisan Review*, May-June, July-August, September-October 1952.

2. Business and Labor

Introduction

Owners, employees, customers: membership in these groups is far from mutually exclusive. All owners and employees are sometimes customers; many customers are part owners of businesses. The groups depend on one another, moreover, for their economic welfare as well as for the necessities of life.

Yet in any given situation, most people identify with one group and believe that the others threaten their best interests. As customers, we demand better quality merchandise at lower prices. If this requires decreased corporate profits or lower wages, so be it. As owners, we seek greater profits, not infrequently by encouraging unwise purchases, marketing goods designed for rapid replacement, or charging unfair prices. Exploitation of labor is uncommon today, but it still exists among migrant farm workers and others with little skill and less organization. As employees, we struggle for higher wages and better working conditions. Of less concern to us are restrained productivity, shoddy workmanship, ruthless coercion of fellow workers for the sake of united action, and strikes which penalize stockholders and inconvenience the public.

The problems that arise from this melee of conflicting interests and from the mediative efforts of government and private agencies are today chiefly domestic. However, increasing penetration of our markets at home and abroad by goods of better quality or lower price produced in other countries may add important international dimensions in the near future.

The speeches and essays in this section call attention to some of the foci of greatest tension between owners, employees, and customers: consumer distrust of business and advertising; management's efforts to achieve a clear political voice comparable to labor's; direct negotiations between labor and management; and abuses of the economic and political powers of labor unions.

BERNARD DEVOTO

Why Professors Are Suspicious of Business

The article from which the following excerpts were drawn was published in Fortune for April 1951. The editors of Fortune had asked DeVoto, "Why are intellectuals like yourself so hostile to business? You obviously are no leftist; what, then, is your case?" DeVoto replied: "I'm not hostile to business; I'm merely suspicious of some things it does. And I'm not speaking as an 'intellectual,' but as a professional who has been trained to evaluation, and feels too often he is being either insulted or shortchanged." The following article elaborates this statement.

Bernard DeVoto (1897-1955) was a brilliant essayist and writer of fiction and history. He was awarded the National Book Award and Pulitzer and Bancroft prizes. For the last twenty years of his life, DeVoto commented on the American scene from "The Easy Chair" column of Harper's magazine.

The professor explains to the Committee of Businessmen that his profession is no more hostile to business than to government, religion, or education—all of which it subjects to inquiring scrutiny. What the committee has set out to examine is rather an attitude of skepticism amounting to distrust, which, he concedes, is so widespread among his colleagues that it may be called characteristic.

He goes on. The word "business" is an abstraction; we must determine which of the images that stand for it in academic thinking arouse distrust. In the board rooms of their corporations the gentlemen frequently hang beautiful photomontages showing such things as mines, railroad and transmission lines, power plants, furnaces, rolling mills, converters, refineries. These are majestic symbols of the industrial order, of opulence, power, and human achievement. The attitude we are examining expends no skepticism on them; it accepts them as, so to speak, *given*. They issue from the cultural heritage, the accumulated knowledge of mankind.

What concerns us is the response of academic minds to the stimuli business offers them every day. The scholar's distrust begins not in his professional field but in the daily contacts with business that he shares with everyone else. It is because he directs his analytical intelligence at the common experience that his attitude is important to business.

It would be arrogant and absurd of the academic profession to doubt the intelligence that has given the United States its industrial plant; there is no finer intelligence or more effective use of intelligence. Nevertheless the academic distrust of business is primarily skepticism of business intelligence as it is manifested elsewhere. The principal begetter of distrust is the advertising agency.

For consider. By trade a scholar undertakes to determine the meaning, significance, and implications of what he encounters. He has an episodic but important relationship as a consumer of goods—but also he has a practically continuous relationship with business as a target of advertising. It demands his attention every time he picks up a newspaper or a magazine, passes a billboard, or turns on the radio. Business has chosen to make advertising its principal spokesman and interpreter, and he must accept it as just that. His first observation is that business appeals for judgment in a torrent of mendacity, imbecility, and bilge.

The agency instantly demurs, we aren't aiming at the professor, we're aiming at the mass market. But they are hitting the professor. The result is annoyance, resentment, anger, or laughter, all cumulative, all disparaging to business. Whatever his professional field, the scholar must deal constantly with fallacies, false evidence, false reasoning, and systems of false knowledge. When his seminar takes up Dr. Velikovsky's ingenious but nonsensical argument that the earth once stood still because a comet was becoming the planet Venus, what happens? Precisely the same thing must be expected to happen when the Googler Co. makes a play for his half dollar by advertising a mysterious ingredient perfected by scientists after years of patient study in its laboratories. (No firm so wretched as to have but one lab!) Such an ingredient goes into Googler's Motor Oil, Googler's Underarm Allure, and Googler's Shaving Cream. Secret processes have been applied to Googler Lawn Seed, Floor Wax, and Sour Mash Bourbon. And five of Googler's competitors have paid other advertising agencies to invent other scientists, mysterious ingredients, and secret processes. What is the professor to make of those responsible for this phenomenon?

Or take the effort of tobacco companies to sell him cigarettes as a remedy for sore throats. The copywriter produces an incantation composed of imaginary medical testimony, fictitious clinical tests, and supposititious fatalities to nonexistent rats. Its content is indistinguishable from the quackeries and logically elaborated nonsense that he has to appraise in his own field. Such stuff is passed off as knowledge in, for instance, astrology, or dowsing, or the cipher supposed to reveal that Bacon wrote Shakespeare's plays. But, whereas the Baconian believes his nonsense, the professor must assume that the manufacturer who pays the advertising agency to lie expensively does not. Or such other advertising rituals as "statistics prove," "research establishes," and "a poll of experts shows." The professor is an expert, research is his trade, and he has mastered statistical method—including statistical fallacies. Tell him that research establishes that 91 out of 104 experts use Googler's Anti-Freeze and you produce a threefold response of professional contempt.

The Googler Co., in fact, is building up a dilemma with exceedingly sharp horns. What is worse, Union Carbide, Johnson & Johnson, International Business Machines, and others of that stature are drawn into the dilemma by association. They do not direct such ritualistic nonsense at him, but they belong to the same business system of which Googler is so fair a flower. When the professor examines the claim of poor whites in the brush country that mysterious ingredients and secret processes give goofer dust the power to ward off witches, he recognizes the assertion as belonging to a system of magic. He recognizes advertising as just that too, a system of magic: its theorems and dogmas are magical; it is put to magical use.

Now magic, like science, is a theory of nature, an explanation of what happens; unlike science, it is a false theory and an erroneous explanation. Googler has hired the tribal witch doctors to market its product. And the basic theorem of the advertising magic is that the customer is simple-minded. One horn of the dilemma is clear: how intelligent is Googler?

This basic theorem the professor traces back to the first world war. His colleagues, the psychologists, announced the results of the first large-scale use of intelligence tests, which they had given to most of the American Army. From them they derived what they called the average IQ, and it fell in a group that the testers decided to designate as having a mental age of twelve years. As an act of classification this was unimpeachable but the words used to designate the group were a disastrous choice.

For the classification did not mean that the average American adult and the average twelve-year-old child have equivalent and interchangeable intelligences. (The testers designated "genius" as the mental age of sixteen years but there are significant differences between Einstein's mind and that of your son who will enter college next fall.) But the witch doctors of the advertising cult, like those of Hollywood, took the metaphor to be a mathematically exact statement of psychological realities, and they spun out of it the systematic magic that they think of as their science. This catastrophic by-product of terminology would have been impossible if the psychologists had used a designation without overtones, if they had called the average IQ λ or S9. A copywriter addressing ten million people whom he had to think of as λ could not possibly suppose he was talking to ten million children, and crucial differences would result. But advertising decided that consumers have the minds of children and has never re-examined its conclusion. . . .

The faculty could have no absolute objection to advertising if it could be regarded as merely formal magic and no more. When the medicine men sing their chant before the seasonal hunt, no one is harmed and perhaps the hunters will do their job all the better for believing that precautionary measures have been taken. But magic may be invoked not only by believers but by those who know it is false yet think they can use it to coerce people to their purposes. Business makes so much of its activity conform to magic that the scholarly mind wonders whether it may not have suffered as a result. Both horns of the dilemma are now clear: the intelligence of business and the good faith of its social philosophy.

The professor's function in society is to appraise, increase, and disseminate knowledge. He believes that the function of business is to make and distribute honest goods—to utilize mankind's cultural heritage in producing the best goods that the present state of knowledge permits and to employ the advance of knowledge in steadily improving them. He suspects that it is wasting some of his patrimony, that it could, in the terms given, make better goods that it does.

The absolute question is the integrity of the end product. In order to manufacture goods business borrows from society's capital funds the accumulated knowledge of mankind. Is it repaying the loan with clipped coins? The professor applies a rough scale that he has derived from his own experience and observation. What matters to business is not whether his measurements are right but that he bases his judgment of business on them.

He believes that, in general, household goods have the least integrity: cutlery, house hardware, furniture, fixtures, gadgets, appliances, the heavier machines. Here business regularly forces on the consumer products of lower quality than it knows how to make. Considerably higher in the scale come such things as glassware, crockery, leather goods, goods used for decoration, products of art and handicraft. Still higher are goods made for sports, games, hobbies, recreation, and, in general, life's private pleasures; the professor believes that he gets an honest (if overpriced) product when he buys, say, a camera, firearms, binoculars, golf or tennis equipment, musical instruments. . . .

He offers in evidence the curious distributional malfunctioning that has permitted the development of a small industry wholly within the confines of a big one—the manufacture of high-fidelity radio-phonograph combinations. Using only parts that the big manufacturers make, the small one produces for about $175 a machine that outperforms anything the big one puts on the market. He cannot make a machine to sell for $50 as the big manufacturer does, but at $175, which is at the bottom of the medium-price range, his product outperforms the big manufacturer's $1,500 machine. This is as if someone were to buy parts from General Motors and, for a third of the price of a Chevrolet, produce automobiles that outperformed a Cadillac. Furthermore, for half of $1,500 he will make a machine that utilizes most of the existing accumulation of knowledge, which is equivalent to the chairman's $20,000 automobile.

More than one aberrant factor is at work here, however, whereas what the professor is talking about can be seen without complication in household cutlery. At no level does there seem to be genuine correspondence between price and value, and at all levels the quality is below what the professor thinks it ought to be. The differences between butcher knives that sell for one dollar, three dollars, and five dollars are chiefly differences in polish and ornamentation. None of the knives performs well the function it is supposed to. . . .

He goes into a store to buy a jackknife. What he wants is one made of steel that will take and hold an edge. What he is offered is one made of steel that can be advertised as rustproof. Enough chromium has been put into it so that it will not hold an edge, but if enough had been put into it to make it rustproof it would not even take one, so that in a week he finds it pock-marked with rust. Business has completely subverted the product and frustrated the consumer; the explanation appears to lie in the tribal magic.

Right here the professor's wife asks to be sworn in. (The sharpest-fanged critic of business is the American housewife; business thinks of her as a listener to soap opera who will believe any incantation the priesthood can think up.) When she sets out to buy one of the kitchen knives the professor mentioned, she wants one she can cut with. Advertising voodoo substitutes one with a blade so shiny she could make up her lips by it, and a handle painted blue on the theory that squaw-like-um pretty beads in tepee. Voodoo offers her a meat grinder whose handle has been streamlined to reduce air resistance. It designs her electric iron to resemble abstract sculpture. It affixes a red light to her vacuum cleaner so that she may know it is in use when she is cleaning a rug with it. The shamans have said that without a red light she would buy a broom. . . .

For her part the worth of the entire business system turns on the point of a needle: either business can no longer make a sharp needle or it is no longer willing to. Nor for at least ten years has she been able to buy thread that would not break when she tried to use it. How long are goods supposed to last, she asks, and is it sanctity or caste she loses when she tries to get them repaired? If a 50-cent belt in the vacuum cleaner wears out, the agency will not replace it in less than six weeks and not then until a series of young men have tried to sell her a new machine, alleging that hers is antiquated. When a burner in the gas range breaks she finds out that the model she bought in 1940 has been superseded and the part is not carried in stock; must she limp along on three burners for want of a five-dollar spare or spend three hundred dollars for a new range? Does business want her to use its stove or replace it? And is business now concentrating on the sheerest nylon stockings because those of coarser gauge wear too long?

His helpmate may be thinking with her grievances, the professor admits, or she may have mistaken a bad run of the dice for the collapse of the industrial order and yet! An oil burner ought to meet the peak load; if business is repaying its social loan, why does his break down every cold spell? Six months ago he replaced a wall switch that had lasted a good many years; the new one is already worn out. The typewriter he bought two years ago is more dilapidated than its predecessor was after fifteen years of use. He has had to put two new escapements into it; meanwhile the ads promise him that the dull paint will protect his eyes from glare. Blotters do not absorb ink. The fountain pen has never yet become a writing instrument—

it is quite accurately taxed as jewelry—and for the steel nib that is a writing instrument, business no longer makes a penholder that will grip it without wobbling. Filing cabinets wear out faster than they used to, so do flash-light bulbs, so do radio tubes, and evidently the manufacturers of razor blades all wear full beards.

How account for these phenomena? The question brings the professor to the brink of dangerous thoughts. During the war manufacturers of consumer goods frequently had to use inferior or substitute materials in order to make goods at all. The goods sold and then went on selling after the war because the ravenous market would accept anything. The manufacturer had reached a critical road fork. He could restore the quality of his product as soon as possible or he could push the inferior product as long as possible. To choose the first course was sagacious for the long run, to choose the second assured a quick cleanup, and the professor believes that some businesses made one choice and some the other. But now he is ready to imagine the king's death. He wonders whether wartime adulteration and substitution did not accelerate an already existing tendency to follow a *third* course.

His earlier hypothesis alleged against business only the mild stupidity of credulously accepting a system of magic. Now, however, he could construct a hypothesis that would explain the system of magic as used intentionally to support a business policy of lethal stupidity. It would commensurate the increasingly sheer nylon stockings, the glareless typewriter, and the vacuum cleaner that the agency declares obsolete when the belt breaks.

His wife will require the entire business system of the United States, from the Mesabi mines on to R. H. Macy's buyers, to stand on the point of a needle. He will summon it to the bar and rest the prosecution's case on a single jackknife. Metallurgy has developed from the cavemen's campfire that melted the red-paint rock, skill from the artisanship of the first maker of stone axes, the profit system from the first cost-accounting method on a stick, financial organization and machine production and the conquest of nature and the convolution of management's forebrain—all these have progressed to the climax of a knife that will do neither what the consumer wants nor what the manufacturer claims.

Business—the Googler Knife Co. and behind it U.S. Steel and the Guaranty Trust—is simply the Neolithic axmaker. Ever since he started to barter his surplus production and so initiated the system of exchange on which civilization rests, there has been an implicit concept: the honest product. Up to the limit imposed by his customer's ability to pay, the caveman would make as good an ax as his material, his knowledge, and his skill permitted. It was one of the three bases of classic capitalism: profits were to be sought in increasing production, improving quality, and lowering price. The Marxian heresy, forsaking profits as the root of all evil, at least retained the implicit concept: production for *use*. The advertising heresy is more revolutionary: production for sale, not use. But the professor's new hypothesis defines a heresy entirely destructive to the implicit concept: production for replacement. It would work by planned obsolescence and the degradation of goods.

How? The Googler Co. offers a new product for sale, the Hoodad. When the market approaches saturation, Googler lowers the price and the Hoodad continues to sell. There comes a point, however, beyond which Googler cannot reduce prices. It therefore brings out a new-model Hoodad, with a teardrop-shaped case, a transparent plastic handle, and the Cyberneticator (pat. reg.), which rings a three-tone chime, flashes wing tip lights, and shuts itself off. At intervals more advanced models of the Hoodad follow.

But what to do when they have exhausted all the possibilities and the next one is going to look pretty much like the first? The theory of production for sale offers no further expedient but there is a flagrant hint in the Hoodad's longevity. Googler has been giving it too much integrity; it lasts too long. A blessed vision lights up, fifty million Hoodads wearing out every two years, every year, every six months, and fifty million customers replacing them. Let Googler degrade its goods. Build a worse mousetrap and the world will be forced to beat a pathway to your retail outlets.

This is not the butcher's hand on the scales, the sand in the sugar, the water in the milk, but a phenomenon of an entirely different kind. We may observe that in arriving at it the professor has not mentioned even one of the goblins that the *New Republic* sees when it thinks about business, or any of those that business sees when it thinks about the New Deal or talks about the American Way. He has simply preached the old-time religion, once the orthodoxy of business itself, which held that its whole duty was to produce the best goods it could and to improve them as progress might permit.

[The professor] leans back in his chair and lights a cigarette, leaving the package on the table to show that it does not MFT. Gentlemen, he says, nothing amazes my profession more than the banshee wails of your vice presidents who address conventions about the threats to free enterprise. Neither you nor we were ordained of God in our present estate or made inherent in nature's order. Society directs us to work in our respective ways with its capital, the knowledge it has piled up, and will maintain or obliterate us as we may serve our functions. All you need do to lose the world is to produce dull needles. All you need do to enter into heaven with the saints shouting hosanna and all the fears of vice presidents stilled forever is to produce sharp ones. The productive plant pictured in your board rooms is the astonishment and admiration of the world. The true genius of American business created it by applying society's knowledge to society's natural wealth. But when the ore has been smelted, the metal refined, the power generated and applied to fabrication, and the sales order countersigned, how sharp a needle do you deliver to the housewife? We hear your customers asking you for a Hoodad with a cutting edge and we see you hiring sorcerers to tell them that Men of Distinction prefer one that cannot rust but does. You must excuse us if as critics of the cultural process we wonder whether you have lost your religion, your conscience, your direction, or your common sense.

As he reaches for his hat, [the professor] adds, One of you asked me if what the academics thought mattered a damn. I am only one consumer and only one voter. But my colleagues and I collectively teach many voters and consumers, and we teach those who teach all there are. It may be that our distrust does you an injustice so cruel as to appall all righteous men and that the bill of complaint we have drawn against you is pure fantasy. But there it is and it is worth answering.

You can't answer it with an advertising campaign.

RICHARD WEIL, JR.

The Merchant Replies

This article was published in **Fortune** for June 1951, under the title, "Says Business to Mr. DeVoto. . . ."

Richard Weil, Jr. (1907-58) served as president of R. H. Macy & Co. from 1949 to 1953.

The professor, with zest, has drawn up a bill of complaint against American business. His taking-off point is fresh. He bases his conclusions about business directly on his and his wife's immediate experiences as ordinary consumers. To these he has directed the "analytical intelligence" of a professor. And the conclusions he has reached, he says, are important to business, right or wrong.

I agree. And since he gives us the specific data on which he has built his conclusions, let's see just how right or wrong he has been.

The professor's wife ". . . will require the entire business system of the United States, from the Mesabi mines on to R. H. Macy's buyers, to stand on the point of a needle."

It seems his wife can no longer buy a sharp needle, and the professor concludes: ". . . either business can no longer make a sharp needle or it is no longer willing to."

Query: What can have happened to needles in America? It was easier for me to find out, I suppose, than for the professor. Macy's sells about 1,500,000 needles a year, and Macy's Bureau of Standards has tested the needles we sell since 1927.

So I talked to our head of stock for needles about it. She told me, rather unexpectedly, that no home-sewing needles are now being made in the United States. Most of the needles housewives buy come from England, others from Germany and Japan, a few from France, Spain, and China. I assume, however, this does not evade the professor's point, since I hope he will agree that importing some foreign goods is as proper a part of American business as manufacturing cars—or cowboy clothes.

I'm told the English and German needles are best; and that many professional sewers from the garment industry in New York buy them regularly from the same counters at Macy's as the housewife does and in the same packages. They report no trouble with the points, nor have our tests found any. Those needles whose points are meant to be sharp seem to be as sharp as ever. But some needles, I learn, are purposefully blunted for millinery sewing, tapestry needlework, and the like.

Why, then, has the professor's wife been stuck with dull needles? It may be that, unaware, she has been getting millinery needles. Or it may be that she has been buying really inferior (and less expensive) needles. But in either case, I am virtually certain she can find sharp needles. I know she can find them at Macy's, and in thousands of other stores in America.

The professor also believes "there are many goods whose value is not commensurate with their price at any level" and as evidence points to ". . . the development of a small industry wholly within the confines of a big one—the manufacture of high-fidelity radio-phonograph combinations. Using only parts that the big manufacturers make, the small one produces for about $175 a machine that outperforms . . . the big manufacturer's $1,500 machine . . . as if someone were to buy parts from General Motors and, for a third of the price of a Chevrolet, produce automobiles that outperformed a Cadillac. . . ."

Several different points plead to be picked out of this one. The least of them is this: why shouldn't the professor give American business an award for producing the high-performing set at the low cost of $175? Isn't the small manufacturer as much a part of business as the large?

Another point: in the professor's eyes, the $1,500 set seems very much overpriced when you can buy one to outperform it for only $175. He ignores at least two things here in explaining to himself this diversity of price: (1) the very different values different people get from their sets; (2) the real possibility that his standard of performance may be too narrow, or even false.

The professor's $175 probably buys a high-fidelity *chassis only,* generally built later into a bookcase by a devotee of fine music who scorns to pay for a cabinet because "you can't play the cabinet." There's no objection to this. It's no more than a matter of taste. Most other people, it happens, would as soon buy a stripped-down radio-phonograph as a stripped-down automobile. They consider their set as much a piece of furniture as an instrument; they *like* the cabinet. And the man who pays $1,500 for his set usually gets a very fine cabinet indeed, as well as other luxury trimmings. The basic costs of these are as great, or greater, than that of the chassis—but they evidently give him satisfactions he is willing to pay for.

Is he paying too much? Remember how free his choice is—and how hard this particular $1,500 set must compete with all the other sets the man can look at and listen to, priced well above and below the $1,500. And remember how free the professor is to buy the $175 chassis he likes. By what reasoning, then (on the part of either business or the professor), could "overpricing" give the $1,500 set an undue profit advantage, in a market where over 100 different manufacturers are competing?

A third point: the professor assumes that the "higher" the fidelity, the better the set. It's a common assumption, but it happens to be wrong.

The professor will find the extensive research evidence for this in the *Journal of Experimental Psychology* (Vol. 35, No. 5, October 1945) and in the *Proceedings of the Institute of Radio Engineers* (September 1945), where a radio engineer and a psychologist combined to report a major study on this very point. Neither of these researchers was interested in the manufacture or sale of sets (both were with C.B.S.). But they were very much interested in the satisfactions people got from listening to all kinds of program material, from classical music to talks, in different ranges of frequency or fidelity.

They set up an experiment with a wide cross section of listeners, including men and women, young and old, well-educated and not, and trained musicians and FM set owners.

As these people listened, the "fidelity" used in transmission was switched, on a planned basis of immediate contrasts, from low to medium frequencies, from medium to high, from low to high.

The people knew when a change occurred (a light flashed) but did not know what the change was. They were asked to express their preference, by reporting which intervals sounded best to them.

The findings: in every subgroup of the cross section—including the groups of trained musicians, those with special interests in music, and FM set owners—a majority of the listeners consistently voted their preference for low vs. medium fidelity, for medium vs. high, and low vs. high. The higher the fidelity, the fewer people liked it!

This explains why there can be a great difference between what the professor calls a "superior" set and what his next-door neighbor prefers. It also explains why manufacturers were concentrating on the production of great quantities of medium- and low-fidelity sets long before they had the benefits of this research: they were being responsive to consumer selection. It's not because the manufacturers "prefer" to make sets of lower fidelity.

It's simply because *most people in America* want just that, even when they can hear all sets, and can pay for high fidelity.

If more people wanted high-fidelity sets, there's little question but that the big manufacturers could produce them for less than they cost now, and certainly more cheaply than the professor's small manufacturer who "puts the parts together" for $175.

The professor also makes a good deal of his and his wife's unhappy experiences in trying to find a knife that will cut. Just that: *cut.* And he comes to another conclusion: business has arrived at ". . . the climax of a knife that will do neither what the consumer wants nor what the manufacturer claims."

Of course there are shoddy knives. Isn't some shoddy stuff the inevitable fringe of any human activity—whether it's business or teaching, housekeeping or book writing, medicine or art? But why has the professor happened into so much of it when buying his household goods?

I can only guess that the professor may have been exaggerating. Or that he is an unusually bad shopper. Or that he looks for his goods only in out-of-the-way stores whose stocks are extraordinarily limited. For the professor's experiences with knives (as with so many other of his complaints) simply do not jibe with our inventory facts-of-life. We now have on sale at Macy's at least 100 different models of bread knives, carving, vegetable, butcher, fish, and utility knives for the home kitchen; for men, we have at least nine different types of hunting knives, seven types of fishing knives, and dozens of different styles of pocketknives.

I *know* that among them are knives which "will take and hold an edge," knives made of steel as fine or finer than any pioneer's knife. And while Macy's, of course, tends to have larger selections than other stores, these are not knives we make in the basement after hours. They are produced or imported by American business, and are available throughout the nation in other stores.

Let me remark parenthetically that I am sending the professor a selection of them taken from regular stock. I can't be sure just what he will slash at with these knives. But I hope it won't be American business. They're sharp.

The professor: Is business now concentrating on the sheerest nylon stockings because those of coarser gauge wear too long?

This would be a funny question if it were not so irresponsible in a serious discussion of business. The simple answer is that it isn't business but *women* who are concentrating on sheer stockings. They do it for one of the oldest reasons in the world. They think their legs look nicer in them.

It would be instructive for the professor to stand by our stocking counters for an hour. He would see that that any woman who cares to (and some do) can find all the "coarser" gauge nylons she wishes. We have them. Certainly these are more durable—but at these same counters the vast majority of women knowingly choose sheers. So manufacturers must produce more sheers, and we must have them in stock, or we would be serving our customers less well.

The professor, I suppose, might reply: "But why doesn't du Pont produce a sheer nylon yarn that will last longer?"

There are at least two answers to this. For the first, one might as sensibly ask the Army why it doesn't produce a small rifle—with the firing power of a cannon. And the second is that more than likely both the Army and du Pont are already working hard on exactly these problems.

If not du Pont, then certainly someone else, out of a simple desire for profit, must be trying to develop a yarn as sheer or sheerer than nylon and stronger. After all, if nylon knocked out silk for stockings, why not X to knock out nylon? The profits would be handsome.

Thus we come full circle. The suspicions the professor has developed about business carry him to the point of shying at shadows, developing fantasies of distrust, seeing evil where there is only the normal play of consumer tastes, accusing business of "deliberate degradation" of goods only because women (as though it were something new) want to look as attractive as they can.

The complaints of the professor are based on "what he has himself observed." What could be fairer? But one must wonder if he isn't trying to judge business too broadly from the narrow plank of a one-man sample of hardly representative experiences. It reminds one of the old joke in logic:

"Indians walk in single file."

"How do you know?"

"Well, the one I saw did."

Happily or unhappily, not even the professor is "an iland entire of it selfe." He lives in a community whose *combination* of values shapes the patterns of merchandise available anywhere in it. This combination of the community's values (somewhat different from his individual pattern) is neither a conspiracy on the part of business nor one against him.

The professor seems to minimize or ignore the "fun" quality that most people get out of the merchandise they buy. Throughout history, the market place has always been a vital, cheerful center of the community's life. It has never housed only the cold logic of a purchasing agent, measuring "utility" alone. As early as the year 1300, the mercers' bazaar of Paris was called the *paradis des femmes*. And neither women nor men have changed much since then.

It does not do, therefore, to berate people directly or indirectly for seeking emotional values in the goods they buy; for buying radio-phonographs, say, with good cabinets even when they "can't hear the cabinets." They get fun and pride out of these cabinets. Nor will it do to blame women or business for the dominance of sheer hose, when any sensible persons knows that thicker hose wear longer. Illogical? Let the professor argue the point with the original Human Design.

I would also remind the professor that the bad things produced by business are directly subject to a tougher discipline than applies in any other major field of human endeavor; to a still very tough competition, not only with more desirable items in their own category but with everything else the customer may choose to spend his money on.

This may not necessarily improve the average person in business—but it certainly tends to improve the average product he offers for sale. And it explains why it is a commonplace—a truism—that one of the toughest projects in the world is to try to make a significant profit out of bad merchandise.

According to the professor, there is a "deliberate degradation" of goods. Blotters, he says, do not blot, his new wall switch wore out in a few months, and he is sure flash-light bulbs, radio tubes, typewriters, filing cabinets, and razor blades are all wearing out faster than ever. Well, I can only report that since we sell all these things, Macy's Bureau of Standards checks them with unsentimental technical procedures. It reports no difficulty in finding good brands of all these articles.

Look at it another way. Any time Macy's thinks it can improve an item, or can lower its cost without depreciating its quality, or can think up a desirable new product, there is nothing to keep us from ordering such merchandise made by our manufacturing resources. As it happens, we do this constantly, and so do other large retailers. (Let me cite the case of mattress covers: quite recently, the only covers on the market were sleazy, shapeless, shrinkable, "buttoned" bags. Nobody had thought to make a better one until one of our buyers specified a new deal in mattress covers in 1948: made of Sanforized cotton of good quality, closed by a zipper. A small matter? It far outsells any other mattress cover we've ever had.)

This is one of a thousand reasons why I know that superior merchandise sells faster than inferior stuff. It has greater value to the customer, and customers very soon discover that. Our manufacturers know it too. They cannot long stand the preference of Macy's customers for the better item. They must meet the competing value, or fade.

That is why the professor's notion that business can generally hold good things back must be considered naïve. And this also helps account for something all economists recognize: that the real productivity of business in the United States has been steadily increasing for many generations now, from 2 to 3 per cent a year, from 20 to 30 per cent a decade. What other aspect of U.S. life has progressed so much?

What, then, might the professor do about business? I offer a suggestion. It is not to ask him to shout hosannas in honor of American business. Quite the contrary. I ask for *more* criticism—as well as more informed criticism.

And I, for one, would like to see the professor apply it where it can do most good: in training the young.

At any rate, here is the suggestion, made by a colleague of mine: "Encourage youngsters to bring to school merchandise that has failed, and there examine it. Discuss the conditions that led to the failure, compare the claims alleged to have been made with its actual performance, consider the likelihood of abuse or misuse as a causative factor . . . teach the class to be cautious of exaggerated claims and promiscuous superlatives. . . ."

This, and much more, was said in a talk as long ago as 1935, by the head of Macy's Bureau of Standards before a group of New York City educators. It still seems to me a useful thing to do, and one of the most direct contributions the professor and his associates could make to the advance of American business.

For the essence of American business is how much more responsive it is to its customers' sense of values than the professor seems to realize. As I have already suggested, business is more closely disciplined—by the millions of choices of what people buy (and do not buy) every day—than anything else in our democracy. And because of this discipline, it stands relatively very high in its continuing performance for the community.

Like the professor, I do not feel this is high enough. Yet generally, American business can rise most quickly only as the pressure of consumer demands and reactions to it rises.

And the more *informed* these demands are, the faster and higher business will rise.

Go to it, professor.

ALBERT LYND

The Advertiser Replies

This article was published in Fortune for June 1951, under the title, "Says Business to Mr. DeVoto. . . ."

Albert Lynd is a member of the New York advertising firm of Batten, Barton, Durstine & Osborn, Inc.

"The Professor," says Mr. DeVoto, explaining the professor's distaste for advertising, "is an expert, research is his trade, and he has mastered statistical method."

Nonsense. Some professors know statistical method and a great many do not. A bright girl in the research organization of a large advertising agency knows more about statistical methods and statistical fallacies than the entire English department of Harvard University. And I'll throw in most of the history department (where I was once a bat boy for professors), the philosophy, classics, and fine arts departments, most of the law faculty, and all of the faculty of theology.

DeVoto identifies a scholar as one who "undertakes to determine the meaning, significance, and implications of what he encounters." Right. If he had applied that definition in a study of advertising-agency procedures, he could not have made the preposterous statement that an advertising writer begins with a "basic theorem" that most people in this country have the mental age of children. No competent copywriter would be silly enough to make that kind of a priori approach to his job.

A good advertising man is a first-class pragmatist. If he has any basic theorem at all, it is that most advertising is an intrusion upon the time and attention of people; a justifiable one but an intrusion nonetheless. The reader has bought the magazine for something other than the ads. Whether his mental age is eight or eighteen or some Greek letter, the advertisers may not expect that he will have any conscious reason for interrupting his concentration on a story, a comic strip, or a word quiz. Therefore the copywriters undertake to stop him in spite of himself.

Most people, according to advertising tests that are in no sense "mythological," are stopped most effectively by appeals to strong instincts like the desire for health, security, or social approval. The people who are so stopped include geniuses, dullards, and the vast majority who are neither. No judgment upon anyone's mental age is involved when an intruder attempts to get attention from a preoccupied person—whether a plumber or a professor—by speaking above a whisper.

The copywriter neither creates nor imagines the intellectual or emotional level at which he will obtain the best response. He *seeks* it with some carefully tested instruments, of which more later. Of course, most appeals are designed for the largest audience, but the mass market has proved as varied in quality as it is massive in quantity. It often happens that certain products sell most effectively when the same appeal is used in Negro newspapers and in Ivy League college newspapers.

With proper allowance for the considerable number of people who are fooling their friends, if not themselves, about their invulnerability, there is of course a minority so highly resistant that advertising has no effect—reverse or otherwise—on them. Mr. DeVoto indicates that he understands there just aren't enough of these to support any significant volume of production of autos or soap or cigarettes. (There aren't even enough of them among the alumni of leading universities, including DeVoto's, to support so pure a product as education. For really tough jobs of fund raising these institutions have called in competent advertising hands.) Mr. DeVoto also knows, perhaps, that professors are able to live better, ride better, eat better, and smell better than they would otherwise on their present incomes because the market created among people who do respond to the usual advertising appeals is as large as it is.

DeVoto's demonstrations of "bad faith" are built on parody. He uses literary exaggeration to charge business with advertising exaggeration. Does he have chapter and verse on specific skulduggery, statistical or other? If free competitive business makes any sense at all, there is no lack of good faith in the effort to increase sales of Googler's product by warning young ladies that without it they may offend young men and vice versa; by coining impressive neologisms for its effective ingredients; by giving truthful evidence of its use by "experts," doctors, or anybody else to whose views many people may defer. The condition of good faith here is the actual efficacy of the product for the advertised purpose. Is it "bad faith" when a publisher, perhaps DeVoto's publisher, plugs a book by selecting the most favorable sentences from the most favorable reviews, after no little effort to secure good reviews?

In the fun of goring Googler with a contrived dilemma, DeVoto may have overlooked the possibility that advertising claims are true. Except in times of shortage every product must have some competitive advantage, or it must sell at a price advantage. The advantage may be in something as subjective as taste, where it *is* so if thinking makes it so. The preferences of many people for one brand of beer or of cigarettes are obvious. Each brand is somewhat different in taste from others, and its fans believe their preferred taste to be the best taste. They are quite right. The manufacturer is entitled to the same opinion, and to the right of trying to induce even more people to share it.

Manufacturers do have laboratories—and in the plural. They do add new and useful ingredients to their products. Some cigarettes are easier on throats than others. (DeVoto has never seen one advertised as a "remedy.") Advertisers must be prepared to prove their claims under sanctions more effective than professional disapproval. The Federal Trade Commission may be set in motion on a *competitor's* complaint. DeVoto may retain his skepticism about the ethics of businessmen; but surely he should credit them with enough sense to be vigilant in watching each other. If he is tempted to think that advertisers may play footsie with each other on claims, the printed cases of the FTC will put him straight. There are other sanctions: the scrutiny of the Food and Drug Administration, the Better Business Bureau, the censorship policies of various media, the industry's own Copy Code of the American Association of Advertising Agencies. Good faith is more than encouraged by good intramural policing.

Are there any misrepresentations in advertising? Of course there are. But the Federal Trade Commission, an agency of a government that has not been madly in love with business, examines many thousands of advertisements—and it finds an average of only 3 per cent that require any "further study."

The ratio of good to bad faith is certainly as high for advertisers as it is, say, for professors. The model scholar and teacher whom DeVoto invokes has a lot of brothers whose principal labor is to rig courses for the benefit of the tuition cashier—and who have not been unaware of the G.I. Bill of Rights. A recent release showed, for example, that there are now 6,728 courses in "advertising, public relations, and marketing" in "degree-granting institutions." Many of them are excellent, I know; perhaps most of them are. But the enrollment in 6,728 courses must be so many times greater than job opportunities in these fields that the piling up of such courses is fraudulent in effect if not in intention.

One could go on about the good faith of professors, about the endless hokum of the schools of education, about some of the courses for which colleges now grant degrees. DeVoto gave me leave to go on when he raised the question of guilt by association. But let's both be sensible. On this line of reasoning one could confect a lot of indignation against the Twelve Apostles. And on the matter of good faith they tested eleven to one.

The second horn of Googler's dilemma is the quality of his own intelligence. As DeVoto puts it, if Googler doesn't believe his own advertising he's in bad faith; if he does believe it he's dumb. The second premise is as false as the first. DeVoto is categorically wrong when he says, "How advertising gets sales is not, in any acceptable sense, *known*." If, as he implies, the claims of advertising research people are "sooth-saying," there are quite a few professors of psychology in universities who must be soothsayers. It is under their tutelage that most advertising test procedures have been set up.

I have no room here for the detailed instruction of Mr. DeVoto in the manifold controls and precautions of copy research, media research, depth studies, coupon returns, hidden offers, split runs, sales checks, inventory audits, and other procedures by which advertising effectiveness is tested. DeVoto can find out how much soothsaying there is in them by calling on a few professors who know something about advertising practice. Perhaps Neil Borden of the Harvard Business School, or Darrell Lucas of N.Y.U., or Harry Hepner of Syracuse can explain to him how it is that methods that are scientific in an academic plant become pseudoscientific when they are used in business for profit. Of course there is much that is not fully known about advertising effectiveness; some things will not be known until the unlikely day when all the secrets of the psyche are revealed to the professors who seek them. But what *is* known is vast. If the sense in which it is known is not acceptable to Mr. DeVoto, it is not because of any lack of help to advertisers from duly ordained members of the profession in whose name he expresses his suspicion of business. I believe that the statistical erudition of professors who do research and consulting work for advertising agencies will satisfy his requirements.

Many professors are indeed suspicious of business. I can confirm that out of my own experience as a professorial novitiate. But the reasons of many are simpler than DeVoto's. Professors are worthy fellows who are usually not well paid. Businessmen are better paid without being noticeably more worthy. Resentment against Googler, then, is understandable, even when Googler sweats on university boards to raise money and invest it wisely in corporations that owe their earnings to advertising in order that there may be income to pay professors who are suspicious of advertising.

I recall another reason for professorial discomfort in the presence of business. The logic of business is hackneyed. The plant and production achievements of American enterprisers (with which DeVoto is not displeased) are essentially related to their merchandising achievements, including advertising. But the repeated statements of this sound as trite as Home, Mother, and other irritants of the sophisticate. They are nonetheless valid, for banality has nothing to do with validity. Yet they are so often intoned by dismal speakers at dull dinners that a sensitive and literate critic may be goaded to snappish suspicion of the whole business of business. Alert businessmen today realize this, and are doing something to improve the esthetics of business talk. But the dull reiteration of a principle has nothing to do with its truth. Many professors are able to diminish their suspicions of business when they can stash away a few common stocks, but their irritation at business dialectic is undiminished.

I'm surprised that Mr. DeVoto didn't acquire a better understanding of the reasons and the rightness of modern merchandising during his own successful business experience as an author of pseudonymous fiction for mass-circulation magazines. That is a very proper activity—but it is truly a business. Its market is analyzed and its merchandise designed by enterprisers who assume what every advertising man assumes: if there is a legitimate profit in selling the most goods to the most people, there is a legitimate activity in hawking the goods as persuasively as possible.

Yet, like most advertising men, I am an admirer of DeVoto. I don't mean merely in respect to his writing, which is always invigorating and which in this case may possibly be good for the souls of some of the more dreary business orators. I admire as much his ability at attention getting (and in the advertising business you get to be a connoisseur of this). With almost any material he gets attention. He could get as much with a pro-business article—and in fact once did, with a sensible spoof of *avant-garde* business haters. When I first saw him in action around Harvard more than twenty years ago, only beardless students were the beneficiaries of his waspishness. But it sold very well, then as now.

He might have made a fortune as an advertising man.

BERNARD D. NOSSITER

Wages and Prices

The article from which the following excerpts were drawn was published in Harper's magazine for July 1959, under the title, "The Hidden Affair Between Big Business and Big Labor."

Bernard D. Nossiter has reported on national economic and labor problems for the Washington Post-Times-Herald since 1955.

A big part of American industry is now quietly reshaping itself into an entirely new kind of economic structure. This pattern is quite different from anything that Adam Smith—or Karl Marx—ever dreamed of. It is also a flat contradiction of both the classical idea of competitive free enterprise, and the Communist theory of class war.

In crude terms, it might be described as a sort of corporate syndicalism, linking big business and big unions into an unacknowledged partnership. The pattern varies greatly, of course, from one industry to another. Even where it is most advanced, the liaison between the supposedly rival institutions is far from solid. It is more often a furtive and uneasy alliance between the top bureaucrats of the unions and the corporations—an arrangement that neither party can publicly admit and that most of the participants insist is just gossip.

But thanks to the longest-continued hearings in Congress—the highly publicized McClellan investigation and the little-noticed Kefauver inquiry—a great body of evidence has been assembled. It points to two unmistakable conclusions:

(1) The tacit collaboration between management and union officers has been thriving all through the period of postwar prosperity, and is still spreading.

(2) It seems to be closely connected with rising prices, persistent unemployment, and slow economic growth. . . .

This new pattern is often described by its beneficiaries in one magic word, "stability." To the big corporation's managers, stability means ever-rising prices and profits, freedom from new competitive threats, and profitable stock options in an ever-rising stock market. To the big union's officers, stability means an ever-rising level of wages and fringe benefits for the members—with suitable rewards for the leader whose wisdom has brought this about. Neither union members nor corporate stockholders complain much. The workers who are employed enjoy ever bigger paychecks that outstrip any rise in prices. The stockholders usually can expect their dividends and the prices of their shares to march upward even faster than the wage gains.

Unhappily, not everyone can rejoice in the pleasures of this brave new world. About ten million Americans own stock; about 165 million don't. Employed union members in the high-wage basic industries are also a relatively small, favored group. Trailing behind are pensioners, farmers, the unemployed, white-collar workers, public employees, and many others. Several economists believe that the recent "paradox"—an economic recession side by side with a rising price level—was caused by the industry-union arrangements and the distortions they created. These theorists also think that the current state of affairs—a comparatively slow recovery (by most measurements, the advance has been slower than that in any of the three postwar slumps), relatively high unemployment (between 5 and 6 per cent of the work force compared to a "normal" 3 to 4 per cent), and slow overall economic growth—can be traced to big industry and big unions taking a disproportionate share of the pie. . . .

But why should the corporate managers be so willing to see prices rise?

A Washington investment adviser, Eugene Havas, recently supplied an answer. Share prices largely reflect earnings and dividends. As earnings go up, stock prices go up. And thanks to stock options, Havas had noted, the corporate managers can get handsome rewards from rising stock prices. They can and often do vote themselves options on large blocks of their company's stock.

For example, U.S. Steel last year gave 120 of its executives options on 151,100 shares at $55. This spring, the stock had risen $40 a share above this. Any time a top Steel executive needed cash, he picked up his telephone, told the company treasurer to issue him a few thousand of his optioned shares, and told his broker to sell them at the market price. Thus our executive cleared $40 a share with two telephone calls—and without investing a cent of his own money. And if he can wait six months and one day before calling his broker, he will be taxed no more than 25 per cent on his profit because it is a long-term capital gain.

Since the stock profit depends on investors' estimates of the corporation's future profits, the managers with options have a vested interest in raising prices to increase their company's earnings.

An instructive case was cited by John Blair, the economist for Kefauver's antitrust subcommittee. He calculates that the net profits per ton for U.S. Steel rose from $7.47 in the first quarter of 1953 to $19.31 in the fourth quarter of 1958. At the same time, U.S. Steel was producing at 102.1 per cent of capacity in the first 1953 quarter and at only 72.7 per cent in the last 1958 quarter. . . .

Against this backdrop, thoughtful actors in the contemporary economic drama began expressing their concern openly last fall. One such was Arthur Goldberg, the wise general counsel for the Steelworkers.

Goldberg has a deserved reputation for attempting to harmonize his client's interests with the public welfare. He is counsel to AFL-CIO's

Ethical Practices Committee and probably did more than any single man to bring about the merger of the two federations in 1955.

Last November, he suggested periodic discussions between corporate and union leaders, with government officials sitting in on the talks. The talks, he said, should deal with inflation, automation, and all the other things that the managers could usefully discuss. But even this modest proposal fell on deaf ears. Some sophisticated managements have shown a speck of interest; a few powerful financiers are enthusiastic; no union manager has yet been willing to endorse it.

But Goldberg appears to be giving his union clients some good advice. It really runs like this:

"Boys, you'd better show some voluntary moderation while you can. If you don't, something like enforced wage-and-price control is on the horizon."

Goldberg, as usual, was a good prophet. In the late winter, Kefauver warned McDonald, Blough & Co. that the forthcoming negotiation was their last chance to arrive at a bargain that would *not* be made the excuse for a price increase. Kefauver said Congress would not stand for another performance of the shopworn drama—big wage demand, a strike, a wage increase, and a price boost. The Washington *Post* said editorially that Kefauver had read not only the temper of Congress but of the nation. Several days later, President Eisenhower virtually repeated Kefauver's theme. However, the steel industry chided the Administration for interfering and the Administration has since adopted a much less interventionist stance.

Taking the Congressional temperature is a difficult task. But reporters on Capitol Hill are sensing a new mood that spills across party lines. Democrats with such diverse constituencies as Senators Clark of Pennsylvania, O'Mahoney of Wyoming, Neuberger of Oregon, Gore and Kefauver of Tennessee, Proxmire of Wisconsin, and Douglas of Illinois are troubled about administered prices and wages. In the House, Democratic Representatives as far apart geographically as Bowles in Connecticut, Reuss in Wisconsin, Udall in Arizona, Johnson in Colorado, and Cohelan in California are similarly troubled.

Several farm-belt Republicans, notably Wiley of Wisconsin, have also grumbled about the price-wage spirals of big business and big labor. He and two fellow Republicans, Langer of North Dakota and Keating of New York, have put in their names as co-sponsors of Kefauver's bill to establish a Department of Consumers.

Some of these legislators may be longer on intelligence than influence. However, if they are reinforced by the collective wisdom of the Federal Reserve Board—a group with a different political orientation but certainly just as dedicated to the public welfare—the economic game could well find itself with some new rules.

In brief, circumstances have dictated what one reporter has called a quiet revolution in economic thought among Washington's most thoughtful officials. This revolution has three leading ideas:

(1) Oligopoly, not competition, has become the dominant mode of American economic life. In their search for profits, oligopolists tend to restrain production and employment and raise prices.

(2) The traditional antagonism between unions and management in oligopolistic or concentrated industries is disappearing. Conscious and unconscious collusion takes its place, lifting wages for some and prices (including stock prices) for others.

(3) The public interest in economic affairs has long ago been established in theory and practice. Business enjoys outright subsidies, plus hidden subsidies like tariffs and tax gimmicks, and makes large sales to government. Unions are also supported by government through complex codes guaranteeing organizing and bargaining rights. Therefore, it is no real departure to insist on a public interest in the key wage and price decisions. . . .

What, then, can be done. . . ? The Capital's better minds have been busy wrestling with this one for months. A respectable but small minority favors the traditional antitrust approach. If concentrations of economic power exist on either the industry or the union side, then break them up and restore free, competitive markets.

This is a Jeffersonian approach that is not only concerned with proper pricing, production, and employment but has a deep commitment to the spiritual values of the independent man. It is attractive and sanctified by tradition. Everybody, including the biggest violators, pays allegiance to the antitrust laws and the glories of competition.

But most of the economists and many lawyers are skeptical of its practical value. They make two objections to the antitrust approach:

(1) Existing laws—the Sherman and Clayton Acts—outlaw collusive arrangements between producers or between employers and unions. But in the sophisticated modern world, you can enjoy all the blessings of a price-fixing conspiracy without violating the law. That's what trade associations, conventions, friendly lunches, and the trade press are for.

(2) New laws to make administered price arrangements illegal probably would lead into a blind alley.

H. Thomas Austern, partner in Covington and Burling, a Washington firm on a par with Wall Street's corporation law factories, has some pertinent observations about any such new law which would necessarily rely on a doctrine of "assumed conspiracy."

"The resulting violation is not readily susceptible to judicial remedy," Austern says. "I cannot see how a court could, by injunction, tell a price leader never to change its prices up or down, or enjoin other producers from following in order to remain competitive.

"Unless our courts are to fall into the trap of regulating prices by continuous judicial supervision of an industry, I cannot fathom what form of injunction they might fashion."

However, the trust-beaters reply, under an "assumed conspiracy" doctrine couldn't the court order divestiture—breaking up one big corporation into many little ones? The Justice Department's antitrust division is exploring this possibility, even without new law and relying on the old Acts.

Conservatives like Austern argue that "even if fragmentation of companies were desirable or feasible, there are many who doubt whether modern mass production could survive under it."

Many more economists, on the other hand, are convinced that mass production would be carried on much more efficiently by more and smaller units. They doubt that total output is increased when one corporation like General Motors dominates everything from autos to buses to diesel locomotives to auto financing. They believe output would be increased if U.S. Steel were not either first or second in producing most major steel products.

Even so, few economists would rely on trustbusting to achieve the major economic goals. They think that dissolution to restore competition will not work and that antitrust laws cannot really bust trusts.

As Galbraith told the Kefauver subcommittee, "To suppose that the antitrust laws will work the kind of revolution which will reconcile full employment with price stability is out of the question. This would mean a wholesale revision in industrial structure—a wholesale disintegration of existing business units."

This does not mean that anyone wants to repeal the Sherman and Clayton Acts. The biggest violators defend them largely because they serve as an excuse to do nothing more. Less interested observers would retain the laws because, as Galbraith said, "They bring the conscience of the community to bear on the problem of economic power. . . . And thus they restrain the strong firm in its relation with weaker customers, suppliers, and competitors."

What then? Thinking in academic and political circles is now being drawn to some form of public intervention in the key price and wage decisions. However there is almost universal opposition to direct controls over wages and prices. Instead a kind of middle ground between free markets and controls is being sought. This would be a remote but non-coercive relative of the processes which now decide public-utility prices.

Galbraith, one of the first to suggest this, lays down three principles for such intervention. It should, he says, be:

(1) LIMITED—it should apply only to firms and unions in concentrated industries which have a decisive share of the market power.

(2) SIMPLE—perhaps a government panel should require these corporations and unions to justify in advance each proposed price and wage in-

crease. The panel would then make specific recommendations in the light of agreed-on national goals.

Just what criteria would be used to determine a "justified" increase is a puzzler. Business critics of the idea have said that inability to spell out these criteria will make the scheme unworkable. Since the corporation will likely argue that it needs the increase to restore a past level of profits or to fatten its present inadequate earnings, the "just" price implies a "just" profit rate. And any such notion frightens the corporate managers.

On the other side, the unions contend that the proposal could lead to great industrial unrest. Smart corporation lawyers, it is said, would tie any price change to periods when wage contracts expire. Then, the union could be foreclosed from getting any increase until lengthy arguments had been settled, perhaps in court. Meanwhile, workers would grumble at being asked to continue work under their expired contract until the lawyers all had their day.

(3) CONCILIATORY FACT-FINDING—at least at first we might rely on panel findings to mobilize public opinion to serve as a restraint on union and corporate managers. If this did not work, then sanctions or penalties would be in order.

Some of the obvious respondents before such a panel would be Donner's General Motors (51 per cent of 1958 auto output) and Walter Reuther's United Auto Workers; Blough's U.S. Steel (29 per cent of ingot capacity) and McDonald's Steelworkers; Ralph Cordiner's General Electric Co. (owned 16 per cent of the electrical machinery industry's assets in 1947, the last year in which data was compiled) and James Carey's International Union of Electrical Workers. Trailing along with the price leaders would likely be Ford, Chrysler, Bethlehem Steel, Republic Steel, Westinghouse, Western Electric (an American Telephone & Telegraph subsidiary), and Radio Corp. of America. With their leaders, they dominate autos, steel, and electrical machinery—the industries that Means has shown accounted for the lion's share of the wholesale price rises since 1953.

So far, big industry and big labor have recoiled in horror from this idea. There are some notable exceptions. Reuther, for example, is a vigorous, long-time supporter. A few executives in one of the smartest steel companies think government intervention is inevitable. Incidentally, this corporation is one of the ten biggest producers.

On Capitol Hill, O'Mahoney, Clark, and Reuss have sponsored bills along Galbraith's line. Neuberger has introduced one authorizing temporary price, wage, and rent ceilings. Kefauver has written one to insure that the general public has an advocate—via a Consumers Department—before any panel.

The idea is in its infancy—or strictly speaking, second childhood, because the voluntary, wartime price fixing before OPA resembles it. There hasn't been enough discussion yet for realistic notions to emerge about its strengths, weaknesses, and the technical details of how it would work.

One obvious argument is that the method interferes with "free" markets. But Galbraith replies that the panels "bring the public interest to bear on what is now private pricefixing. It is obvious that if private discretion did not exist, the problem would not arise."

Another argument holds that prices would never be reduced if an industry always had to justify an increase.

To this proponents answer that concentrated industries almost never cut prices anyway. Moreover, Kefauver's Consumer Department might petition for a price decrease and set the panels in motion whenever it decided that output, employment, and price stability would benefit thereby.

Finally, the critics point to the long history of federal regulation. They note that in time, the "independent" commissions become willing vassals of the industry they are regulating. The Federal Communications Commission, for example, is suspected of having been far too friendly to the radio and television networks; one of its former commissioners has been accused of selling his vote to a TV license applicant. Similarly, the airlines and the Civil Aeronautics Board are thought to have had unprofessional relations. In New York, Governor Rockefeller thinks his racing "czar" has enjoyed too many favors from track owners. The sensation-minded Harris Committee on Legislative Oversight (Sherman Adams and Bernard Goldfine were its two major diversions) scratched a little of this surface. Another subcommittee on the Senate side, under John Carroll of Colorado, may complete the abortive Harris inquiry. And Harris himself is readying another investigation.

However, the march toward rationalization—an industrial structure with fewer corporations and considerable private planning—appears unlikely to be halted. All over the globe, men are planning their material arrangements to overcome the obsolete problem of material want. In India, Puerto Rico, the United Kingdom, in Europe's coal-steel community and the Common Market, in all the Communist nations, men have turned from reliance on impersonal market forces to some conscious and public planning of investment, prices, and wages.

More of this already goes on in the United States than is generally understood. Tax laws play a potent part in investment decisions. The planning of a General Motors, U.S. Steel, or a Standard Oil (N.J.) plays a decisive part in the nation's economy. The question now posed is whether these private corporations will be allowed to continue making decisions of vast public consequence without some kind of informed public surveillance.

GLEN PERRY

Businessmen As Politicians

This speech was delivered to the Greater New Brunswick Chamber of Commerce, New Brunswick, New Jersey, on March 15, 1960.

Glen Perry has been assistant director of the public relations department of E. I. du Pont de Nemours and Company since 1944.

Several centuries ago an attractive young girl who wanted to become a nun went to see Vincent de Paul for advice. The priest, later to become a saint, was very old and very wise, and he gave her some very profound counsel. This is what he told her:

"You must love the poor very much, or they will hate you for giving them bread."

You might wonder why I quote St. Vincent in introducing some thoughts on the responsibility of the businessman. I quote it because it seems to me that it contains the answer to many of the problems that are bothering us so much in our human relationships today.

The responsibility of the businessman is a broad field. At its broadest it could be said that the responsibility of the businessman is to keep the United States a going concern. The reason is that the United States, which started out in life as an agricultural country, about sixty or seventy years ago entrusted its fate to an industrial economy. It is too late to change back even if we wanted to, and so we've got to sink or swim with what we have.

It is because this almost terrifying responsibility has been placed on his shoulders that the businessman is so vitally important in our scheme of things. Of course, this big responsibility can be broken down into a number of subdivisions. There is the responsibility to provide a product or a service and to make a profit while doing it. There is the responsibility to operate legally. But the responsibility I want to talk about tonight lies in this field of human relationships.

My reason for choosing it is twofold. First, it seems to me that it is in this area that business and industry face their most critical problems. I believe there are few sales, research, or production problems so difficult that business cannot cope with them. If we get into trouble, I shouldn't expect to see it come from those directions. Our peril lies in the field of human relations—in what are commonly called public relations, employee relations, community relations.

Here there are no hard and fast rules. You cannot tell how you are doing by adding up a column of figures, or by looking at a chart. That is probably why so many businessmen are a little uneasy in this field; why they tend to be skeptical about the men who work in it. But, uneasy or skeptical, the fact remains that it is in these human relationships that business will ultimately win big, or lose big. That is my first reason.

My second reason is that from where I sit some businessmen are embracing very dangerous programs, based on what I believe is unsound thinking. The way many of them are leaping into the political arena is part of it—an important part. I mean to talk about this a little later. For the moment I'll content myself with saying that this does not mean that I think we have no business in politics. We have. But there is no reward for doing it in such a way as to make enemies. As you people in New Brunswick know well, the real aim of politics is to make friends, for your chances of getting what you want are obviously better that way.

Turning from this subject for a moment, let me say that business and industry exist and prosper only by sufferance of the American people. This means that business and industry must do an effective job of winning public support. It is at this point that the more hard-boiled businessman says (as he has said to me more than once), "Phooey! What difference does it make if people don't like me as long as they buy my product? What can they do to me?"

The answer is: plenty. Why do you think the S.E.C. exists? Who do you suppose was responsible for the Federal Trade Commission? Do you believe the Antitrust Division just happened? Do you really think that the present income tax rates in the upper brackets are intended to produce revenue, in the face of the belief held by so many tax experts that the returns would rise if the top rates were lowered? The fact is these rates were intended to be punitive, and the reason was the unpopularity of those with large incomes—the idea that people with low incomes would be more willing to hold still for a twenty per cent tax if the Government took ninety-one per cent from the rich.

No, business could make no worse mistake than to assume that the American people are helpless to punish those whom they dislike or mistrust. The government in any democracy exists to do what the majority of the voters want. It follows that the government will fear and dislike anyone the people of the country fear and dislike, and will make the fact evident in any number of unpleasant ways.

Considering the importance of this area, the businessman will do well to approach it with the same care he would spend on some more easily measurable problem. I admit there has been a great deal of provocation to take an emotional and a hasty, unconsidered approach. Because they have been pushed around ever since the Great Depression by the Government, by organized labor, and by opinion leaders, businessmen have a strong and natural urge to come out swinging.

The bull in the corrida, goaded by the matador, does the same thing. He paws the earth. He lowers his head and charges blindly, and pretty soon he's dead and is being dragged out of the arena, leaving a trail in the dust, while his tormentor struts around receiving the plaudits of the crowd. It seems to me there is a lesson here for the businessman. It could be put very simply, like this: There is no law against using your head, and it is sometimes a very good idea.

So let's try to figure out, first, what we want to accomplish, and, second, how we can do it. I suggest that we want people to approve of us, to like us, and to trust us, because business can have the conditions under which it can operate most effectively only if it enjoys public liking and trust.

Can we accomplish this by fighting with people, by charging around like a Malay running amuck? I don't think so, and I don't think you do either. It is like a man courting a girl. If he is smart, he doesn't try to be as disagreeable as possible. I just don't think business can fight its way into public regard and trust. To me the pugnacious approach is a poor way for the businessman to discharge his responsibility in this field of human relations. For hate breeds hate, hostility breeds hostility. Neither one breeds understanding or confidence.

I am convinced that there are two things business must do: first, it must earn and deserve public favor; second, it has got to see to it that the public knows it deserves it. It's a lot easier to say either than it is to do it, but there isn't any other way.

One point I want to make: this is not peace-at-any-price thinking. I do not advocate turning the other cheek and hoping some day they'll get tired of slapping us around. Far from it. We are talking tactics, not strategy, and my concern is that what we do must be effective. It will profit us nothing if what we do leaves us no better off than we were before, with a real chance that it may leave us worse off.

And this brings me back to the matter of political activity. In touching on it, I realize I am doing so before an audience that includes some of the most advanced thinkers in this field in the entire country. New Brunswick has made very important contributions. What has been done here is both logical and legal, and my information is that it is producing results. Since this is so, I'd expect you to agree with me on what I want to say next. That is that it worries me when I hear a business leader say that business must become active in politics because it is the only group with the power to fight the political might of union labor. It worries me because, frankly, I don't think we have that kind of political power; and if we act on the assumption that we do have it, we are likely to throw some pretty fancy boomerangs. Perhaps our difficulty here stems from the oversimplification implicit in saying a company must engage in political activity. I think what we really mean is that the management group must do it; and that is, votewise, a very different thing. In the companies I know anything about, the wage-roll employees greatly outnumber the management. It follows, other things being equal, that in any event that is to be decided by counting noses management is licked before it starts. It can hope to win only if it can win friends outside its own ranks. This it must do by persuasion. I do not think it can do it by force.

Evidence bearing on this point was furnished in the recent steel strike. At the start the emphasis was on fighting inflation, and all signs were that union members were not especially involved emotionally in the strike. After all, inflation control was in their interest, too. But pretty soon the union propagandists, using the work rule proposals, took the play away from the steel companies, and emphasis was centered on the survival of the United Steel Workers. Once this issue reached major status, there was no longer any question about the emotional involvement of the steelworkers. They clearly regarded an attack on the union as an attack on themselves, and no one could doubt their determination to fight until hell froze over.

It also concerns me whenever I see evidence that large corporations regard their wage-roll employees as their enemies. To me such an attitude—and fortunately it is not prevalent—is shocking. I work for a company that believes its wage-roll employees are, individually, the good friends of management. They are men and women without whose efforts we'd be nowhere at all. They are important to us, as we are to them. We respect them, and we like them. We believe they respect us and like us. You may have noted that I said we believe our wage-roll employees are, individually, the friends of management. I used the word individually because that is the key. We don't think of them as a group. We don't treat them as a group.

This is a question of attitude. To paraphrase Saint Vincent, if you don't like your employees very much, they won't thank you for the fringe benefits, the pay increases. They'll take them, yes, but they won't like you any better for extending them.

There are, of course, times and situations where there is no alternative to fighting one's employees, just as family life is never one everlasting era of peace. And, fortunately, a fight doesn't mean eternal enmity, unless it is that kind of a fight. When it is over, the erstwhile opponents can shake hands and take up the old relationship. It has been our experience that management can talk to its employees as friends, and if performance matches the words, their respect and their regard can be won and held in the face of the effort of the most powerful unions to alienate them. Management, I believe, must set the tone, and it must do this without ever losing sight of its objective. That, I take it, is to maintain the sort of relationship with its employees that makes for the most effective operation of the organization. It is much easier to keep one's temper, even in the face of extreme provocation, when you have clearly in mind what you are trying to accomplish.

Relating this to politics, it seems to me that the aim should be not to seek the essentially negative goal of defeating the unions, a course that always carries with it the danger of disaffecting wage-roll people generally, but rather to approach the very positive goal of winning support for the management position.

Let me turn to another point. I spent seventeen years in newspaper work, and a good many of those years were devoted to covering politics at the local, state, and national levels. I realized early that politics is a game for professionals. I can recall no amateur, beginning with the late Wendell Wilkie down through silk-stocking candidates for the New York City Board of Aldermen, who was any sort of a match for the highly talented professionals. While for a couple of weeks in 1940 I'll confess I thought differently, it was clear in retrospect that Mr. Wilkie never had a chance of defeating the Champ.

Despite all this, one of the stock items in the American credo is that anyone can make a successful career in politics. More than that, the credo would have you believe that a man can, if he is a business executive, do it in his spare time and with rather less thought than he gives to his golf game.

This is a dangerous illusion. Politics cannot be practiced successfully in odd moments by those who have no real acquaintance with it, no real experience, and if you come right down to it, no real interest in anything but results. Granting the occasional exception, it is especially hard for business executives, who already have plenty of problems, to find the time to do a really effective job in this field. On the other hand, labor leaders seem to find plenty of time for this sort of thing.

More than that, the whole approach to life of the businessman and the politician differs radically. It's not easy for them to get on the same wave length, to communicate with one another in the real sense of the word. This is especially true because I have learned from experience that the average business executive feels deep in his heart that there is something unworthy about politics, that it is a dirty business. Again, I concede exceptions. Matching this is the fact that the average politician considers the business executive to be naive, uninformed, and hopelessly impractical when it comes to politics.

As an example, there was the 1958 election in Ohio, in which the business leaders insisted that a right-to-work measure be introduced and supported by the Republican Party. I was in Ohio shortly before the election and found those with a real knowledge of politics scared to death about what would happen on Election Day because of the presence of the right-to-work measure on the ballot. You will perhaps remember that their fears were amply justified, for the Republicans lost heavily in their Congressional delegation and also in the State Legislature. Impartial analysts attributed a great deal of the result to the effect of the right-to-work measure on the electorate.

In this connection let me quote Vice President Nixon: "All that the right-to-work movement accomplished in 1958 was to serve as a red flag in bringing out a tremendous organized labor vote which was predominantly Democratic. Those who supported right-to-work with their time and money would have been far better advised to have contributed to the election of candidates for the state and national legislatures who could be counted upon to consider and vote for necessary labor legislation fearlessly and intelligently."

Here was a situation in which the professional politicians knew the dangers that lay ahead, but were unable to persuade the overenthusiastic amateurs in the business ranks who were contributing a great deal of the money.

Another point: We might as well face the fact that business is in a poor position opposite labor, politically speaking, for two other reasons. In the first place, management cannot help being set apart from the rank and file of employees and their families. Management, in its regard for the soundness of the business and the welfare of the stockholders, has sometimes got to take positions that will not sit well with the wage-roll group.

In addition to giving orders, an occupation seldom very popular with those taking them, management is in a very real sense an umpire, determining how sales revenue shall be divided among the employees, the owners of the business, and the customers. I know of no game in which anyone has much affection for the umpire. So, you might say that union leaders have a built-in advantage over management here.

In the second place, politics is a way of life for any union leader. This is true because he has to be elected, and having won the office, he has got to remain sufficiently popular to be able to win re-election. The result is that the union leader is a very practiced and experienced political operator; he must be in order to survive. It is second nature for him to carry these skills from the field of union politics to the field of state or national politics.

One could contrive a similar situation in the ranks of management only by providing that the executives of a corporation would have to stand annually for election by the employees. I guarantee that, if this were the case, you would find management developing skilled political leaders by the thousands, instead of producing a comparative handful. This is another way of saying that the average businessman has the latent ability to be a very fine politician, indeed. But he has never developed this talent and really lacks the incentive to do so.

All that I have said so far is admittedly on the negative side; and if I were to let it go here, I guess I'd be a ringer for Charlie Wilson's hound dog that just sat on its fanny and howled. I am not going to, however. I do not feel for one minute that business and businessmen have got to sit back and do nothing as the only alternative to doing the wrong thing. Our hands are not tied, and I see no necessity for our losing by default.

I haven't the time to outline a complete program of political activity here, nor would it be especially relevant to my subject. Anyway, you businessmen around New Brunswick have done a very fine job of it yourselves. But I would like to conclude my remarks with some heartfelt comments on the positive side of the picture. I think that business must start with the premise that the greatest ambition the politician has is to get elected, or alternatively, to get re-elected. He does this by trying to please the voters. If he thinks it will please the voters for him to make things hard for business, then you can depend upon it that he will do his best to make businessmen wish they had all become beachcombers or practitioners of yoga.

On the other hand, if the politician feels that to adopt such an attitude would be unpopular with the voters, he will be so considerate of business that industrialists will probably think the millennium has set in. Since I have always felt that when you want to get results you should go to headquarters, I suggest that the politician's boss is the voter and that it is the voter, rather than the politician, that business should be thinking about when it comes to political activity.

It has been my experience that the general public is really not hostile to business. The trouble is that it lacks the information on which to base intelligent judgment. Its ideas of how business operates, why it operates, and who gets what because of it are generally about half a century behind the times. The average man is inclined to think of business as it actually was before World War I. And if business could do nothing more than create in the minds of sixty per cent of Americans the picture of business as it actually thinks and operates today, it would solve half its troubles. I don't see why we can't do this.

As a step in doing it, I think businessmen ought to get better acquainted with the real power elite of the United States, by which I mean the men who do more than anyone else to form opinion in this country: newspaper columnists, radio and television commentators, college professors, ministers. The sad fact is that the overwhelming majority of these people simply don't know what they're talking about when they get on the subject of business and industry, and it's our fault.

I can tell you that men like Walter Reuther and other labor leaders embrace every opportunity to make contact with people in this group, to talk to them, to get to know them, and to sell their ideas to them. The average businessman, if he has ever even met them, seldom or never seeks them out; and if you want to know where the battle is really being lost by default, it is here.

In the short range, business may, faced with immediate crisis, try to persuade politicians of the justice of its cause, just as the fire department rushes to handle any blazes that come along. But even here one should move with care and without forgetting the objective. Beyond that, fire prevention, rather than fire extinction, must be the long-range aim.

It is also true that business can serve both itself and the country by encouraging its employees to take an interest in the political parties of their choice. I think Johnson and Johnson has done an especially fine job of this. Courses in civics can play a useful part. But I'd hesitate to go much beyond this.

I admit it's a dramatic concept to picture one's self sitting back and pulling strings to decide who will run the country and what they will do. But it just doesn't work. I am convinced that the determined effort on the part of business to live right, to identify its interests with those of its employees and of the public, and to try to create popular understanding of these facts is the only long-range political activity by business that is sure to pay off. The reason is that it is the only one aimed at the very heart of our problem.

Business, that is, must state its case—effectively. For it will never be in a truly secure position until both major political parties thoroughly understand the importance of business to the country and the importance to business of having an atmosphere under which it can work most effectively. The urgency for this becomes more pressing with every passing day. For the fact is that the technology of European countries is rapidly equaling and in some cases surpassing our own. Their wage levels are considerably lower than ours, so that they can compete successfully against us, not only in their home markets but in our home markets as well, tariff or no tariff.

As I said at the outset, the United States has staked its future, for better or for worse, on the success of its business and its industry. We are entering a period of life-and-death competition, not among ourselves but with the business and industry of other countries, some of which mean to bury us and have said so. If the American people truly understood this; if organized labor truly understood this; then I don't think you would see demagogic politicians trying to make it harder for business to operate successfully, or doing everything they can to reduce the incentives for individual businessmen to succeed.

It's about time that we businessmen devoted ourselves to an intelligent, planned effort to make the American people understand what the stakes are today and what it will mean to them if either through carelessness or by design they create a situation in which the United States loses the economic war in which it is engaged. That, ladies and gentlemen, is a positive program, and it is a program that will produce results. It is in this respect that it differs from some of the more dramatic programs I have heard a few business leaders discussing these days.

Now, I started with St. Vincent de Paul, and I suppose I had better get around to him once more as I conclude my remarks. For the more I think about it, the more convinced I am that he epitomized the responsibility of the businessman in a few words. As I read him, what St. Vincent has to say to the modern-day businessman is this: no matter what you do for your employees, it will not be enough unless you do it because of deep and sincere respect and regard for them. And if it is not enough for your employees, it will not be enough for the American people.

CLARK MOLLENHOFF

Organized Labor and the Future

This speech was delivered before the 63rd Congress of American Industry, sponsored by the National Association of Manufacturers, at New York City on December 4, 1958.

Clark Mollenhoff has been reporting the Washington scene for the Des Moines Register and Tribune and other Cowles' publications since 1955. He was awarded a Pulitzer prize for national reporting in 1958, largely because of his work in exposing corrupt practices within the Teamsters union.

In the face of the hearings of the McClellan committee, there can be no doubt of the economic and political strength of labor unions in America today. The power held by the International Brotherhood of Teamsters overshadows anything the business barons of 60 years ago could have envisioned.

This is a power over every business in the nation. It is a power over every other union in America. It is a power that touches every home in America.

I asked Jimmy Hoffa if he wasn't afraid of anyone having such power as he possesses, and he shrugged it off with the comment that "I don't abuse it."

There is a tremendous power in the Teamsters union without any help from special laws, but we have this power augmented by large tax-exempt treasuries and special laws that make the operations immune from the anti-trust laws.

And, it should be clear that the special laws that give labor organizations the advantages they hold are a result of the political power that labor exerts.

What is the source of this tremendous political power that unions hold?

Some of it is the legitimate use of the force of the numbers of persons in organized labor, and the pressure that any large number of voters exerts in a democratic society.

But, the McClellan committee has demonstrated dramatically that much of the power flows from the millions of dollars that flow into political campaigns from union treasuries.

The Federal Corrupt Practices Act prohibits the use of union funds in federal campaigns. But, we have seen that union funds are used extensively in city, county and state political campaigns. And, some of this union money

—collected on a compulsory basis from union members—also finds its way indirectly into the federal campaigns from time to time.

These are tax-exempt funds. Under our present tax laws they should not be used for political campaigns, but it is being done. And, so far, the Internal Revenue Service has continued on its long-time lax policy of doing little or nothing about it.

Although this use of tax-exempt funds in politics is widespread, the operations of the Teamsters union, and specifically of Jimmy Hoffa, represent the most dramatic example of the evils inherent in allowing any union official a free hand in using union funds in politics.

James R. Hoffa, twice-convicted of labor law violations, has a million-dollar treasury in his home area of Detroit. He is given authority to use this money in politics, or in any other way that he feels benefits the Teamsters union. This has given Jimmy a lot of rope.

James R. Hoffa—who tolerates thugs, robbers, thieves, arsonists and dope peddlers in union office—has a million-dollar kitty for political donations to help mayors, sheriffs, judges, prosecutors and judges in the campaigns for office.

Examine how Hoffa and his Teamsters have used this money:

Hoffa used $42,000 to contribute to a campaign to try to elect his union attorney as governor of Michigan. That move was unsuccessful.

Hoffa and his organization contributed $17,500 to the successful 1956 campaign of Governor Herschel Loveless of Iowa, a Democrat.

But, Hoffa's organization is bipartisan, and can prove it. His Central States organization tossed more than $10,000 on Fred Hall, a Republican candidate for governor in Kansas, and Governor Docking, a Kansas Democrat, got a similar amount.

There were at least five states in which Hoffa admitted to the McClellan committee that he had money riding on one or both candidates for governor.

Hoffa took $22,000 in union funds and put it into a public relations firm that paid political campaign costs and $100 a week to a Wayne county Michigan judge. The contribution came during a period when the judge had a key role in a criminal prosecution involving some of Hoffa's closest associates in the Teamsters union.

This year, Hoffa put $11,000 into the campaign of a Democratic candidate for county attorney in Wayne County, Michigan.

The McClellan committee has brought out testimony showing what such contributions can do to law enforcement, prosecution and the attitude of the courts.

Union members as well as employers have told their stories of the lack of effective law enforcement where union violence was involved. Bombings, beatings and arson went unpunished in many cases because of a lack of law enforcement.

Police and prosecutors were shown to be lax in following up crimes when there was a union angle. Officials who weren't dishonest, were simply afraid to stir up the hornet's nest that would be involved in aggressive action.

It took the McClellan committee to bring out evidence of a $30,000 pay-off by the Teamsters union to a Tennessee judge in connection with a criminal case involving one of Hoffa's top leaders in the South. The Tennessee judge was finally impeached.

This was a judge who had control over all criminal prosecutions in his county—he had the reins over the grand jury.

Once that pay-off was made, the court was forever beholden to the crooked Teamsters who made it. Union members and employers had little or no chance for a square break in that court, regardless of the facts or the law.

Union members have told the McClellan committee of their futile efforts to get aggressive law enforcement when they were beaten, or threatened for challenging the entrenched union leadership.

Employers and lawyers have testified that there were areas in which it would do them no good to try to assert their rights to injunctions because the courts were stacked against them.

Uncontrolled money power can corrupt politics, and we have seen the documented examples of how it has corrupted politics. Such huge contributions carry an obligation that should not be ignored.

Adequate control over union funds is more important to employers and union members than the so-called right-to-work law.

Control of union funds strikes at the heart of the political corruption that has gone hand in hand with the power to throw huge amounts of tax-exempt money into a crucial campaign.

There is a close connection between the fight against union racketeers and union corruption and the union power that management is so concerned about. I've heard management people scoff at the exposure of union racketeering and union corruption, and add that it is the power of unions that must be controlled.

Unions should be brought under responsible control. The power should be curbed, without engaging in union-busting. But, the first step is to control the tax-exempt union funds—that is the source of political power, and the source of corruption.

If you relieve the pressure of big union contributions from politics—aside from those collected on a voluntary basis—you will make more public officials susceptible to reason.

The first step in this direction should be an effort to make the Internal Revenue Service enforce the law on tax-exempt organizations. The laxity of the IRS has allowed tax-exempt funds to be used for politics under this administration, and under prior administrations. It is time that some of our federal tax officials are forced to administer the law properly.

The McClellan committee has brought forth testimony showing how Hoffa's organization has given almost cradle to grave protection to the hoodlums in the Teamsters.

There was testimony that Hoffa instructed a Teamster official to bring him reports obtained from spying on the work of a Michigan grand jury that was studying Teamster-racket connections.

There was testimony that Hoffa had some of his thugs talk to a key witness, and persuade him to leave the state of Michigan.

There was testimony that Hoffa made a threat to kill or injure a Teamster union official who had been brave enough to testify against him.

There was testimony that Hoffa tried to coerce the prosecutors who were taking aggressive action against his union.

There was testimony that when indictments were returned against some of the members of Hoffa's Hoodlum Empire, he arranged to supply them with the best attorneys at union expense. This was when some of the individuals were charged with selling out their own union members.

There was testimony that Hoffa made political contributions to the campaign of a judge who made key rulings on the criminal cases of his Teamster pals.

And, when all of this activity didn't prevent some convictions, Hoffa used hundreds of thousands of dollars in union funds to continue the salaries of the convicted labor crooks while they were in prison.

And, the Hoffa Empire hired some labor crooks upon their release from jail, or helped arrange jobs for others.

Certainly this is a sordid picture of the way union power and union money have been used to distort our administration of justice. It raises the question of why the American people are not totally enraged at the arrogant display of power exhibited by Hoffa and others.

The answer is simple: The full story of corruption as spelled out by the McClellan committee has not gotten across. It takes time for the American people to become aware of what the work of Hoffa and some of his lawyers is doing, and has done, to our system of government.

I believe the full story will get across eventually, and for this reason I feel that the McClellan committee should be continued.

While the full story has not been assimilated by the public generally, there has been a significant change of attitude in the country on labor matters in the last two years.

If no labor reform legislation is ever passed, the McClellan committee work has changed the atmosphere. If you have a legitimate case against labor abuses, you can get some public attention today. You can speak of your grievances before a college group without being frowned on as an anti-labor reactionary. This would not have been the case three years ago.

This change in atmosphere is due largely to the work of two men—Chairman McClellan and his chief counsel, Robert F. Kennedy.

The AFL-CIO has tried to claim credit for the big reform campaign in labor, but this would not have taken place if it had not been for the work of McClellan and Bob Kennedy. This doesn't mean that George Meany didn't want to clean house, but he wouldn't have had the facts or the public pressure for the job if it hadn't been for the McClellan committee. What Meany has done in ousting the Teamsters and some others has been excellent public relations. He has given a public impression of sharp action to curb corrupt labor, and this is the major reason that organized labor has not been more seriously damaged by the McClellan committee revelations.

But, the AFL-CIO can't claim credit for helping to get the McClellan committee started, for their lobbyists were against it in January, 1957.

Neither can management groups claim any credit for getting McClellan started, nor for the success that he and Bob Kennedy have enjoyed. Many management groups have refused to cooperate, and others have done so reluctantly. Some management representatives were fooled into taking positions that nearly wrecked the committee in the Spring of 1958.

Neither the Republican leadership nor the Democratic leadership can make any great claim to credit for what the McClellan committee has done. It is largely the result of the independence and courage of McClellan, the hard work and the integrity of Bob Kennedy, and the willingness of Senator Irving Ives (Rep., N. Y.) to cooperate in establishing the committee and running it.

The leadership on both sides of the aisle had been ducking its responsibility in the labor racket area for some time.

The future of legislation in the labor field is contingent upon the operations of the McClellan committee this year. . . . But, legislation is only a part of the picture. There are signs that the NLRB has paid attention to the McClellan committee, and there are a number of Supreme Court decisions that have been as important as legislation in curbing the abuse of union power.

There is nearly unanimous agreement that a major problem exposed by the McClellan Labor Racket Committee is the lack of proper law enforcement by local and state government units. You know something about the situation in your own community, but the McClellan committee has documented that there is a widespread laxness in enforcing criminal laws where unions or union leaders are involved. It was true in Tennessee, in Pennsylvania, in Ohio, in Michigan, in Wisconsin and in Illinois. In some cases, the police made little or no real effort to catch the labor crooks. In other cases, the prosecutors let the union-connected thugs off without prosecution. In other cases, union money was used freely to help the political campaigns of judges—the Teamsters even made such contributions while a judge was sitting on a criminal case involving Teamsters officials.

The same use of union money that tends to corrupt prosecutors and influence courts in criminal cases, is also a factor in weighing—or fixing—civil cases in favor of the union.

Employers in Wayne county, Michigan, told the McClellan committee that their lawyers advised that although they had a good case, it would do them no good before most of the judges. They were told that union political power and union political funds had stacked the courts against them.

It makes no difference what kind of state criminal laws are on the books, if business stands idly by and allows—yes, and frequently helps—union labor to corrupt police, prosecutors and sheriffs.

It makes no difference what rights employers and unions are granted under the civil laws, if the courts have been influenced to interpret those laws so that one side is always the winner.

You have a big stake in honest and impartial law enforcement on the local and state levels. But, the chances are that you employers are doing little or nothing about correcting the corrupt conditions that exist.

There is something businessmen can do to expose and eradicate the union-gangster alliances that have grown up in many communities.

As individuals citizens in your communities—not as members of NAM—you can establish and support a totally nonpartisan crime commission. I emphasize that this should not be a politically partisan crime commission. Every effort should be made to keep it away from the machinery of either the Democratic or Republican parties.

This labor racket problem is not one that is restricted to one party or the other, despite what some political figures may tell you on this subject at election time. The really big union crooks are totally bi-partisan—they'll pour money into the campaigns of either Democrats or Republicans if they can buy or neutralize the courts and law enforcement.

The crime commission needs enough funds to hire one or two top notch former FBI agents, or persons with comparable experience. The size of the office staff depends on your community.

The director of your crime commission should be totally isolated from political pressure from either party.

It should not be an employer-dominated operation. It should not be an organization to investigate unions as such. Its reports should not be documents condemning unions as unions.

It should follow all major criminal activity, and all forces tending to corrupt or pervert law enforcement or the judicial processes.

If the crime commission is diligent in pursuing all major criminals, it will also handle any labor-connected criminals in your locality.

If the crime commission is diligent in pursuing the forces that seek to interfere with honest administration of justice, it will naturally follow the activities of those elements of labor who try to fix or coerce the courts.

What can a crime commission do? Here are a few things:

1. It can provide expert investigators to examine the shootings, beatings and other violence in your area. It can serve as a double check on the honesty and efficiency of police. It can make reports on arrests and the dispositions of cases.

2. It can search out the criminal records from the police departments and from congressional committee reports or other sources, and expose the factual background of those crooked labor elements that occasionally drop into a community.

3. It can serve as a central point for newspaper reporters, congressional investigators or others who are searching for an objective report on activities in your community, and who would consider reports from straight labor or management groups to be biased.

There are those areas in the country where dishonest management has corrupted the law enforcement or courts as much as labor. In other areas, formerly honest management may be frantically trying to corrupt the courts or other officials while rationalizing that this is the way the game is played, and so they must also be dishonest to survive against dishonest labor.

Many of these management people are in the process of doing the very thing they despise in some union labor officials. This is not the answer to your problems. If you engage in such dishonesty, you are no better than the lowest Teamster renegade. In addition, you are making it impossible for you to fight dishonest labor, and you are flirting with public exposure.

Most of you say you believe in the American Way, and that you are great supporters of democracy. If you really believe in the American Democracy, you will try to put forth some effort to make it work.

If you are satisfied with fair play from the police and the courts, then don't try to corrupt them. Put some money and work into the job of making the system honest.

A crime commission isn't the whole solution, but if it is administered properly it can go a long ways toward eliminating much of the racket influences from law enforcement and the courts.

There are employers and others who have told me that the majority of the union members don't care if they are tied to a yoke of compulsory unionism, or if their officials are corrupt. There are some union members like that.

There are union men and officials who tell me the root of the trouble is in the business community. They say the majority of the businessmen don't care about honesty in government or business, worship the almighty buck, and are even eager to do business with crooked labor. We must admit there are some employers like that.

I do not believe that the majority in labor or management have fallen to the state where right and justice mean nothing. I do not believe that the majority of the people in this country are unconcerned over the power and the gangster domination of the Teamsters union as it exists today.

I will not accept as fact the thesis that the American Democracy cannot protect itself against the ravages of Big Labor or Big Business.

I believe that the American Democracy can operate honestly, and is not doomed to fall before the power or corruption of racketeers. But, I know that the American Democracy does not function automatically. It needs aggressive and honest people who will work as hard for its success as the crooked elements are working for its destruction or perversion.

If you really believe in this system of government, you will do something to make it work.

Critical Note on Mollenhoff

Should Mollenhoff have made greater use of appeals from his own prestige?

During the years immediately preceding this speech Mollenhoff had devoted his journalistic skills to discovering and publicizing corruption within labor unions, especially the Teamsters Union. Robert F. Kennedy, then chief counsel for the Senate committee which investigated Teamster presidents Dave Beck and James Hoffa, said of Mollenhoff: "It was probably you more than anyone else who is responsible for this investigation." Mollenhoff's series of articles on the operations of Dave Beck had earned for him a Pulitzer prize and a general reputation as an authority on labor racketeering. Because of these experiences, he could hardly have avoided acquiring a stock of striking anecdotes and personal observations which could be incorporated into his speeches. It is curious, under these circumstances, that the speech is so impersonal in its use of evidence.

This quality of impersonality becomes even more striking when we consider Mollenhoff's audience. The National Association of Manufacturers has repeatedly supported stringent control, both legal and economic, of labor unions. To this audience, Mollenhoff would appear as something of a hero: a man who had provided confirmation of their long-festering suspicion that some unions are corrupt. They would tend to accept his assertions as oracular, as emanating from so authoritative a source that the speaker's own word was proof sufficient. Almost certainly, this audience was favorable to his propositions before he even began to speak.

Many speakers, facing such a favorable audience, would concern themselves with stimulating the audience to more intense conviction. Such speakers would exploit all the resources of emotionally charged language and would seek to enhance their prestige still more by recounting their relevant personal experiences. But Mollenhoff spoke in relatively restrained language, and he cautiously qualified his assertions. Only once, in the third paragraph of the speech, did the speaker intimate that he possessed first-hand knowledge. Otherwise, the audience's acquaintance with Mollenhoff's background would have to have come from the chairman's introduction of the speaker. The speech itself provides no suggestion of the speaker's long experience with his subject. Should Mollenhoff have made greater use of appeals from his own prestige?

Such appeals are not entirely absent from the speech, of course. Perhaps some auditors formed a favorable impression of the speaker because of his choice of clear statement over emotionality, or because of his carefully hedged and elaborately qualified proposals. Yet, these are options open to almost any speaker. The unique advantage which Mollenhoff enjoyed was that of an authoritative reputation created in advance of the speech, a reputation which would have disposed many members of his audience to believe almost anything he said on his subject because *he* said it. It was an advantage which Mollenhoff chose not to employ in the speech. Should he have?

Questions

To what extent does government now protect the interests of consumers? Is there sufficient need to justify further activity in this direction? Do you believe industry deliberately designs consumer goods to fail in a short time? Do you know of any examples of such practices? Are product improvements deliberately spaced to encourage purchase of new models? Is the primary obligation of a business to its owner or to its customers? Does a business concern have the right to "charge what the traffic will bear"? Does the public have the right to regulate prices and profits in the drug industry? Prices and profits of a dairy? Of a cosmetics' manufacturer?

Does "misleading" advertising really mislead anyone? Assuming that businesses are concerned primarily with sales, could they improve the effectiveness of present advertising? How important is advertising to the American economy? Is government regulation of advertising sufficiently strict at this time? Does the Post Office Department subsidize mass mailing of advertising material? Advertising lines our highways with bill boards and pays for broadcasts of the Metropolitan Opera Company. On balance, is advertising's contribution to society good or bad? How do you explain the apparent contradiction between the often held propositions that advertisers are very sensitive to consumer reactions and that consumers dislike much advertising? If you wanted to sell a face cream, a cough syrup, an automobile, or some similar product, how would you bring it to the attention of consumers? Do you object to advertising that is directed at children?

Should the federal government establish compulsory arbitration in some industries? Is there a better way to avoid bitter and expensive strikes? Should firemen, policemen, or teachers be permitted to strike? Should the employees of private companies which provide essential public services (transportation, water, gas) be permitted to strike? Should the federal government control profits in some industries? Is the control of corporations vested in the owners or the managers?

Does present corporate tax policy inhibit the growth of business? Is personal income tax policy punitive with respect to the higher tax brackets? Are you aware of any important injustices in federal, state, county, or local tax laws? If your state, county, or municipality required additional funds, would you favor raising them through a property tax, sales tax, income tax, excise tax, direct levies, bond issue, or other means? In what situation, if any, do you believe agencies of government should follow a "pay-as-you-go" policy? Do gasoline taxes favor truckers at the expense of those who drive automobiles?

Should corporation funds be used to support political candidates? Should corporation executives, in their role as representatives of a company, support political candidates? Should they speak out in this role on questions of public policy? Would the public interest be served, for example, if we knew whether or not General Electric favored an economic boycott of Cuba?

Discord is the exception between owners and managers, the rule between managers and workers. Is this because the interests of management are identified more closely with the interests of owners than those of workers? Because the owner's voice is weak and the workers' voice is strong? Can labor-management tensions be alleviated, or are they inherent in the system? Have profit-sharing plans improved the situation? Would tensions decrease if inflation were controlled?

Do we need stronger laws to decrease the possibility of corruption within labor unions? Should the political and economic power of unions be curbed? Do unions in fact exercise considerable political power? To what extent are unions democratic? Do you favor "right-to-work" laws? Do you favor unions among teachers? Clergymen? Is law enforcement lax in the locality you are most familiar with? Elsewhere in the nation? Do most people want the law strictly enforced? Would you pay five dollars for the privilege of attending the Annual Policeman's Ball with the added inducement of a torn-up speeding ticket? How widespread is petty theft from employers or petty fraud on income tax returns?

Suggestions for Further Reading

Aiken, Thomas, Jr. "The Double Image of American Business Abroad," *Harper's*, August 1960, p. 14.

Beirne, Joseph A. *The Communications Worker and the Economy*. Communications Workers of America pamphlet, 1960.

————. *The Job Revolution in Telephones*. Communications Workers of America pamphlet, 1959.

————. *Union's Role in Helping Productivity*. Communications Workers of America pamphlet, 1958.

————. *Wages as a Factor in Inflation*. Communications Workers of America pamphlet, 1959.

Berle, Adolph A., Jr. *Economic Power and the Free Society; A Preliminary Discussion of the Corporation*. Fund for the Republic pamphlet, 1957.

Buchanan, Scott. *The Corporation and the Republic*. Fund for the Republic pamphlet, 1958.

Bureau of Labor Statistics. *The Extent and Nature of Frictional Unemployment*. (A study paper prepared for the Joint Economic Committee, 86th Congress, 1st Session.) Washington, D.C.: Government Printing Office, 1959.

Conrad, Alfred H. *The Share of Wages and Salaries in Manufacturing Incomes, 1947-56*. (A study paper prepared for the Joint Economic Committee, 86th Congress, 1st Session.) Washington, D.C.: Government Printing Office, 1959.

Consumer Reports publishes frequent, well-reasoned and well-supported criticisms of various aspects of American business. The following is a sampling:

"Advertising," September 1959, p. 494; November 1959, p. 595; October 1960, p. 550.

"Consumer Protection," February 1959, p. 74; February 1960, pp. 47, 64, and 96; June 1960, p. 289; September 1960, p. 477.

"Credit," March 1959, p. 140; September 1959, p. 488; January 1960, p. 43.

"Obsolescence," April 1959, p. 206; January 1961, p. 6.

"Packaging," August 1959, p. 434; September 1960, p. 488; January 1961, p. 41.

"Profits," November 1958, p. 597.

Eckstein, Otto, and Gary Fromm. *Steel and the Postwar Inflation*. (A study paper prepared for the Joint Economic Committee, 86th Congress, 1st Session.) Washington, D.C.: Government Printing Office, 1959.

The European Common Market and Its Meaning to the United States. Committee for Economic Development pamphlet, 1959.

Ferry, W. H. *The Economy Under Law*. Center for the Study of Democratic Institutions pamphlet, 1960.

Hacker, Andrew. *Politics and the Corporation*. Fund for the Republic pamphlet, 1958.

Halsey, Van R. "Fiction and the Businessman: Society Through All Its Literature," *American Quarterly*, Fall 1959, p. 391.

Harris, Seymour E. "Can We Prosper Without Arms?" New York *Times Magazine*, Nov. 8, 1959, p. 20.

————. *The Incidence of Inflation: or Who Gets Hurt?* (A study paper prepared for the Joint Economic Committee, 86th Congress, 1st Session.) Washington, D.C.: Government Printing Office, 1959.

Honthakker, H. S. *Protection Against Inflation*. (A study paper prepared for the Joint Economic Committee, 86th Congress, 1st Session.) Washington, D.C.: Government Printing Office, 1959.

Kerr, Clark. *Unions and Union Leaders of Their Own Choosing.* Fund for the Republic pamphlet, 1957.

Meyers, Frederick. *"Right to Work" in Practice.* Fund for the Republic pamphlet, 1959.

Miller, Arthur S. *Private Governments and the Constitution.* Center for the Study of Democratic Institutions pamphlet, 1959.

Morse, Wayne. "Speech Opposing the Landrum-Griffin Labor Bill," *Congressional Record,* 86th Congress, 1st Session, Sept. 3, 1959.

Nossiter, Bernard D. "The Teamsters; Corrupt Policemen of an Unruly Industry," *Harper's,* May 1959, p. 70.

Raskin, A. H. "Do Public Strikes Violate Public Trust?" New York *Times Magazine,* Jan. 8, 1960, p. 24.

Redford, Emmette S. *Potential Public Policies to Deal with Inflation Caused by Market Power.* (A study paper prepared for the Joint Economic Committee, 86th Congress, 1st Session.) Washington, D.C.: Government Printing Office, 1959.

Schultze, Charles L. *Recent Inflation in the United States.* (A study paper prepared for the Joint Economic Committee, 86th Congress, 1st Session.) Washington, D.C.: Government Printing Office, 1959.

Stieber, Jack, W. E. Oberer, and Michael Harrington. *Democracy and Public Review; An Analysis of the U.A.W. Public Review Board.* Center for the Study of Democratic Institutions pamphlet, 1960.

Tyler, Gus. *A New Philosophy for Labor.* Fund for the Republic pamphlet, 1959.

Wilson, Thomas A. *An Analysis of the Inflation in Machinery Prices.* (A study paper prepared for the Joint Economic Committee, 86th Congress, 1st Session.) Washington, D.C.: Government Printing Office, 1959.

3. Civil Rights

Introduction

Marked advance of Negroes toward true equality was perhaps the major development in American society during the fifties. Today the advance continues. Yet Negroes are still very far from enjoying their full rights as citizens. The legal guarantee of rights leaves discriminatory attitudes and beliefs largely untouched, and many other citizens who are members of national, cultural, or religious minority groups suffer disabilities similar to, if less severe than, those imposed on Negroes.

There is surprisingly little disagreement on the rights to which people are entitled. Those shadowy groups in American society which would suppress one minority or another have produced no articulate spokesmen to influence the course of public discussion. Rather, the speed with which civil rights should be impartially secured for all, and the means of securing them, have become the issues of controversy. The selections that follow reflect this shape of the public discussion.

RALPH MCGILL

The Meaning of Lincoln Today

The speech from which the following excerpts were drawn was delivered at the Cooper Union, New York City, on February 12, 1960.

Ralph McGill has been editor of the Atlanta Constitution since 1942. In 1959 he was awarded the Pulitzer prize for editorial writing.

Commemorative addresses ideally honor a person or event in the past and illuminate an idea significant in the present. Speakers seldom succeed as well in both aims as McGill does here.

A hundred years, lacking but a few days, have passed since Abraham Lincoln here delivered the speech which was the pivot of his life and the nation's.

His whole life was a span of but 56 years. When on that damp and snowy night, a century ago, he quit this auditorium to go back to his hotel, limping because one of his new boots pinched, there were roughly five years left to him.

This life, so richly and fortuitously prepared, saved the Union and perpetuated the nation.

But a few days hence we will pause in reverent memory to honor George Washington, whose steadfast faith and courage made possible the birth of this nation. In a few weeks we will commemorate Thomas Jefferson, the majestic Virginian, whose hand was in both the immortal Declaration of man's inalienable rights, and in the Bill of Rights. The words of both are as plainly and permanently written as the Commandments fetched by Moses from Mt. Sinai.

Yet, as deeply and sincerely as we honor and revere these two, in acknowledging our eternal indebtedness to them, it is somehow Lincoln who seems closest to us. It is so with peoples around the world. This man from our prairies is in our hearts. The mystery of him, the humanity of him, the many facts and legends of his brief life, are a part of the flesh and blood of our national folklore and culture, of our faith in the nation and the people who make it. For all that we reverence Washington and Jefferson, they remain somehow the marble and bronze men in halls of fame, in the pantheon of our heroes. But Lincoln—we can see him plainly across the arches of a hundred years—and more. We know what he felt, and believed. His sorrows and joys; his incredible faith, in people, the union; his patience and gentleness; his courage and his weaknesses, are all known to us.

We can see him, here, a century ago, tall and gaunt in his new, ill-fitting suit of black broadcloth, wrinkled from having been folded in the valise for the long journey from Springfield, Illinois to New York. . . . He had taken no public opinion polls in search of principles or convictions. They had come to him through his senses, through his eyes and his ears, and the workings of his sensitive mind. He had seen the conditions of the frontier. He noted life and contrasts on the long river journey to New Orleans. There he saw the slave markets and witnessed the inhumanity of them. His principles and convictions had been refined and toughened in the Douglas debates. They were his. He, himself, had acquired them. He held to them. They gave him the compass course for his life. When the Whig party deserted his principles he quit that party. When the Republican party was born and proclaimed principles which matched his own, he joined it.

So, when he came East—to Cooper Union—he brought his principles with him. Neither he nor they were then well known. When he had finished, the crowd here gave both an ovation.

We can look at the speech and the man and see what he did was to close an essential gap—a cultural time lag. It was then necessary to persuade society to take great strides.

This has meaning for us today. We like to think that only for us has it become necessary to close the gap between technology and the moral sciences—between the scientific and the social sciences.

Today's national problem is to find the inspiration and the leadership which will enable us to have great convictions and to fuse moral considerations with social inventiveness.

So it was when Lincoln spoke here in February, 1860. Slavery had been brought about by agriculture, mainly cotton. But already machines ginned, spun, and wove cotton. One day, men were saying then, machines would pick it. Machines were appearing in the wheat fields. Machines were then grinding sugar cane. Railroads were being built and projected in dreams to the Pacific. There were then, more than now, sensitive problems of property interests in a changing economy. Iron and coal had come to rivers, rails and the seas. In Lincoln's time pig-iron production had vaulted, or so it seemed, from almost nothing to almost a million tons a year. Iron plows were ripping the prairie soils. Steam transportation, with coal in the fire boxes, was settling up the Northwest. Pigs and corn came one way on steamboats and in freight cars. Plows, reapers, furniture, and the new machines went the other.

There was something else in those freight cars and on the decks of riverboats. It was the new political and economic power, symbolized by the Northwest. In the South, billions of dollars were enslaved by slavery. This capital was confined, by the system, to ownership of slaves and slave-labor supplies. In the East and Northwest there was a wage-labor system. In such a system the dollars were free to circulate as operating capital. This was the new power which was even then breaking the political hold of the South on the government in Washington.

Then, as now, the people wanted bread and jobs, land and roads, freedom and answers to their questions. A civil war was coming on. Then, as now, the people had to be reached to make public opinion. The gap which Lincoln had to close between technology and the social sciences was greater than today.

This has meaning for us today. Nor is it lacking in irony. When Lincoln came here to speak, government in the United States was deadlocked on the issue of slavery in the new territories. But elsewhere the cause of freedom was advancing around the world, thrilling millions and giving hope to the oppressed. Most impressive, in that time, was the fact that the long struggle to liberate the serfs in Russia was reaching its climax. On the day before Lincoln was inaugurated, the czar's official decree was published setting all serfs free.

This was a great leap forward in human rights. And it turned, of course, the eyes of the world to this country with its shining principles and its guarantee of human rights written into the Constitution.

In the South, the moderate's voice had long been all but silenced. In Virginia, for example, the *Southern Literary Messenger* repudiated, as ignorant and erroneous, the principles of the Declaration and the Constitution and stigmatized Jefferson's statement that in any contest between masters and slaves, Divine Goodness must take the side of the downtrodden. A leadership which might have clung to Jefferson turned instead, in a sort of compulsive madness, to excitement of fears and passions.

All this was a part of the gap before Lincoln's feet.

Yet, the speech here a century ago was not anti-Southern. It was firm in developing its central point. It was that the United States could no longer remain a slaveholding republic. It was, in essence, the speech of a moderate. Patiently, with great wisdom, Lincoln insisted that this country must not evade its moral responsibilities. He could see, as could others, that we were losing our position of democratic leadership in the world.

So, he spoke with calm, charitable reasonableness. He wanted to allay Southern fears. The Southern people, he said, were just as reasonable as any. He would, he said, concede as much as a sense of duty permitted.

He paused, and reporters noted only the hissing of gas lights was heard until he resumed, saying that the difficulty was that duty forbade a surrender of principle. It was a calmly analytical address, legalistic as to the Constitution, but it is plain what Lincoln hoped to achieve. He wanted a national dialogue—not the excitements of extremists. And he was complaining, ever so politely and calmly, but complaining still, that no one in the South would debate what he thought the issues were. He addressed himself to the South and the Republican party.

> Even though the Southern people will not so much as listen to us, let us calmly consider their demands and yield to them if, in our deliberate view of our duty, we possibly can.

Now, it may be argued that the historical situation had by February, 1860, so deteriorated as to make a national dialogue impossible. But this is utterly refuted by many succeeding events, including the facts of the Democratic convention at Charleston, South Carolina, in the spring. It would have been possible, even then, to have prevented a split of the party and the nation. But folly's voice was strong, and the conservative feared to speak.

And here we come to what perhaps is the crux of the meaning of Lincoln for us today.

Regardless of how possible or impossible Lincoln's point was at the moment of his Cooper Union speech, the idea of a national dialogue on the race question was a critical one then just as it is now.

It was a failure, or inability, call it what you will, to conduct such a dialogue which was responsible for the quick descent into civil war. That the war and ensuing radical reconstruction policies for years postponed any possibility of subsequent dialogue on the same question is inescapable. But here we are today. And we are still not engaging in a really national dialogue on it. On racial questions there is still the old poison of extremisms, little diluted, in both perspective and action. There is a great, conservative body of opinion, North and South, which knows that we cannot have full citizenship for some and part citizenship for others. The business community everywhere knows this. But it has not played its part.

To be sure, the situation is not as bad as before. We do not deal with human slavery, but with the highly important problems of equal citizenship and of an end to discriminations already too long permitted. And, once again we are in a time when a great gulf is to be bridged. Once more there are fears that this nation has slipped somewhat backward in its position of democratic leadership in the world. . . .

Both parties have dodged an honest national dialogue on the subject of simple, legitimate civil rights. Both parties have indulged in mutual togetherness and an almost incredible unwillingness to face the facts and to see the gulf which must be closed between the technical and social sciences of our time.

Is Lincoln's Cooper Union appeal for a national dialogue to be historically rejected generation after generation?

This raises the question of who, or what groups, in any society can conduct a dialogue. It must be, of course, those on each side of a question who have a sense of the vital role of communication, who are more interested in building bridges of communications than in destroying them.

The greatest failure to join in the dialogue has, it seems to me, been on the part of all that is wrapped up in the word business.

We of late have had a great deal of talk about business men getting into politics. This has been urged, I believe, by various persons and committees of the National Association of Manufacturers, the U.S. Chamber of Commerce, and heads of some of the larger corporations. But from the beginning they have revealed a fatal flaw in their image of what getting into politics means. They have had the narrow one of merely electing someone they thought would best represent them locally.

Getting into politics means much more than that. Politics demands a public philosophy. This is basic. If, for example, we allow public education to be destroyed in several states, the reverberations of it will echo in every state. It will poison the legislative wells of necessary federal assistance to education. It will take up the time of the Congress in acrimonious debate which will stir up extremist, hate groups in every state in the Union. It already has done something of this.

The whole issue has been left to the politicians. They have had the assistance of church groups and of several organizations and individuals. But, here is something which will harm the nation and its economy unless it is resolved nationally. The South has been blamed for something in which the North has an almost equal blame. The South has no exclusive franchise on prejudice.

Lincoln said here that moral right makes might. That, I believe, is yet true. If the nation's business leadership will get into politics in the fullest and best sense we can make real progress. The Committee for Economic Development, for example, has recently released a study and recommendation on education. That is business statesmanship. Here is a public philosophy on education by leaders of the nation's productive economy. We can use it in other fields. If we leave it only to the politicians, then the instinct for survival will allow most of the talking and interpretation to be done by the extremists. We are all citizens of this country or we are not. The sooner we make up our minds about it, with help from the Chambers of Commerce, the sooner this nation will bridge the gap which is presented to us in this last half of the 20th century. Let us repeat—getting into politics requires a mature public philosophy if the political system is to be backed by a healthy public opinion.

Because of our failure to do this in the field of race we see again the dangers present at the time of Lincoln's speech. The extremists of action and perspective have been too much in the fore.

Yet, there is hope, and some progress, even though Deep South extremism, because it declines to accept the authority of courts and the decisions of the U.S. Supreme Court as law, cannot be exonerated any more than could that of 1860 which appealed to fears and appetites rather than rational, logical principles.

"The Southern Moderate" is a phrase much maligned and abused. Some, indeed, who have so identified themselves, merely have held up pious hands in deploring violence. Others believed themselves moderates because, while admitting inevitability, they proposed a cooling off period of a few vague years after the court's 1954 school decision. But there were, and are, Southern moderates who said that the Supreme Court decision was law, that it was wisely written with its recognition of the several degrees of the problem of compliance, that the decision was past due, and that the task was to bring the best minds together and work out a legal process meeting the court decision. That there are now but four states in which no beginning of compliance has been made must not cause us to ignore the clear and definite progress in others. The processes of law grind slowly, but they grind.

There have been moderates in the pulpit, press and among people in general, especially women. These invariably have been subjected to abuse, often vile, and to threats. Several ministers have been deprived of their pulpits in manners crude and vulgar. A sort of guerrilla fighting goes on in the Deep South states' public opinion. It is not merely that the U.S. Supreme Court has ruled discrimination among citizens unconstitutional. This revolution coincided with dislocations and aroused emotions growing out of the revolutionary effect of an agricultural system in transition. Industry was coming, cities expanding. An old order was dying, resisting mightily. The birth pangs of the new were great. A failure, with the usual exceptions, of press and public leadership, too often has left interpretation to those who defended the status quo with appeals to fear and hate.

The Southern moderate paid, and still pays, as does the nation, for the folly of not having had a dialogue in 1860—and after.

When Lincoln spoke here he destroyed, for example, the myth of state sovereignty. Yet, the mythology since built around the word sovereignty is almost unbelievable. The states, for example, may not secede; they cannot determine the composition of their citizens; they cannot forbid exit and entry; they cannot coin money, or make war; they cannot enact laws which conflict with federal laws. These are but some of the many illustrations of nonsovereignty. Yet, at this hour, as in 1860, one of the confusing elements in attempts to have a national dialogue has been the insistence, by extremist leadership, on state sovereignty. There was dug up in Virginia, in late 1954, the old idea, interred with John C. Calhoun, of interposition. This proposed that a sovereign state would interpose its sovereignty between itself, the federal government and the Supreme Court. This was not possible before 1860. It also conveniently ignored Appomattox. Yet, many good people, hoping for a way out, were deceived.

One of the features of Southern politics has been a magnificent irrelevancy, often entertaining. But nothing has been so fantastically irrelevant as the Virginia interposition theory in the year after the court's school decision. Much of the press took it up. It was one of the things which made impossible any rational discussion. Here again was leadership which may not be exonerated.

Nor is this all. Perhaps even more serious is another example of mythology and deceit which has prevented logical discussion. This is the charge, repeated over and over by a shocking number of Deep South political leaders, some members of the press, pulpit and laymen, that the Constitution of the United States is not law—that a constitutional decision does not have the effect of law.

The nation could not have been formed without the indispensable ingredient of federal law, the Constitution and its amendments being superior to state law. No lawyer is needed to know that. Nor is any legal acumen required to know that there would have been no need to go through the great travail of ratifying the federal Constitution if it were not to establish its primacy.

Article VI, Clause 2, of the U.S. Constitution plainly says that, "This Constitution, and the laws of the United States which shall be made in pursuance thereof . . . shall be the supreme law of the land, and the judges in every state shall be bound thereby, anything in the Constitution or laws of any state to the contrary notwithstanding."

That alone is plain enough. Without it, there is no national sovereignty.

Yet, even now, a great many thousands of persons have been sold the idea that the Supreme Court acted illegally, that the Constitution is not law, and that the states are not really bound by it.

Still another bit of mythology which has been hard-pushed to the detriment of rational discussion is the assertion that the U.S. Supreme Court can't make law. The facts are that it interpreted the 14th amendment in the school decision as it had made interpretations on numerous occasions when corporate rights were in dispute. Actually, some of these decisions begin in almost the same language as the school decree. Lawyers know, though this fact has not been widely advertised by those seeking orderly compliance, that one of the earlier acts of the Congress itself was to give to the Supreme Court sovereignty over state law. In the judiciary act of 1789 the Congress enacted legislation giving the Supreme Court jurisdiction when the courts of a state have upheld the action of that state in a case involving interpretation of the federal Constitution.

There has been but one casualty in the lists of obscuring barriers to reasonable discussion. Not long after the court decision, some gentlemen who leaped before they looked, began hearings in Washington to prove that if the children from segregated schools were admitted to desegregated schools they would pull down the educational levels of all grades because they were not as far advanced. They proved this over and over with obvious pleasure. And they were right. The children from a given grade in the District of Columbia's segregated Negro schools were not, as a rule, as far advanced as those in the others. But one fine day the hearings abruptly were ended. The gentlemen suddenly realized they daily had been proving exactly what the Supreme Court had said in its decision—namely, that segregated schools were not equal and were, in fact, a discrimination.

All of these, and others, have combined to create public confusion and misunderstanding in the Deep South states. It is not fair to indict the Southern people. A great majority of them dissented from the court decision. But they are not disloyal. From the start they were given a biased perspective.

Now, as in 1860, there is a great want of discussion of the moral or lawful issues involved. There has been much talk of states rights, little of moral rights.

Now, as in 1860, there have been continually agitated appeals to appetites and fears.

Now, as in 1860, it is necessary as resolutely to put the nation first. We are first of all a union of citizens and laws. And who honestly can deny that federal laws must apply equally to all citizens in all states? A biased jury or judge making a fair trial impossible, the denial of the right to vote, failure to apply the equal protection of the laws as guaranteed by the 14th amendment, are the nation's business—not that of any one state. It would be a most unhappy prospect if we had to live in one state without the equal protection of the Constitution of our country.

Out of experience comes the beginning of wisdom. We learned from the travail in Arkansas and Virginia that not until the full leadership of a community is willing to participate can there be a dialogue productive of results.

From the beginning there have been hopeful omens. Contrary to 1860, most of the national and regional organizations of the Christian church called for support of the U.S. Supreme Court and the processes of law. Here and there, particularly in some of the rural areas, there have been individual clergymen who declared that the Bible condemned the court and the government. A shocking number of ministers, though the total is relatively small, have been forced out of their pulpits for declaring that Christianity is not a private club. But on the whole, the official voices of religious organizations have been heard on the side of Christian principles and the processes of law.

There have been some few newspapers, organizations and individuals who have not retreated into the myths of state sovereignty and the unconstitutionality of the Constitution. But Little Rock, and then Virginia, showed us that not until the business leadership joins in the public debate and has its say will the debate produce effective results. So long as it is left to the extremists, to those who make a profit out of merchandising prejudice, and to those who put themselves and their political position ahead of the welfare of school children and the nation itself, just so long will we have excitement to violence, chaos, a breakdown of law and the national integrity. . . .

WILLIAM L. DAWSON

Segregation in the Armed Forces

This speech was delivered in the House of Representatives, April 12, 1951.

William L. Dawson has represented the First Congressional District of Illinois in the House of Representatives since 1943.

Dawson spoke in support of a motion made by Representative Melvin Price of Illinois. Representative Graham A. Barden of North Carolina had proposed an amendment to the Universal Military Training and Service Act of 1948, then under reconsideration by the House. One effect of the Barden amendment would have been to force the military services to reinstitute segregated troop units (which had been abolished by presidential order in 1948). Price moved to amend the amendment by striking out references to segregated units. The House agreed to the Price amendment on April 12.

Speakers can achieve ethical appeal by producing either direct or indirect evidence of their competence, integrity, and good will. Dawson's speech is filled with clear examples of direct evidence. Indirect evidence supporting the speaker's ethos is also present in such sentiments as "Deny to me today, if you will, all that American citizenship stands for, I will still fight to preserve our nation. . . ." Because the speaker here makes a choice of which the audience approves, he gains some

stature in their eyes. All things considered, indirect evidence tends to be stronger than direct, partly because it seems less calculated, partly because its effect on the audience is largely subconscious and relatively immune to listener resistance.

Mr. Chairman, I was born in the South. I lived there all during the days of my young manhood. When World War I broke out I was above the draft age. I did not have to go, but I believed then as I believe now that it was the duty of every citizen, when the welfare of the nation in which he claims citizenship is at stake, to rally to the call and to give his life if need be, for the preservation of the nation.

I went to war. I was commissioned William L. Dawson, first lieutenant of infantry. I led Americans in battle—black Americans. This mark you see here on my forehead is the result of German mustard gas. This left shoulder of mine is today a slip joint. I cannot raise this left arm any higher than the shoulder unless I lift it with the other hand. That would have been a good joint, hospitalization would have been available, if I had not been a Negro American. I served in a segregated outfit as a citizen trying to save this country. How long, how long, my confreres and gentlemen from the South, will you divide us Americans on account of color? Give me the test that you would apply to make anyone a full-fledged American, and by the living God, if it means death itself, I will pay it. But, give it to me. Why should this body go on record at a time when we are fighting a world war to brand a section of its citizenry as second class?

I have sat in the well of this House and I have seen you gentlemen from the South, and rightly so, stand up and applaud members of other races, nonwhite races, who were darker than I am. I have seen you applaud them, yet you will take me, a citizen of the United States, of your own flesh and blood, and brand me with second-class citizenship. If there is one place in America where there should not be segregation, that place is in the armed services, among those who fight for this country. Oh, I know how some of you feel, but there is but one God. I did not make myself black any more than you made yourself white, and God did not curse me when he made me black any more than he cursed you when he made you white. I would give up this life of mine to preserve this country and every American in it, white or black. Deny to me today, if you will, all that American citizenship stands for, I will still fight to preserve our nation knowing that someday under the Constitution of the United States all of these restrictions will be removed, and that we will move forward before the world as one people, joined in a democracy which shall set the pattern for all the world.

I say to you who claim to love America, in this hour of its stress that the greatest argument the Soviet Union is using among the black peoples of this world to turn them against you is your treatment of me and Americans like me.

No; I do not believe this body means to go off on this tangent, and I believe you who come from the South, if you would look back a little bit, would never, never again take a step to handicap any one of God's children for what they are. I believe that the South is big enough for all of us to live in together in peace and in happiness if we can but have understanding; but we cannot have understanding if you array one against another because of color.

I hope you will vote for the Price amendment.

THOMAS R. WARING

The Southern Case for Segregation

The following abridgement is based on an article published in **Harper's** magazine for January 1956.

Thomas R. Waring has been editor of the Charleston **News and Courier** since 1951.

The considerable striking force of Waring's article stems chiefly from its specificity and concreteness. Vivid, precise pieces of amplification compel audience attention and resist casual refutation. But a given set of illustrations, no matter how excellent their quality, will sustain only those general ideas to which they are relevant. Waring's argument is irresistible so long as he maintains that certain beliefs do exist and that the existence of these beliefs makes Southern white resistance to integration understandable. When his phraseology begins to suggest that the attitudes justify the resistance, he is on less firm ground.

Although the Supreme Court has declared that separation of the races in public schools is unconstitutional, few white Southerners are able to accept the prospect of mingling white and Negro pupils. Resistance to the court decree is stiffening throughout the region.

Many white Northerners are unable to understand the depth of feeling in the Southern states, whose area is about a sixth of the nation and whose population is roughly a fourth of the total. The purpose of this article is to try to put before the open-minded readers of this magazine the point of view of the Southerner—whom the rest of the United States apparently cannot believe to be open-minded at all on the subject of race.

At the outset it is only fair to warn the Northern reader that he may be infuriated before he reaches the end. This, I suspect, is just as inevitable as the outraged feelings of the Southerner when he reads the Northern press with its own interpretation of the American dilemma. Both sides have been shouting at each other so loudly that it is difficult any longer to hear facts through the din of name calling. If, in the course of speaking for the South, I should raise blood pressure among some Northerners, I apologize for causing pain—with the hope that I may be able to reach Northern minds that are truly open so that some good may come along with the discomfort.

The reader outside the South may, unfortunately, react in still another way. He may find it difficult, if not impossible, to believe much of what I say. To this I can only reply that as editor of a South Carolina newspaper with a circulation of 56,000, with twenty-eight years of journalistic experience in both the North and the South, I have had to be in possession of accurate information on this as on any other subject covered in my work. Across an editor's desk pass, day by day and year after year, reports, letters, statistics—in other words, facts. By means of these facts, plus personal conversations with people from all over the world, an editor manages to keep in touch with public opinion.

It is the public opinion of the South that I am about to report. That opinion is a fact. It exists, and can be demonstrated. What I am saying is documented by facts and statistics. If these should seem to the reader to add up merely to bias, bigotry, and even untruth, I shall regret it. Facts, however, remain facts. . . .

Southerners believe they have valid reasons, aside from "prejudice" about the color of skin, for their insistence on sending white children to exclusively white schools. Without debating superiority of either race, they are keenly aware of cultural differences. In some ways the standards of white people are none too high. The same economic conditions that have held back Negroes have worked against the whites. The increasing prosperity of the South is removing some of these disadvantages for both races, though not necessarily in precisely the same way.

Whether all the differences will eventually be removed, or enough of them to make mixed education acceptable to a substantial number of white people, the differences are too great *at present* to encourage white parents to permit their children to mingle freely in school. This has nothing to do with the frequent practice of children of both races of playing together when young, or with cordial relationships in many other contacts of ordinary life.

Volumes could be written on racial differences from many angles, including anthropology and sociology. I shall merely try to summarize five of the differences that most immediately come to the minds of white parents in the South. These are health; home environment; marital standards; crime; and a wide disparity in average intellectual development.

Health. Negro parents as a whole—for reasons that white people may sympathetically deplore but which nevertheless exist—are not so careful on the average as their white neighbors in looking after the health and cleanliness of their children. The incidence of venereal disease for instance is much greater among Negroes than among whites.

Statistics to document this statement are difficult to come by, though the statement itself would be generally accepted in the South. The U.S. Public Health Service some years ago quietly stopped identifying statistics by races. South Carolina figures, available for 1952-53, give a clue to the situation in that state; it probably is much the same elsewhere in the South. Out of a population 60 per cent white and 40 per cent Negro, 6,315 cases of syphilis were reported, of which 89 per cent were among Negroes. Infection with gonorrhea was found in six Negroes to one white person, but some physicians report that many cases of gonorrhea among Negroes go unrecorded.

During the same period—1952-53—a campaign against venereal disease was carried on, county by county. A spot check of four representative counties in different parts of South Carolina showed that cases of syphilis were found among 1.3 per cent of the white persons examined. This was a fairly constant percentage. The percentage of infection among Negroes ranged in the same counties from 8.5 to 10.8 per cent, averaging more than 9 per cent.

Fastidious parents do not favor joint use of school washrooms when they would not permit it at home—and there's no use to tell them that it is unlikely that anyone will catch venereal disease from a toilet seat. They just don't want to take risks of any kind with their children.

Home environment. For most colored children in the South the cultural background is different in many ways from that of their white neighbors—and while these differences may have various explanations, they add up in the public's mind as racial. Slavery is so long in the past that nobody thinks about it any more, but the master and servant, or boss and laborer, relationship between whites and Negroes is still the rule rather than the exception. The emergence of a middle class among the Negroes has been extremely slow—again, the reasons count for less in the minds of white parents than the fact itself. Indeed, the professional and commercial class among Negroes is so small that its members are in perhaps the most unenviable position of all. They have progressed beyond the cultural level of the vast bulk of their own people, but are not accepted among the whites, who fear to let down any dikes least they be engulfed in a black flood.

Someone may suggest that here is an opening wedge for integration in the schools, by admitting a few well scrubbed and polished colored children of cultivated parents. In reply, let me say that this would be no more acceptable to the colored people than to the whites. The solution, perhaps —as it is among upper-bracket white people who do not send their children to public schools—might be private schools for prosperous Negroes as for prosperous whites. In any case, white people feel that cultural gaps on other levels should be filled in before discussing integrated schools.

Marital habits. Among many Southern Negroes they are, to state it mildly, casual—even more so, in fact, than among the often-divorced personalities of Northern café society. Many Negro couples—the statistics are not readily available, for obvious reasons—do not bother with divorce because there was no actual marriage in the first place. Statistics on the results of such casual unions, however, are available. On the average one Southern Negro child in five is illegitimate. It is possible the figure may be even higher, since illegitimate births are more likely to go unrecorded. Even among Negroes who observe marriage conventions, illegitimacy has little if any stigma.

Many white people believe that morals among their own race are lax enough as it is, without exposing their children to an even more primitive view of sex habits. Moreover, while these parents do not believe there is any surge of desire among their offspring to mate with colored people, they abhor any steps that might encourage intermarriage. They believe that lifting the racial school barriers would be such a step. Miscegenation has been on the wane of recent years. Whatever mixing of blood may have occurred—and admittedly that was due largely to lustful white men seeking out acquiescent Negro women—has been without benefit of either law or custom. On some levels of society, breaking the racial barriers might lead to mixed marriages. The mixture of races which white Southerners have observed in Latin American countries gives them a dim view of legalizing cohabitation with Negroes.

Crime. For many years, crime in the South has been more prevalent among Negroes than among white people. Though the Northern press no longer identifies criminals by race, white Southerners have reason to believe that much of the outbreak of crime and juvenile delinquency in Northern cities is due to the influx of Negro population. They believe the North now is getting a taste of the same race troubles that the South fears would grow out of mixed schooling, on a much bigger scale. They want no "Blackboard Jungles" in the South.

Maintaining order is a first concern of Southerners. What they have heard about the fruits of integration in the North does not encourage them to adopt the Northern race pattern. In Chicago, three hundred policemen have been assigned for a year or more to guard a nonsegregated housing project, with no bigger population than a Southern village where a single constable keeps the peace. In the County of Charleston, South Carolina—with 190,000 population, nearly half Negro—the total law enforcement manpower of combined city and county forces is 175.

While the homicide rate in the South is high, it is due in large measure to knifings and shootings among the colored people. Interracial homicide is relatively rare. (One of the reasons why the ghastly killing of Emmett Till in Mississippi made hot news—and some of that news was superheated and garnished with prejudice for the Northern press—was the very fact that it *was* unusual. No lynching, as even most Northerners now realize, has occurred in years.)

With racial bars down and rowdies of both races daring one another to make something of the vast increase in daily contacts, opportunities for interracial strife are frightening. Conservative, law-abiding people—and believe it or not, they constitute the bulk of the Southern whites—are deeply fearful that hatred and bloodshed would increase without separation of the races.

And they know that, in the long run, if there is riotous bloodshed it will be for the most part Negroes' blood. The thin tolerance of the ruffian and lower elements of the white people could erupt into animosity and brutality if race pressure became unbearable. Schools would be a focal point for such disturbance, first among pupils themselves and later by enraged parents. Instead of learning out of books, the younger generation would be schooled in survival—as several Northern sources have told me already is happening in some areas of New York, Philadelphia, and Washington, D.C.

Intellectual development. Again for whatever the reasons may be, Southern Negroes usually are below the intellectual level of their white counterparts. *U.S. News and World Report*—the fairest nationally circulated publication I am acquainted with in its treatment of the race issue—has reported that in Washington, colored children are about two grades behind the whites in attainment. This discrepancy, I believe, is about par for other communities. In Washington it was found that there were even language difficulties to surmount. The children used different terms for some things.

Some advocates of integration say the way to cure these differences is to let the children mingle so that the Negroes will learn from the whites. The trouble with this theory is that even if it works, a single generation of white children will bear the brunt of the load. While they are rubbing off white civilization onto the colored children, Negro culture will also rub off onto the whites.

Few Southern parents are willing to sacrifice their own offspring in order to level off intellectual differences in this fashion. They reason that their children will get along better in later life if they have, as youngsters, the best available cultural contacts. Such an attitude is not, I understand, altogether unknown in the North. Many parents in New York City, for example, make considerable financial sacrifices to send their children to private schools, to spare them the undesirable associations and the low-geared teaching standards of most public schools.

If this sounds snobbish to a Northern reader, let me ask you to examine your own conscience. Can you honestly say that you are eager to send your own child to a classroom where the majority of other pupils will be considerably more backward in their studies, and extremely different in social background and cultural attainments? Which would you *really* put first: your theory of racial justice, or justice to your own child?

HOWARD ZINN

A Fate Worse Than Integration

This article was published in Harper's magazine for August 1959.

Howard Zinn is chairman of the history department at Spelman College, Georgia.

Even before this year's court decision compelling Virginia's schools to open on an integrated basis, parents in Norfolk County were carrying placards which read:

"We are not for integration or segregation but we want our schools open."

They may also have been carrying with them the hint of a solution to the largely unvoiced but fundamental dilemma over integration which has been worrying both the Negroes seeking entry into the schools and white liberals in both the North and the South.

I say "unvoiced" dilemma because there is no issue on which liberals are more certain than that of racial equality. They may disagree about Formosa or Suez or regulating the unions, but concerning racial discrimination they are unified and altogether free of doubt. At least outwardly. Underneath, however, liberals have often been more uneasy than they will admit. They know that the vast majority of Southern whites favor segregation, that the enforcement of integration below the border states may well cause mob protests, beatings, dynamiting, and other forms of violence. And even those who are able to suppress their qualms about bloodshed cannot escape practical doubts about success: "How in the world are we going to have integration in South Carolina, Georgia, Alabama, Mississippi—Supreme Court or no Supreme Court—if local leaders and the population are fiercely opposed?"

The placard displayed in Virginia suggests, I believe, the solution to this dilemma: *that white Southerners are not in effect for segregation when it means losing something they value even more than the separation of the races.* In their unconscious hierarchy of values, segregation does not hold the highest rank. This is the crucial fact which has permitted integration to take place in many areas of Southern life and which promises to soften the determination to put up "massive resistance" even in the Deep South.

Any pollster, any white Southerner, or any Negro will tell you that white Southerners are overwhelmingly for segregation if the question is put to them in isolation. What is often overlooked, however, is that, like everyone else, the white Southerners cherish a large number of values; that these values are arranged roughly and unconsciously on a kind of ladder of importance; and that although the Southerner may not consciously acknowledge it, segregation is scarcely ever at the top.

This should not be too surprising. Human beings constantly choose to do unpleasant things simply because not to do them would be even more unpleasant. And because the choice is, at least on its face, "voluntary," the psychological effect is altogether different from what it would be if the act were compelled by force. Millions of people every day wake at an unpleasant hour and go to an unpleasant job, because to do otherwise would have consequences far more painful—going hungry, or becoming a welfare case, or taking a job even more distasteful. They are being compelled, of course, by the rigorous limit on available choices. Yet, this indirect compulsion does not produce the growling rebellion that would result from being herded to the factory or office at bayonet point.

Public-opinion polls are very poor guides to questions like integration because they present so narrow a choice of alternatives. When people state their attitude on a single issue, they must ignore the complexities of real-life decisions, which are more like multiple-choice tests than true-or-false quizzes. For instance, when a group of bus-drivers in a Northern city were polled on the prospective employment of Negro drivers on their routes, their response was overwhelmingly negative. But when the Negroes were actually put to work, not one white driver resigned, there were no unpleasant incidents, and the transportation system went on as smoothly as before. A group of restaurant owners, all of whom had served a Chinese couple without comment, were polled several weeks later on whether they would serve any Orientals, and 80 per cent of them replied that they would not. In both cases, reactions were tested in isolation from the realities of choice-making. In the case of the bus-drivers, defying the employer was obviously not preferable to accepting Negro drivers. In the restaurants, the greater evil may have been simply making a scene, or alienating the white person who accompanied the Chinese couple.

All this has crucial implications for Southern white resistance to integration. If we explore the full range of Southern preferences and values realistically, the strategy necessary for successful integration becomes clear and the weirdly illogical and uneven pattern of segregation in the Deep South becomes more comprehensible. Here are some examples of the values which white Southerners may consider more precious than continued segregation:

THE MOST OBVIOUS IS MONEY—THE SIMPLE DRIVE TO MAKE A PROFIT. The power of the boycott, directed against the bus companies in Montgomery, and the white tradesmen of Tuskegee, needs no elaboration. In a number of Southern cities, the bus companies have been unashamedly willing—in some cases anxious—to speed progress toward integration.

But beyond this, the fact that segregation does not strictly apply, even in the deepest South, to paid daily labor is so deeply established that it is often overlooked. A white plumbing contractor will hire a Negro helper and sit beside him on the front seat of his half-ton truck rather than hire a white helper and pay ten dollars more per week. The wage differential accounts, in thousands of instances, for the hiring of Negro employees on jobs for which whites are available, even though the two races must sit or work together. A diligent statistician could probably work out the prevailing market price of segregation—it does not appear to be worth more than about ten dollars a week to the white Southern employer. Whites work alongside Negroes in factories and on construction jobs, not always in superior capacities, for the good old-fashioned reason that "it's my job." Segregation is not worth the cost of a job to most Southern whites.

Negroes, it should be noted, are often respected customers in the stores of the Deep South. Their very preponderance, which segregationists often cite as a reason for their fears, operates to break down racial barriers. Negroes and whites stand on the same lines in the supermarkets, handle the same food, encounter for the most part the same courteous service which is a special pride of the South. (At the Motor Vehicle Bureau, lines are separate, but this is the state, and no private profit is involved.) At Rich's in Atlanta—the South's largest department store—Negroes and whites rub shoulders at the crowded counters. Women of all shades try on the same hats, the same dresses, and even the same foundation garments.

This was not true fifteen years ago, and growing Negro purchasing power is certainly a good part of the explanation. More and more, the Southern white retailer places a higher value on winning a new customer than on asserting his racial superiority. White salesmen will occasionally say "yes sir" to a Negro purchaser in Atlanta, something unheard of a decade ago.

Another proof of the power of economic pressures to break down racial barriers is the increasing amount of service being given to middle-class Negroes by white menial laborers. The old servant-employer relationship is being reversed as the Negro bourgeoisie expands. There are countless examples: the white telephone repairman wiping his feet as he enters the home of a Negro businessman; the white employees of a contractor digging ditches on the campus of a Negro university; the white deliveryman unloading his wares at the back entrance of a Negro lawyer's home. In every one of these cases, the simple value of "making a living" overrides whatever scruples these whites may have.

No one is more segregation-conscious than the General Assembly of the state of Georgia. Two years ago these legislators considered a bill to outlaw any integrated sports activity in the state. But this would have been a financial blow to the Atlanta "Crackers," and would have deprived Georgia of the business stimulated by major-league farm clubs. So, in the very same session which called for the impeachment of seven Supreme Court Justices, the sports segregation measure was buried.

The incident points up another key value—THE IMPORTANCE AMERICANS

ATTACH TO THEIR SPORTS. Many Southerners will not cling to segregation if it means giving up popular sports. Georgia Tech students showed this three years ago by their near-violent reaction when it appeared that segregation would cause cancellation of an important game. And the successful integration of golf courses in Atlanta was possible because whites refused to give up golf to keep Negroes away.

The high cost of segregation to Southern taxpayers has long been known and it may be argued that Southerners are not easily influenced by economic concerns because they have been willing to pay it. This is true, but for the same reason that factory workers will go on strike against a pay reduction but do nothing against an income tax which is far more costly. When the economic burden is indirect and distant, it becomes psychologically less oppressive. When it is felt immediately at hand, people will attempt anything to avoid it, even if that means making a sacrifice.

There are still other values more treasured in the South than segregation. ONE OF THESE IS SOCIAL PEACE, OR "LAW AND ORDER." Even in the most flagrant cases of violent opposition to integration—Little Rock, Clinton, the Nashville school dynamiting, the Autherine Lucy affair—only a small minority of Southerners has preferred violence to quiet if unhappy acceptance. More and more Southerners who strongly defend the idea of segregation are resigning themselves to compliance as the legal structure erected by the courts becomes increasingly formidable. There are still Southerners who talk in terms of "last-ditch resistance." But greater numbers are succumbing to the doctrine of inevitability. Many who *talk* uncompromisingly withdraw in silence when the time comes actually to defy the laws. Of course, for that tiny minority which values segregation above the peace of the Community, it may be necessary to use compulsion.

THE TRADITIONAL SOUTHERN QUALITIES OF HOSPITALITY, COURTLINESS, AND GOOD MANNERS come into conflict with segregation at many points, and increasingly they triumph. Many Northerners have noted with surprise a phenomenon which the South takes for granted: a vociferous segregationist, in personal contact with a Negro, can often be gentle and courteous. Such displays of courtesy had no real effect on living conditions in the South so long as the Negro remained "in his place." But as the Negro dares to appear in places and situations where he has never been, the courtesy will face a genuine test for the first time. And in many cases the individual white, facing a situation where he must violate ordinary rules of courtesy in order to defend racial separation, will maintain his conduct at the cost of permitting a breach in racial tradition.

Thus, particularly daring Negro college students will sit where they are "not supposed to" on a bus, and no one, including the driver, will say a word. Negroes will ask for a book at a "white" library, where the rules specifically bar them, and they will get it because the librarian does not want to be rude in a face-to-face situation. As more lines are crossed, the conflict between traditional Southern values of courtliness and racial arrogance will deepen. More people will have to make painful choices, and a good number, it is safe to say, will choose courtesy.

There are many sacrifices, it appears, which white Southerners simply will not make in order to maintain segregation, as much as they cherish it. Harry Golden once demonstrated that many Southerners will not even give up a drink of water to preserve their "way of life." When an "out of order" sign was put on a "white" drinking fountain, there was a brief period of hesitation, but soon everybody was drinking from the "colored" fountain. And since the recent desegregation of buses in Atlanta, there has been a slow but steady increase in the number of instances where whites will not give up the comfort of a seat to avoid sitting next to a Negro.

POLITICAL POWER IS ANOTHER VALUE THAT MAY PROVE MORE IMPORTANT THAN SEGREGATION—at least so far as Southern leaders are concerned. So long as few Negroes voted, Southern politicians could successfully exploit the race issue. But with the increase in Negro voting, the South is beginning to approach the point where political power may depend more on concessions to the Negro than on the kind of demagoguery that John Rankin and Eugene Talmadge made their specialty. The friendly new attitude of city officials in Atlanta is attributable in large part to their dependence on the Negro electorate. In the recent primary elections the city's white candidates flocked with their wives and children to the leading Negro Baptist Church to declare their friendship for the colored race. The same legislator who had supported the bill calling for impeachment of the Supreme Court appeared that evening to plead for support at the polls. And since that time, he has introduced a bill in the Georgia state legislature, asking the removal of all Constitutional references to segregation. As more Negroes vote, white politicians will increasingly find their hunger for office in conflict with their racial views.

NOW, TO MANY SOUTHERN PARENTS, THE EDUCATION OF THEIR CHILDREN IS BEGINNING TO SEEM MORE IMPORTANT THAN THE MAINTENANCE OF SEGREGATION. The petitions circulated in Little Rock, the placards borne in Virginia, were only the advance signs. The states of the Deep South—which depend on the closing of the public schools as their last legal weapon—have been shocked by the Virginia court decisions into the realization that the maintenance of tradition may require too great a sacrifice. Not only the Atlanta *Constitution's* Ralph McGill, but editorial writers in Macon, Gainesville, and other Georgia cities, are questioning the wisdom of closing down the public schools. There has been a stream of "letters to the editor" in the Atlanta newspapers asserting that desegregation is preferable to wiping out the school system. Some of the first letters were signed "Coward"—revealing testimony to the social and economic risks of nonconformity in the Deep

South today. One writer suggested forming a "Cowards Club" for people of like mind. But more and more people are giving their names as they realize the extent to which their fellow Atlantans share their sentiments.

It is possible that we have come to a turning point in the evolution of the integration controversy. Up to this point, integration has proceeded successfully in a good many instances, in both North and South, supported by *unconscious* preferences of the segregationists. From here on, as we face the last entrenched fortresses of Deep South resistance, the values which take precedence over segregation can be exploited *consciously* in order to bring about racial equality as quickly and as painlessly as possible. The Eisenhower Administration moved in this direction when it chose to hold back temporarily and wait for the effects of school closure on popular opinion in Little Rock, Norfolk, and Arlington. In Atlanta today, a new organization called HOPE (Help Our Public Education) is deliberately avoiding the bitter issue of segregation or integration by placing before the half-million people of that city a much lesser choice: integrated schools or no schools at all. Thus far the response has been heartening, and can be attributed to that strange ladder of values deep in the Southern mind, on which segregation is by no means the highest rung.

The South undoubtedly has a long way to go before it solves its race problems and it would be false to pretend that the way will be easy. But, as I have tried to show, many of the values to which Southerners are deeply attached are operating to remove the barriers between races in the South and not violently to reinforce them—even while the cries for continued segregation remain loud and bitter. This principle is a powerful one: whether or not it is used deliberately to deal with crises over Negro rights as they arise, I believe it must ultimately assert itself throughout the South. For the white Southerner it is becoming increasingly clear that there are many fates worse than integration.

WILLIAM P. ROGERS

The Right to Vote

This speech was delivered before the Economic Club of Detroit on February 8, 1960.

William P. Rogers was Attorney General of the United States from 1957 to 1961.

It is a privilege for me to appear at the Economic Club of Detroit. Because of the calibre of your membership and the energy of your officers your organization is an outstanding national forum.

You symbolize the growing awareness of all thoughtful Americans that the people of our nation must be interested not only in the problems that immediately affect them or in matters that touch their daily lives. Their interest must also extend to all national and international problems. The harm to our national standing and prestige as a result of the brutal lynching of Mack Charles Parker in Mississippi is of as much concern to us as anything which might happen in our own home towns or our own state. What happens in some remote province in India tomorrow may change the entire course of our lives. Never before in the history of our nation has it been so important that we have an awareness that we live in a world community and that we put aside personal prejudices and look beyond our immediate self-interests. Because this forum recognizes that fact, I want to discuss with you a national problem of considerable magnitude that has been largely brushed under the rug for more than 80 years.

We are beginning a new decade in America with pride in our democratic way of life. This fall we will go to the polls to elect our state and national leaders. Many thousands of American citizens, however, who are fully qualified under our laws to take part in that process will be denied that right because of their color. This is a serious matter and it concerns every person in our country whether he be Negro or white.

It is basic in a free society that the individual shall not only be free from oppression, but that he shall enjoy, in full measure, the means of self-expression. A fundamental method of expression depends upon the right to choose his representatives. Governments, as stated by the men who declared this nation's independence, derive "their just powers from the consent of the governed." Voting is the principal means by which the will and the consent of the governed may be manifested. Its practical bite is sharp. Those who vote have leverage. Thus, it is axiomatic that when minority groups exercise their franchise effectively, they realize, in greater measure, other fundamental protections and freedoms.

The right to vote free from invidious discrimination has been part of our constitutional fabric for 90 years. The 15th Amendment states unequivocally:

> The right of citizens of the United States to vote shall not be denied or abridged by the United States or by any State on account of race, color, or previous condition of servitude.

Despite this mandate, which falls equally on state and nation, we must acknowledge with candor that after almost a century this constitutionally protected right has remained largely unfulfilled in a few areas of our country for many of the citizens who were intended to be its principal beneficiaries.

What are some of the particulars of this contradiction between our principles and our practices?

In ten of our states, as a recent report of the Commission on Civil Rights discloses, only about 25 per cent of the Negroes of voting age are registered as contrasted with 60 per cent of the white population of voting age. In five of these states there were fifteen counties in which not one Negro of voting age was registered despite the fact that these citizens comprised more than 50 per cent of the population in each county. Similarly, there were more than 100 counties in which fewer than 5 per cent of the Negroes of voting age were registered. And, in not one of these ten states did Negroes comprise more than 14 per cent of the enfranchised population.

First, I think it may be helpful to analyze the problem briefly in terms of the respective responsibilities of state and nation. There is a persistent confusion, in this and related fields, concerning "states' rights," on the one hand, and the role of the federal government on the other.

The idea advanced by some that "states' rights" mean that a state has a right to do what it wants to do regardless of the federal constitution is fallacious and dangerous. Our nation learned the futility of such thinking under the Articles of Confederation. It is accurate to say that a state has a right to exercise powers not delegated to the United States—but it is inaccurate if you neglect to add that the state has a *responsibility* to exercise those powers in conformity with the Constitution of the United States.

It is for this reason that when we speak of "states' rights" we should add the words "and responsibilities." Every state has a responsibility to exercise its rights in conformity with the Constitution of the United States. It is this constitutional responsibility, solemnly imposed on each state, which makes our nation the United States of America.

So, under our constitutional system a state has a right to conduct elections and to establish qualifications for voters. However, it has a corresponding responsibility under the Constitution of the United States to do these things without discrimination on account of race or color—either by law or by administrative action.

In considering elections, a state may set the voting age at 18 or 21 or some other figure. It may prescribe other reasonable requirements—citizenship, residence, literacy, and the like. One proposition is, however, plain. Race or color is not a proper ground for disqualification. It is arbitrary, unreasonable, and unconstitutional.

Let us consider for a moment some of the techniques which have been used over the years to keep Negroes from voting in some areas.

One of the earliest devices was the enactment of registration laws containing so-called "grandfather clauses." These laws prescribed formidable registration tests but exempted those whose ancestors had been entitled to vote prior to the Civil War. This discriminatory technique was struck down when it came before the Supreme Court but the disappearance of one device has been regularly followed by the appearance of a variety of substitutes. Indeed, a latter-day version of the "grandfather" approach has appeared recently in the form of a state statute which gives permanent status to all persons currently registered and prescribes new and difficult tests for future registrants. The obvious aim is to "freeze" the existing voting pattern.

Some state qualification laws call for the applicant to prove a grasp of civics, a familiarity with current affairs and even an ability to interpret abstruse clauses of the Constitution. One such statute, for example, requires the answer to such questions as: "What is a republican form of government? What is the definition of a felony? Who is the Solicitor General of the Judicial Circuit in which you live? What does the Constitution of the United States provide regarding the suspension of the writ of habeas corpus?" Not all qualifying examinations are necessarily unreasonable, but it is apparent that they may be used as a means of racial discrimination. A biased registrar who gives an oral test to an applicant can readily translate his prejudice into a failing mark for the candidate.

Other discriminatory techniques have been widely employed in some areas. There are registrars who make themselves highly inaccessible to Negroes or who somehow never get around to processing their applications in time.

A somewhat more subtle discriminatory device is the requirement that a would-be registrant bring with him two persons already registered to "vouch" for him. The effect in communities where no Negroes are registered is apparent. Thus, in one county, a court found that for 31 years the registrar had failed to register any Negroes because no Negroes were registered and no one else would "vouch" for them. In other areas, the requirement has been given added teeth by refusing to permit any person to "vouch" for more than two other people in any given year.

We have witnessed, therefore, almost a century of persistent and successful efforts by some states to avoid their constitutional responsibilities and to defeat the objectives of the 15th Amendment. When the forces of a state officialdom are marshalled to deny constitutional rights to some citizens, the problem becomes one of national significance and demands national attention.

In the years preceding 1957, it had become unmistakably plain that the legal weapons available to the federal government were inadequate. At our disposal were several criminal statutes enacted in the post-Civil War years. However, they were of little practical value in securing and protecting the right to vote. It was virtually impossible to convince grand juries and petit juries that they should indict or convict state officials whose conduct reflected attitudes prevalent in the community.

Civil suits brought by private complainants to protect their individual rights had also proved largely ineffectual as a means of altering the pattern. To require a Negro to institute a suit against a state official was a high price to pay for the privilege of voting and few who were discriminated against had either the means or the inclination to pursue such a course.

Realizing these things, President Eisenhower took a vitally important step in the field of civil rights by recommending to the Congress what is now known as the Civil Rights Act of 1957. It is the first statute to be passed in more than 80 years to protect the Negro in exercising his right to vote.

It authorizes the Attorney General to bring an action in the name of the United States on behalf of Negroes who have been discriminated against on account of race or color by state officials. If the court finds that the state officials have so discriminated they may be enjoined from continuing such practices and may, upon refusal to comply, be sentenced to jail for criminal contempt.

Let me mention two of the cases which the United States has brought under the Act.

One of the cases before the court arises out of a suit to enjoin the registrars of Terrell County, Georgia, from discriminating against Negro applicants on the pretext that they are illiterate. The government offered to prove in that case that among those turned down on the ground of illiteracy were four Negroes who were graduates of Georgia colleges and teachers in Georgia's public schools. One of the four also held a master's degree from New York University. This case is now before the Supreme Court on the question of the constitutionality of the statute.

In another case which the Supreme Court will soon consider, the District Judge has ordered the registrar of a Louisiana parish to restore to the rolls some 1,400 Negroes whose names have been stricken because of trivial deficiencies in the registration forms. It was established in that case that there were similar deficiencies in most of the forms covering white voters. Challenges, however, were directed almost exclusively at Negro voters pursuant to an organized campaign which the trial court characterized as "massively discriminatory."

The experience of the last three years indicates that the 1957 Act should be strengthened in important respects.

Several states have recently passed statutes authorizing or requiring the destruction of voting records. This, of course, would lead to the disappearance of evidence which might be vital to proof of racial discrimination. We have accordingly recommended to the Congress an amendment which would require state registrars to preserve election records and would authorize the Attorney General to inspect them.

The Administration has also proposed an amendment to the Civil Rights Act of 1957 which would provide that in a case where a Federal District Court finds a "pattern of discrimination" it may appoint a "voting referee." He would be responsible to the court and, with the approval of the court, could authorize qualified Negroes to vote in any election. This bill would avoid the necessity of separate and lengthy litigation for each voter or each group of voters.

If Congress enacts these important and worthwhile bills the United States will proceed with utmost vigor and perseverance to enforce them. As head of the Department of Justice, I believe that we have a solemn duty to our country to make the Constitution of the United States mean what it says to all its citizens in every part of our country.

Up to this point I have been speaking of law enforcement. Possibly the most important question of all is whether there are any other ways to accomplish the objective except by law enforcement methods. The answer is that if the states concerned lived up to their responsibilities to the nation they would not be necessary. Unfortunately, as I have said, in some states this has not been the case. This was forcefully brought home by Judge Wright in the Louisiana case I referred to earlier when he concluded his opinion by suggesting "that instead of challenging the constitutionality of the Civil Rights Act of 1957, these defendants should be searching their souls to see if this charge is well founded."

It is most distasteful for the United States to be proceeding against states or state officials for refusing to comply with the Constitution of the United States. But what is the alternative? Must we continue to close our eyes to the inconsistency of our national position in this regard?

There is only one answer that makes sense either for the states concerned or the nation. The practice should be stopped by voluntary action of the states and state officials concerned. Although law enforcement will finally succeed, it will be costly to our national prestige and to our national self-respect.

Why shouldn't responsible leaders of the areas involved urge voluntary action to remove this blot? Why shouldn't this voluntary action be forthcoming? All concerned know that there is no justification for continuing racial discrimination in the voting process and that it will ultimately be removed. But wouldn't it be a great national blessing if the change could be made voluntarily rather than by the difficult and disruptive processes of law enforcement?

If this were done—if good faith efforts were being made to give Negroes an equal opportunity to vote—there would be no necessity for federal action and none would be taken. But until this happens, particularly because the Negro has been made to wait so long, the United States must, by legislation and law enforcement methods, move forward with the greatest possible speed.

In conclusion, let me say that there is considerable hope that a meaningful civil rights bill will be enacted by this Congress. But it is important that any new measures in this field meet two tests—will they stand up under court challenge and will they be effective? We can ill afford to atone for 90 years of failure by enacting legislation effective in theory but impractical in application.

In our thinking on this problem we must consider the image that racial discrimination presents to a largely non-white world. Naturally doubts will arise about whether our system holds forth the greatest hope for individual freedom and dignity when we exclude from our voting process some of our own citizens on account of color.

Prime Minister Macmillan stated the other day before the South African Parliament that the "wind of change" throughout Asia and Africa is blowing. These nations have not committed themselves to either Western ideas of democracy or to Communism. But they are watching. "What is now on trial" he said "is much more than our military strength or our diplomatic or administrative skill. It is our way of life."

Throughout the world, today, the word "democracy" is a rallying cry. It expresses men's basic desires for dignity and the fullest utilization of human potential. The concept of democracy, indeed the word itself, is a source of such powerful inspiration that even its greatest enemies cynically attempt to use it by designating themselves "peoples democracies."

This nation, both at home and abroad, has consistently espoused the principles of equality before the law and the worth of every individual. To keep faith with ourselves, to live up to our national ideal, we must be unremitting in our efforts to secure to all our citizens the full opportunity to exercise those basic rights which are the common heritage of all free peoples.

JOHN STEINBECK

Atque Vale

This article was published in the Saturday Review for July 23, 1960.

John Steinbeck is best known as a novelist (The Grapes of Wrath won a Pulitzer prize in 1940), but he also makes frequent comments on contemporary affairs.

I am constantly amazed at the qualities we expect in Negroes. No race has ever offered another such high regard. We expect Negroes to be wiser than we are, more tolerant than we are, braver, more dignified than we, more self-controlled and self-disciplined. We even demand more talent from them than from ourselves. A Negro must be ten times as gifted as a white to receive equal recognition. We expect Negroes to have more endurance than we in athletics, more courage in defeat, more rhythm and versatility in music and dancing, more controlled emotion in theatre. We expect them to obey rules of conduct we flout, to be more courteous, more gallant, more proud, more steadfast. In a word, while maintaining that Negroes are inferior to us, by our unquestioning faith in them we prove our conviction that they are superior in many fields, even fields we are presumed to be trained and conditioned in and they are not.

Let me give a few examples.

In the Alabama bus boycott we knew there would be no Negro violence —and there wasn't. The only violence was white violence.

In the streets we expect courtesy from Negroes even when we are ugly and overbearing.

In the prize ring we know a Negro will be game and will not complain at a decision.

In Little Rock we knew that any brutality would originate among the whites.

For a long time whites would not compete against Negroes for fear they might lose. It was said that their coordination—it was called animal co-ordination—was better and their physical responses quicker.

If there is racial trouble, we are convinced that Negroes will not strike the first blow, will not attack in the night, will not set off bombs, and our belief is borne out by events.

We expect Negroes to be good-tempered and self-controlled under all circumstances.

But our greatest expectation is that they will be honest, honorable, and decent. This is the most profound compliment we can pay any man or group. And the proof of this shows in our outrage when a Negro does not live up to the picture we ordinarily have of him.

With thousands of burglaries, muggings, embezzlements reported every day, we are upset when a Negro is found doing what so many whites do regularly.

In New York, with its daily reports of public thefts, deceits, and assorted political and fiscal raids on public money and treason against public trust, one Negro who succumbs to the temptation to do what many white people do fills us with dismay and the papers are full of it. What greater compliment can we pay to a people?

Finally, let me bring it down to cases.

I have children, as many of you whites who read this have. Do you think your children would have the guts, the dignity, and the responsibility to go to school in Little Rock knowing they would be insulted, shoved, hated, sneered at, even spat upon day after day, and do it quietly without showing anger, petulance, or complaint? And even if they could take it, would they also get good grades?

Now I am a grown, fairly well-educated—I hope intelligent—white man. I know that violence can produce no good effect of any kind. And yet if my child were spat on and insulted, I couldn't trust myself not to get a ball bat and knock out a few brains. But I trust Negroes not to, and they haven't.

I think so much of those school children in Little Rock—a small handful who carry the will and conscience, the hopes and futures of millions in their arms. They have not let their people down. I think, what quiet pride their grandchildren can have in them knowing they came of such stock.

And then I think of the faces of the mob that tried to keep them out, faces drooling hatred, cursing and accursed faces, brave only in numbers, spitting their venom at children. And some of those faces, masked, sneaking in the night to plant a bomb—the final weapon of a coward.

What pride can their descendants take in their ancestry? But of course they will forget, or lie, or both.

When Martin Luther King was stabbed by a hysterical woman, he might well have felt some anger or hurt or despair. But his first words on coming out of the anesthetic were: "Don't let them hurt her. She needs help."

Perhaps some of the anger against Negroes stems from a profound sense of their superiority, and perhaps their superiority is rooted in having a cause and an unanswerable method composed of courage, restraint, and a sense of direction.

JOHN JAY CHAPMAN

Coatesville Address

On August 14, 1911, John Jay Chapman, lawyer, essayist, and reformer, read in his New York City newspapers an account of a particularly brutal lynching of a Negro in Coatesville, Pennsylvania. Although he was not personally associated in any way with the persons or place involved in the atrocity, Chapman brooded on the event. As the first anniversary of the lynching approached, Chapman announced to his family that he was going to Coatesville to hold a prayer meeting and to deliver a speech commemorating the terrible occasion. In Coatesville, Chapman encountered a population suspicious of his motives and growing increasingly sensitive to the approaching anniversary. After frustrating attempts to find a hall in Coatesville suitable for his meeting, Chapman finally succeeded in renting an empty store. He placed advertisements in the local paper, and held his prayer meeting on Sunday, August 18, 1912. This speech was his sermon. He delivered it to an audience of three persons: a lady friend who had accompanied Chapman to Coatesville, an elderly Negro woman, and an unidentified man, believed to have been a local spy.

We are met to commemorate the anniversary of one of the most dreadful crimes in history—not for the purpose of condemning it, but to repent of our share in it. We do not start any agitation with regard to that particular crime. I understand that an attempt to prosecute the chief criminals has been made, and has entirely failed; because the whole community, and in a sense our whole people, are really involved in the guilt. The failure of the prosecution in this case, in all such cases, is only a proof of the magnitude of the guilt, and of the awful fact that everyone shares in it.

I will tell you why I am here; I will tell you what happened to me. When I read in the newspapers of August 14, a year ago, about the burning alive of a human being, and of how a few desperate, fiend-minded men had been permitted to torture a man chained to an iron bedstead, burning alive, thrust back by pitchforks when he struggled out of it, while around about stood hundreds of well-dressed American citizens, both from the vicinity and from afar, coming on foot and in wagons, assembling on telephone call, as if by magic, silent, whether from terror or indifference, fascinated and impotent, hundreds of persons watching this awful sight and making no attempt to stay the wickedness, and no one man among them all who was inspired to risk his life in an attempt to stop it, no one man to name the name of Christ, of humanity, of government! As I read the newspaper accounts of the scene enacted here in Coatesville a year ago, I seemed to get a glimpse into the unconscious soul of this country. I saw a seldom revealed picture of the American heart and of the American nature. I seemed to be looking into the heart of the criminal—a cold thing, an awful thing.

I said to myself, "I shall forget this, we shall all forget it; but it will be there. What I have seen is not an illusion. It is the truth. I have seen death in the heart of this people." For to look at the agony of a fellow-being and remain aloof means death in the heart of the onlooker. Religious fanaticism has sometimes lifted men to the frenzy of such cruelty, political passion has sometimes done it, personal hatred might do it, the excitement of the amphitheater in the degenerate days of Roman luxury could do it. But here an audience chosen by chance in America has stood spellbound through an improvised *auto-da-fé,* irregular, illegal, having no religious significance, not sanctioned by custom, having no immediate provocation, the audience standing by merely in cold dislike.

I saw during one moment something beyond all argument in the depth of its significance. You might call it the paralysis of the nerves about the heart in a people habitually and unconsciously given over to selfish aims, an ignorant people who knew not what spectacle they were providing, or what part they were playing in a judgment-play which history was exhibiting on that day.

No theories about the race problem, no statistics, legislation, or mere educational endeavor, can quite meet the lack which that day revealed in the American people. For what we saw was death. The people stood like blighted things, like ghosts about Acheron, waiting for someone or something to determine their destiny for them.

Whatever life itself is, that thing must be replenished in us. The opposite of hate is love, the opposite of cold is heat; what we need is the love of God and reverence for human nature. For one moment I knew that I had seen our true need; and I was afraid that I should forget it and that I should start schemes of education, when the need was deeper than education. And I became filled with one idea, that I must not forget what I had seen, and that I must do something to remember it. And I am here today chiefly that I may remember that vision. It seems fitting to come to this town where the crime occurred and hold a prayer-meeting, so that our hearts may be turned to God through whom mercy may flow into us.

Let me say something more about the whole matter. The subject we are dealing with is not local. The act, to be sure, took place at Coatesville and everyone looked to Coatesville to follow it up. Some months ago I asked a friend who lives not far from here something about this case, and about the expected prosecutions, and he replied to me: "It wasn't in my county," and that made me wonder whose county it was in. And it seemed to be in my county. I live on the Hudson River; but I knew that this great wickedness that happened in Coatesville is not the wickedness of Coatesville nor of today. It is the wickedness of all America and of three hundred years—the wickedness of the slave trade. All of us are tinctured by it. No special place, no special persons, are to blame. A nation cannot practice a course of inhuman crime for three hundred years and then suddenly throw off the effects of it. Less than fifty years ago domestic slavery was abolished among us; and in one way and another the marks of that vice are in our faces. There is no country in Europe where the Coatesville tragedy or anything remotely like it could have been enacted, probably no country in the world.

On the day of the calamity, those people in the automobiles came by the hundred and watched the torture, and passers-by came in a great multitude and watched it—and did nothing. On the next morning the newspapers spread the news and spread the paralysis until the whole country seemed to be helplessly watching this awful murder, as awful as anything ever done on the earth; and the whole of our people seemed to be looking on helplessly, not able to respond, not knowing what to do next. That spectacle has been in my mind.

The trouble has come down to us out of the past. The only reason slavery is wrong is that it is cruel and makes men cruel and leaves them cruel. Someone may say that you and I cannot repent because we did not do the act. But we are involved in it. We are still looking on. Do you not see that this whole event is merely the last parable, the most vivid, the most terrible illustration that ever was given by man or imagined by a Jewish prophet, of the relation between good and evil in this world, and of the relation of men to one another?

This whole matter has been an historic episode; but it is a part, not only of our national history, but of the personal history of each one of us. With the great disease (slavery) came the climax (the war), and after the climax gradually began the cure, and in the process of cure comes now the knowledge of what the evil was. I say that our need is new life, and that books and resolutions will not save us, but only such disposition in our hearts and souls as will enable the new life, love, force, hope, virtue, which surround us always, to enter into us.

This is the discovery that each man must make for himself—the discovery that what he really stands in need of he cannot get for himself, but must wait till God gives it to him. I have felt the impulse to come here today to testify to this truth.

The occasion is not small; the occasion looks back on three centuries and embraces a hemisphere. Yet the occasion is small compared with the truth it leads us to. For this truth touches all ages and affects every soul in the world.

Critical Note on Chapman

Ostensibly, the Coatesville Address is an example of ceremonial speaking. Its aim is the commemoration of an historical event, and its circumstance is an occasion when the event is being remembered. These are the typical attributes of a ceremony, and in sharing these attributes, the Coatesville Address is in the same general category as a Fourth of July oration, a commencement speech, or a funeral eulogy. However, it is only in these characteristics that Chapman's speech resembles the ceremonial discourse.

The typical ceremonial speech is devoted to enhancing and amplifying some of the beliefs and values common to the speaker and his audience. For example, the Fourth of July orator usually praises something which he calls "freedom." He is careful not to define "freedom" with any precision; he merely praises it, and all the members of his audience nod their heads in agreement. The members of the National Association of Manufacturers agree, and the members of the AFL-CIO agree. Tipplers and Prohibitionists agree. Saints and executioners agree. Everybody is in favor of "freedom," whatever he means by it. Thus, when the ceremonial speaker praises "freedom," he offends no one; he gains an almost universal assent.

The occasion of Chapman's Coatesville Address was ceremonial: the anniversary of an historical event. But there are certain characteristics of Chapman's speech which mark it as quite an exceptional kind of ceremonial speech, indeed, as an extraordinary and singular speech. First, instead of praising or condemning some event, idea, or condition toward which the speaker and his audience share the same attitude, Chapman explores with relentless honesty an episode that is painfully embarrassing to the people of Coatesville, his intended audience. Second, the idea which Chapman presents as his rhetorical apocalypse is far from being a harmless ambiguity or a notion initially attractive to the intended audience. It is one which the people of Coatesville would not even have understood. And yet the speech is strong: vivid, memorable, exciting. Why?

In answering this question we first must look at the speaker's personality as it is reflected by the speech and by the circumstances of its delivery. The impression of Chapman which the people of Coatesville probably would have received was that of a crank, a nosy fanatic, a troublemaker, perhaps a madman. But we have the advantage of a half-century's perspective on the speech and on the event which provoked it. We are able to see the man behind the speech as one with an acutely sensitive conscience and a fervent concern for morality, willing to risk his safety and his "respectability" in service to his principles. Whatever else we may think of Chapman's act in traveling to Coatesville, we are bound to grant that it was an act of courage. And once Chapman's courage and moral sensitivity communicate themselves through the medium of his speech, it is no longer possible to dismiss him as a "mere" fanatic, or a crank, or a madman.

Second, we must note the general point of view lying behind the speech, the whole system of judgments and attitudes that made the speech possible. When we witness any act of heroic goodness or shocking evil, our impulse frequently is to ask, What sort of man would do this? What sort of man would risk his reputation for an ideal? What sort of man would participate in a lynching? From what men do, we infer what they are. Similarly, the current reader of Chapman's speech is brought to ask himself, What general point of view, what conclusions about human nature and the world would bring a man to say the things that Chapman said?

The fact is that we cannot discern in this speech all of the moral and sociological doctrines upon which it stands. What we do discern is that Chapman had original and complicated convictions about the nature of evil, the pathology of American society, and the character of religious insight. These convictions are by no means made clear in the speech. But through the speech we are compelled to infer that these convictions were there, in Chapman's mind, enabling him to make this speech, and to say just the things that he said.

We can find a rhetorical parallel in Lincoln's famous Second Inaugural Address, delivered during the bloody fury of the Civil War. In this address, with its celebrated "malice toward none—charity for all" passage, Lincoln rose above the bellicose partisanship of his immediate audience. This audience, agitated by war, was in no mood for compassion. The ceremonial speaker who rattled his saber, who vindicated their indignation, and who promised punishment for their enemies, would have been enforcing his listeners' common beliefs. But Lincoln, from a frame of reference radically different from his audience's, spoke of charity and of peace. His speech still lives, not because it gave an audience what that audience wanted to hear, but because it rose above that audience and disclosed a moral system which transcended any single time or place.

In the same way, Chapman's speech has power because it is the rhetorical symptom of a profound and intricate morality. We have to rely on other writings of Chapman to learn what that morality is. In this speech we see only its shadow. But that shadow alone is enough to give the speech strength and to confirm that Chapman's vision "touches all ages and affects every soul in the world."

Questions

Dawson maintains that those who fight for the United States are entitled to full citizenship. Do you agree? Should conscientious objectors who refuse to fight lose all or part of their rights as citizens?

Do you believe that color or religion should be a factor in choosing a physician? A roommate? A co-worker? Does one have a moral right to make race or religion a factor in such choices?

Should interracial marriages be prohibited by law? Is there any evidence that such marriages follow upon integration? Should government have the right to impose any restrictions on the choice of a marriage partner? Religious restrictions? Racial restrictions? Age restrictions?

Should the owner of a hotel be permitted to refuse accommodations to Orientals? A theater manager refuse admittance to Negroes? A dairy refuse to sell milk to Puerto Ricans? A university restrict the proportion of Jews among its students? If you owned a business and had to choose between employing and serving a minority group, and suffering economic losses, which would you choose? Which would be the moral choice?

How can integration in the South best be accomplished? If Negroes secured their full voting rights, would other civil rights follow more easily? Is it better to move slowly toward integration and create as little "tension" as possible, or to move quickly and vigorously, and end segregation as soon as possible?

Do the Democratic and Republican parties differ significantly in their views on integration? Should any pressures other than legal pressures be brought to bear on segregated areas? Is "education" the most effective solution to racial problems? What educational program would you recommend?

How can integration in the North best be accomplished? Is the number of Negroes in northern universities disproportionately small? Should minority groups be represented in educational institutions in proportion to their size? In business occupations? In residential areas?

Suggestions for Further Reading

"America, His Hope, His Future. . . ." New York *Times,* Jan. 17, 1960, section 10.
Anshen, Ruth N. *Freedom: Its Meaning.* New York: Harcourt, Brace, 1940.
Dykeman, Wilma, and James Stokely. " 'The South' in the North," New York *Times Magazine,* April 17, 1960, p. 8.
East, P. D. "How to be a Man of Distinction," *Harper's,* January 1959, p. 11.
Forster, Arnold. *A Measure of Freedom: An Anti-Defamation League Report.* New York: Doubleday, 1950.
Hand, Learned. *The Spirit of Liberty.* Ed. by Irving Dilliard. New York: Knopf, 1953.
Konvitz, Milton R. *The Constitution and Civil Rights.* New York: Columbia University Press, 1947.
Lewis, Anthony. "Human Background of the Civil Rights Issue," New York *Times Magazine,* Feb. 14, 1960, p. 10.
Lowenstein, Edith. *The Alien and the Immigration Law.* New York: Oceana, 1958.
Millis, Walter. *Individual Freedom and the Common Defense.* Fund for the Republic pamphlet, 1957.
Morgan, Robert W., Jr. "Over the Bridge," *Atlantic Monthly,* Feb. 1959, p. 73.
Newman, Edwin S., ed. *The Freedom Reader.* (Docket Series, Vol. 2.) New York: Oceana, 1955.
———. *The Law of Civil Rights and Civil Liberties.* New York: Oceana, 1949.
Rowan, Carl T. *South of Freedom.* New York: Knopf, 1952.
Shoemaker, Don S., ed. *With All Deliberate Speed.* New York: Harper, 1957.
Slawson, John. *Social Discrimination: The Last Barrier.* American Jewish Committee pamphlet, 1955.
Smith, Stanley H. *Freedom to Work.* New York: Vantage, 1955.
"Special Report on Civil Rights Legislation," *Congressional Quarterly,* May 6, 1960, p. 749.
United States House of Representatives Committee on Un-American Activities. *Preliminary Report on Neo-Fascist and Hate Groups.* (Document Y4 Un 1/2: L11.) Washington, D.C.: Government Printing Office, 1954.

4. Education

Introduction

Pressure from two distinct sources has come to bear on the American educational system within the last decade, engendering wide public concern over education and forcing a critical re-examination of our educational institutions and practices.

One scource of pressure has been the Soviet achievements in technology, especially in space exploration. Our chief international rival, in exhibiting the fruits of a proficient system of technological training, has projected the subject of education onto the arena of the Cold War, thereby dramatizing to the American public some of the deficiencies of our own educational system.

A second pressure bearing on American education is the generation of "war babies" now engulfing our colleges. The sheer numbers of students, seeking entrance into institutions equipped for a much smaller population, are straining our educational resources and forcing us to difficult decisions concerning who may be educated and what will constitute an education.

The speeches and essays in this section focus on some of these decisions. Our legislators and professional educators are preoccupied with finding additional support for education. But even more important than finding money is determining how it should be spent: whether on education for the superior few or the average many; whether on technology, with its promise of material rewards, or on the humanities, with their less measureable consequences.

As the speech by Woodrow Wilson demonstrates, some of our vexations over education are older than Sputnik, but the exigencies of our time give them special urgency.

WOODROW WILSON

The Spirit of Learning

Wilson, then president of Princeton University, delivered this speech on July 1, 1909, before the Phi Beta Kappa chapter of Harvard University.

When this address was given, Wilson was in the midst of a bitter debate at Princeton over his plan to abolish the private residential clubs for students (Princeton's equivalent of fraternities) and to substitute for them dormitories in which all students would be required to reside. Older tutors would reside in the dormitories with the students and bring "the spirit of learning" into the university's residential facilities. Wilson ultimately failed in his efforts to implement these proposals and, in the year after this speech was given, he resigned the presidency of Princeton to become governor of New Jersey.

The "college" referred to in the speech can be understood as the college of liberal arts.

We have fallen of late into a deep discontent with the college, with the life and the work of the undergraduates in our universities. It is an honorable discontent, bred in us by devotion, not by captiousness or hostility or by an unreasonable impatience to set the world right. We are not critics, but anxious and thoughtful friends. We are neither cynics nor pessimists, but honest lovers of a good thing, of whose slightest deterioration we are jealous. We would fain keep one of the finest instrumentalities of our national life from falling short of its best, and believe that by a little care and candor we can do so.

The American college has played a unique part in American life. So long as its aims were definite and its processes authoritative it formed men who brought to their tasks an incomparable morale, a capacity that seemed more than individual, a power touched with large ideals. The college has been the seat of ideals. The liberal training which it sought to impart took no thought of any particular profession or business, but was meant to reflect in its few and simple disciplines the image of life and thought. Men were bred by it to no skill or craft or calling: the discipline to which they were subjected had a more general object. It was meant to prepare them for the whole of life rather than for some particular part of it. The ideals which lay at its heart were the general ideals of conduct, of right living, and right thinking, which made them aware of a world moralized by principle, steadied and cleared of many an evil thing by true and catholic reflection and just feeling, a world, not of interests, but of ideas.

Such impressions, such challenges to a man's spirit, such intimations of privilege and duty are not to be found in the work and obligations of professional and technical schools. They cannot be. Every calling has its ethics, indeed its standards of right conduct and wrong, its outlook upon action and upon the varied relationships of society. Its work is high and honorable, grounded, it may be, in the exact knowledge which moralizes the processes of thought, and in a skill which makes the whole man serviceable. But it is notorious how deep and how narrow the absorptions of the professional school are and how much they are necessarily concentrated upon the methods and interests of a particular occupation. The work to be done in them is as exact, as definite, as exclusive as that of the office and the shop. Their atmosphere is the atmosphere of business, and should be. It does not beget generous comradeships or any ardor of altruistic feeling such as the college begets. It does not contain that general air of the world of science and of letters in which the mind seeks no special interest, but feels every intimate impulse of the spirit set free to think and observe and listen—listen to all the voices of the mind. The professional school differs from the college as middle age differs from youth. It gets the spirit of the college only by imitation or reminiscence or contagion. This is to say nothing to its discredit. Its nature and objects are different from those of the college—as legitimate, as useful, as necessary; but different. The college is the place of orientation; the professional school is the place of concentration. The object of the college is to liberalize and moralize; the object of the professional school is to train the powers to a special task. And this is true of all vocational study.

I am, of course, using the words liberalize and moralize in their broadest significance, and I am very well aware that I am speaking in the terms of an ideal, a conception, rather than in the terms of realized fact. I have spoken, too, of what the college did "so long as its aims were definite and its processes authoritative," as if I were thinking of it wholly in the past tense and wished to intimate that it was once a very effective and ideal thing but had now ceased to exist; so that one would suppose that I thought the college lost out of our life and the present a time when such influences were all to seek. But that is only because I have not been able to say everything at once. Give me leave, and I will slowly write in the phrases which will correct these impressions and bring a true picture to light.

The college has lost its definiteness of aim, and has now for so long a time affected to be too modest to assert its authority over its pupils in any matter of prescribed study that it can no longer claim to be the nurturing mother it once was; but the college is neither dead nor moribund, and it has made up for its relaxed discipline and confused plans of study by many notable gains, which, if they have not improved its scholarship, have improved the health and the practical morals of the young gentlemen who resort to it, have enhanced their vigor and quickened their whole natures. A freer choice of studies has imparted to it a stir, an air of freedom and individual initiative, a wealth and variety of instruction which the old college altogether lacked. The development of athletic sports and the immoderate addiction of undergraduates to stimulating activities of all sorts, academic and unacademic, which improve their physical habits, fill their lives with interesting objects, sometimes important, and challenge their powers of organization and practical management, have unquestionably raised the tone of morals and of conduct in our colleges and have given them an interesting, perhaps valuable, connection with modern society and the broader popular interests of the day. No one need regret the breaking-up of the dead levels of the old college, the introduction and exaltation of modern studies, or the general quickening of life which has made of our youngsters more manly fellows, if less docile pupils. There had come to be something rather narrow and dull and morbid, no doubt, about the old college before its day was over. If we gain our advances by excessive reactions and changes which change too much, we at least gain them, and should be careful not to lose the advantage of them.

Nevertheless, the evident fact is, that we have now for a long generation devoted ourselves to promoting changes which have resulted in all but complete disorganization, and it is our plain and immediate duty to form our plans for reorganization. We must re-examine the college, reconceive it, reorganize it. It is the root of our intellectual life as a nation. It is not only the instrumentality through which we must effect all the broad preliminary work which underlies sound scholarship; it is also our chief instrumentality of catholic enlightenment, our chief means for giving widespread stimulation to the whole intellectual life of the country and supplying ourselves with men who shall both comprehend their age and duty and know how to serve them supremely well. Without the American college our young men would be too exclusively shut in to the pursuit of individual interests, would lose the vital contacts and emulations which awaken them to those larger achievements and sacrifices which are the highest objects of education in a country of free citizens, where the welfare of the commonwealth springs out of the character and the informed purposes of the private citizen. The college will be found to lie somewhere very near the heart of American social training and intellectual and moral enlightenment.

The process is familiar to every one by which the disintegration was brought about which destroyed the old college with its fixed disciplines and ordered life and gave us our present problem of reorganization and recovery. It centered in the break-up of the old curriculum and the introduction of the principle that the student was to select his own studies from a great variety of courses, as great a variety as the resources of the college and the supply of teachers available made possible. But the change could not in the nature of things stop with the plan of study. It held at its heart a tremendous implication: the implication of full manhood on the part of the pupil, and all the untrammelled choices of manhood. The pupil who was mature and well informed enough to study what he chose was also by necessary implication mature enough to be left free to *do* what he pleased, to choose his own associations and ways of life outside the curriculum without restraint or suggestion; and the varied, absorbing college life of our day sprang up as the natural offspring of the free election of studies.

There went along with the relaxation of rule as to what undergraduates should study, therefore, an almost absolute divorce between the studies and the life of the college, its business and its actual daily occupations. The teacher ceased to look upon himself as related in any responsible way to the life of his pupils, to what they should be doing and thinking of between one class exercise and another, and conceived his whole duty to have been performed when he had given his lecture and afforded those who were appointed to come the opportunity to hear and heed it if they chose. The teachers of this new regime . . . have never thought of the university as a community of teachers and pupils: they think of it, rather, as a body of teachers and investigators to whom those may resort who seriously desire specialized kinds of knowledge. . . . They do not think of living with their pupils and affording them the contacts of culture; they are only accessible to them at stated periods and for a definite and limited service; and their teaching is an interruption to their favorite work of research.

Meanwhile, the constituency of the college has wholly changed. It is not only the bookish classes who now send their sons to college, but also men of business and of affairs, who expect their sons to follow in their own footsteps and do work with which books have little connection. In the old days of which I have spoken most young men who went to college expected to enter one or other of the learned professions, expected to have to do with books and some of the more serious kinds of learning all their lives. Books were their proper introduction to the work that lay before them; learning was their natural discipline and preparation. But nowadays the men who are looking forward to the learned professions are in a minority at the college. Most undergraduates come out of an atmosphere of business and wish a breeding which is consonant with it. They do not wish learning. They wish only a certain freshening of their faculties for the miscellaneous contacts of life, a general acquaintance with what men are doing and saying in their own generation, a certain facility in handling themselves and in getting on in the incidental associations of college life rather than in the main intellectual occupations of the place. They want to be made men of, not scholars; and the life led at college is as serviceable for that as any of the tasks set in the classroom. If they want what the formal teaching offers them at all, it is for some definite and practical purpose connected with the calling they expect to follow, the business they expect to engage in. Such pupils are specially unsuitable for such teachers.

Here, then, is our situation. Here is the little world of teachers and pupils, athletic associations, musical and literary clubs, social organizations and societies for amusement, class-room and playground, of which we must make analysis, out of which we must get a new synthesis, a definite aim, and new processes of authoritative direction, losing nothing that has been gained, recovering what has been lost. All the fresh elements we have gained are valuable, many of the new points of view are those from which we must look upon the whole task and function of the college if we would see it truly; but we have fallen upon an almost hopeless confusion and an utter dispersion of energy. We must pull the whole inorganic thing together under a new conception of what the college must be and do.

The chief and characteristic mistake which the teachers and governors of our colleges have made in these latter days has been that they have devoted themselves and their plans too exclusively to the business, the very commonplace business, of instruction, to well-conceived lectures and approved class-room method, and have not enough regarded the life of the mind. The mind does not live by instruction. It is no prolix gut to be stuffed. The real intellectual life of a body of undergraduates, if there be any, manifests itself, not in the class-room, but in what they do and talk of and set before themselves as their favorite objects between classes and lectures. You will see the true life of a college in the evenings, at the dinner-table or beside the fire in groups that gather and the men that go off eagerly to their work, where youths get together and let themselves go upon their favorite themes—in the effect their studies have upon them when no compulsion of any kind is on them and they are not thinking to be called to a reckoning of what they know.

The effects of learning are its real tests, the real tests alike of its validity and of its efficacy. The mind can be driven, but that is not life. Life is voluntary or unconscious. It is breathed in out of a sustaining atmosphere. It is shaped by environment. It is habitual, continuous, productive. It does not consist in tasks performed, but in powers gained and enhanced. It cannot be communicated in class-rooms if its aim and end is the class-room. Instruction is not its source, but only its incidental means and medium.

Here is the key to the whole matter: the object of the college, as we have known and used and loved it in America, is not scholarship (except for the few, and for them only by way of introduction and first orientation), but the intellectual and spiritual life. Its life and discipline are meant to be a process of preparation, not a process of information. By the intellectual and spiritual life I mean the life which enables the mind to comprehend and make proper use of the modern world and all its opportunities. The object of a liberal training is not learning, but discipline and the enlightenment of the mind. The educated man is to be discovered by his point of view, by the temper of his mind, by his attitude towards life and his fair way of thinking. He can see, he can discriminate, he can combine ideas and perceive whither they lead; he has insight and comprehension. His mind is a practised instrument of appreciation. He is more apt to contribute light than heat to a discussion, and will oftener than another show the power of uniting the elements of a difficult subject in a whole view; he has the knowledge of the world which no one can have who knows only his own generation or only his own task.

What we should seek to impart in our colleges, therefore, is not so much learning itself as the spirit of learning. You can impart that to young men;

and you can impart it to them in the three or four years at your disposal. It consists in the power to distinguish good reasoning from bad, in the power to digest and interpret evidence, in a habit of catholic observation and a preference for the non-partisan point of view, in addiction to clear and logical processes of thought and yet an instinctive desire to interpret rather than to stick in the letter of the reasoning, in a taste for knowledge and a deep respect for the integrity of the human mind. It is citizenship of the world of knowledge, but not ownership of it. Scholars are the owners of its varied plots in severalty.

If we recognize and accept these ideas, this conception of the function and the possibilities of the college, there is hope of a general understanding and accommodation. At present there is a fundamental misunderstanding. The teachers in our colleges are men of learning and conceive it their duty to impart learning; but their pupils do not desire it, and the parents of their pupils do not desire it for them. They desire something else which the teacher has little thought of giving, generally thinks it no part of his function to give. Many of the parents of our modern undergraduates will frankly tell you that what they want for their sons is not so much what they will get in the class-room as something else, which they are at a loss to define, which they will get from the associations of college life: and many more would say the same thing if they were equally ingenuous. I know what they mean, and I am free to say that I sympathize with them . . . , but I agree with them only if what is to be got in the class-room is nothing more than items of knowledge likely to be quickly lost hold of. I agree with them; but I see clearly what they are blindly feeling after. They should desire chiefly what their sons are to get out of the life and associations of the place; but that life and those associations should be freighted with things they do not now contain. The processes of life, the contagions of association, are the only things that have ever got any real or permanent hold on men's minds. These are the conducting media for every effect we seek to work on the human spirit. The undergraduate should have scholars for teachers. They should hold his attention steadily upon great tested bodies of knowledge and should insist that he make himself acquainted with them, if only for the nonce. But they will give him nothing he is likely to carry with him through life if they stop with formal instruction, however thorough or exacting they may make it. Their permanent effects will be wrought upon his spirit. Their teaching will follow him through life only if they reveal to him the meaning, the significance, the essential validity of what they are about, the motives which prompt it, the processes which verify it. They will rule him, not by what they know and inform him of, but by the spirit of the things they expound. And that spirit they cannot convey in any formal manner. They can convey it only atmospherically, by making their ideals tell in some way upon the whole spirit of the place.

How shall their pupils carry their spirit away with them, or the spirit of the things they teach, if beyond the door of the class-room the atmosphere will not contain it? College is a place of initiation. Its effects are atmospheric. They are wrought by impression, by association, by emulation. The voices which do not penetrate beyond the doors of the class-room are lost, are ineffectual, are void of consequence and power. No thought will obtain or live there for the transmission of which the prevailing atmosphere is a non-conducting medium. If young gentlemen get from their years at college only manliness, *esprit de corps,* a release of their social gifts, a training in give and take, a catholic taste in men, and the standards of true sportsmen, they have gained much, but they have not gained what a college should give them. It should give them insight into the things of the mind and of the spirit, a sense of having lived and formed their friendships amidst the gardens of the mind where grows the tree of the knowledge of good and evil, a consciousness of having taken on them the vows of true enlightenment and of having undergone the discipline, never to be shaken off, of those who seek wisdom in candor, with faithful labour and travail of spirit.

These things they cannot get from the class-room unless the spirit of the class-room is the spirit of the place as well and of its life; and that will never be until the teacher comes out of the class-room and makes himself a part of that life. Contact, companionship, familiar intercourse is the law of life for the mind. The comradeships of undergraduates will never breed the spirit of learning. The circle must be widened. It must include the older men, the teachers, the men for whom life has grown more serious and to whom it has revealed more of its meanings. So long as instruction and life do not merge in our colleges, so long as what the undergraduates do and what they are taught occupy two separate, air-tight compartments in their consciousness, so long will the college be ineffectual. . . .

If you wish to create a college, therefore, and are wise, you will seek to create a life. . . . It is the duty of university authorities to make of the college a society, of which the teacher will be as much, and as naturally, a member as the undergraduate. When that is done other things will fall into their natural places, their natural relations. . . .

No doubt there are many ways in which this vital association may be effected, but all wise and successful ways will have this in common, that they will abate nothing of the freedom and self-government which have so quickened and purified our colleges in these recent days of change, will have no touch of school surveillance in them. You cannot force companionships upon undergraduates, if you treat them like men. You can only create the conditions, set up the organization, which will make them natural. The scholar should not need a statute behind him. The spirit of learning should not covet the support of the spirit and organization of the nursery. It will prevail of its own grace and power if you will but give it a chance, a conducting medium, an air in which it can move and breathe freely without effort of self-consciousness. If it cannot, I, for one, am unwilling to lend it artificial assistance. It must take its chances in the competition and win on its merits, under the ordinary rules of the game of life, where the most interesting man attracts attention, the strongest personality rules, the best organized force predominates, the most admirable thing wins allegiance. . . .

My plea, then, is this: that we now deliberately set ourselves to make a home for the spirit of learning: that we reorganize our colleges on the lines of this simple conception, that a college is not only a body of studies but a mode of association; that its courses are only its formal side, its contacts and contagions are its realities. It must become a community of scholars and pupils—a free community but a very real one, in which democracy may work its reasonable triumphs of accommodation, its vital processes of union. I am not suggesting that young men be dragooned into becoming scholars or tempted to become pedants, or have any artificial compulsion whatever put upon them, but only that they be introduced into the high society of university ideals, be exposed to the hazards of stimulating friendships, be introduced into the easy comradeships of the republic of letters. By this means the class-room itself might some day come to seem a part of life.

JOHN ELY BURCHARD

The Engineer—A New Perspective

This speech was the first in a series of addresses and panel discussions devoted to the general topic, "The Development of Creative Leaders," at the Cooper Union, New York City, October 8, 1956. The speech was later published in Brainpower Quest: A Report on a Convocation Called by The Cooper Union for the Advancement of Science and Art to Find New Sources from Which to Draw Tomorrow's Leaders in Science and Engineering, edited by Andrew A. Freeman (New York, second printing, 1958).

Burchard is dean of the School of Humanities and Social Science at the Massachusetts Institute of Technology, a member-at-large of the American Council of Learned Societies, and a past president of the American Academy of Arts and Sciences. He has been instrumental in liberalizing the engineering curriculum at M.I.T.

I have been asked to talk about the engineer's contribution to society. I have tried to relate this topic to the problem of finding creative leaders but I shall speak almost entirely about engineers and scientists.

I would not like anyone here to think that I am unaware that there are other kinds of creative leaders but I shall leave them out for the most part because we live in a world, at least in our country, where great concern is never expressed about the shortage of painters or the shortage of sculptors or the shortage of philosophers. Some shortage of teachers is deprecated but we talk most about the shortage of engineers. And it is to that present crisis that I want to direct your attention today.

It seems neither possible nor useful to attempt, in satisfaction of this topic, to give you a conspectus of the achievements of the engineer viewed across the wide span of history. But a little recent history may be rewarding.

Peter Cooper, as many of you know, was a characteristic leader of the unfolding nineteenth century, the century which witnessed the beginning of the explosive changes that have now come upon us through increasing technology. He had practically no schooling. He was a hard worker, and shrewd. It took him, for example, only three years of work for another who made machines to shear cloth, before he himself was making machines. He tried the furniture business and the grocery business and the glue and isinglass business. It is more than a century and a quarter since he built the Canton Iron Works at Baltimore, the foundation of his fortune.

When Trevithick's early experiments with steam propulsion, made just at the beginning of the century, matured in Hedley's "Puffing Billy," George Stephenson's "Blucher" and the Stephensons' prize-winning "Rocket" of 1829, and very soon after the Delaware and Hudson had imported three of the British locomotives, Cooper designed and built the experimental "Tom Thumb" for the Baltimore and Ohio, which, if small, was yet the first locomotive built in the United States.

Cooper's life was full of firsts—the rolling mill which he erected in New York in 1836 and moved to Trenton in 1845, rolling the first American iron beams there in the same year; the Bessemer process was tried by him for the first time in the United States in 1856. At about the same time, he was substantially interested with Cyrus Field in the project to lay the first Alantic cable. His engineering intuitions, his daring to try the new, his unquestioned success as manufacturer and innovator probably far exceeded his political acumen, else it is hard to understand how he, a hard-money Democrat, came to stand unsuccessfully for the presidency as the Greenback candidate in 1876.

He lived to the age of ninety-two; but before he was seventy, and in the year 1859, he founded this Union, and in his opening statement made it clear what he had in mind. The endowment he hoped would be "forever devoted to the advancement of science and art, in their application to the varied and useful purposes of life."

It is not too difficult a historical hazard to guess what Cooper meant by "useful." It is not hard to imagine that in his day he would not have regarded an application of art as useful or perhaps a product of art at all, if it were the kind of thing that came from the hand of a Klee or a Picasso, or even if, objectively, it were a social commentary. He would probably have had difficulty in supporting science of the kind which can no longer be explained to the non-scientist or from which the possible applications could not, at least in theory, be foreseen. But so would any other man of his age; so would many men of the present age too, if the truth were known.

Later on, this institution received benefits from many other men, many of them very practical men, men like Andrew Carnegie. It is to the everlasting credit of the various administrations of this Union that, without forgetting the importance of the usefully applied arts, they have ever widened the scope of their interests until we see the institution as it is today, an institution which has witnessed turning-point addresses by such different people as Abraham Lincoln, John Tyndall, Robert Ingersoll, Victoria Woodhull; an institution whose present president has for years been a leader in the effort to establish the essential relations between studies in the humanities and social sciences and studies in the useful arts.

From this short excursion into biography we might reflect on how terms change with times; neither science nor art meant to Peter Cooper what they mean to us today, just as they meant even different things to the men who founded the American Philosophical Society and the American Academy of Arts and Sciences in the eighteenth century. And we all know how much more broadly we would seek to interpret the word "useful," how much we are interested now in promoting studies which have only potential utility and which would have seemed absurd by the earlier standards.

I do not know whether Peter Cooper was ever called an engineer or whether he ever fancied himself one, but it is certain that his training and the way he went at putting through innovations, including the promotion of others' inventions, was very different from the training and the way of life of the engineer of today. He lived in the age when invention was a reality and not a myth, when one could sometimes with complete justice attribute the whole or almost the whole of a successful move to a single individual. One suspects that he was not much of a team man unless he was the captain, that there was little of the "other-directed" personality in him. Those traits of imagination and persistence and courage to do the unexpected which served him so well in the nineteenth century would no doubt serve him well today. In almost every other respect he would now have to be a different man. It seems to me more profitable to examine some of the challenges confronting that different man than to provide a summary of technological history which has been written in many books.

I intend here only to ask some questions. To most of them I can profess no sort of answer. They are not rhetorical. They bother me. I suspect they bother you. If they do not, I am sure they ought to.

Let me begin by mentioning four things that I have noted in the last fortnight. They are all in some way related to each other and to the question that ought to trouble us.

The *New York Times* for Sunday, September 23, 1956, carried about ten and a half pages of advertisements exclusively intended to solicit applications for engineering jobs. Excluding the few who wanted salesmen or managers, there were 108 such advertisements, many very large. Most of the companies did not indicate what kind of innovations they wanted men to work on. The few that did made it pretty clear that the center of interest was in problems relating to missile guidance, radar navigation, and bombing systems. If you know what companies do and something of what their commitments are, you can make a pretty shrewd guess about many of the undefined jobs. Many of the advertisers have widely flung research interests and production interests not at all military in their significance, but it is not hard to guess the preponderance of the military pressure in this frantic quest.

It was interesting also to note the nature of the inducements offered, when any were made specifically. By all odds the greatest inducement was pay and chance for advancement in pay; security was a close second, coupled with opportunities for advanced study, that is, advancement. A great deal was made of the nature of the community in which the work would be done, that is, whether it had parks, swimming pools, golf courses, even a chance to play polo, good schools. On the whole the least attention was paid to the fundamental interest of the job; few said, as one did, that with them you could rub shoulders on a shirt-sleeve first-name basis with first-class scientists. One company, which specifically listed the questions they were asked by potential employees, named five: advancement, salary, location, benefits, and nature of work. The excitement possible in the problems of the company which did this was hardly portrayed dramatically in the answer to the last question. Either the men who make the job advertisements do not understand their clientele or we have here something to think about—two things to think about. What do we want all our engineers for, so badly that the shortage is so great; and what do we regard as the important incentives to a young engineer in taking a job? Are we looking for a horde of skilled technicians to buy for the same kind of high price paid in the USSR?

Two days later, and two months ahead of time, the new Atlantic cable was completed, linking London with Ottawa and New York. At last the three countries were provided with inter-communication by telephone permitting a consistently loud and clear signal unprejudiced by the caprices of the atmosphere. The first world news round-up story over this new facility carried an interesting reminder by the reporter speaking from London. When Samuel Morse first sent a message on the telegraph from Washington to Baltimore on May 24, 1844, he remarked, "What hath God wrought!"

The first commercial message on the first Atlantic cable was preceded by a congratulatory message from Queen Victoria to President Buchanan, on August 16, 1858. President Buchanan replied, perhaps over-optimistically: "It is a triumph more glorious, because far more useful to mankind, than was ever won by conqueror on the field of battle. May the Atlantic Telegraph, under the blessing of Heaven, prove to be a bond of perpetual peace and friendship between the kindred nations and an instrument destined by

Divine Providence to diffuse religion, civilization, liberty and law throughout the world."

There were salvos of a hundred cannon fired at daybreak and at noon in City Hall Park in New York, bells pealed from the churches, factory whistles were blown; there were other demonstrations, dinners, parades, not witnessed again for an event of this kind unless at the return of Charles Lindbergh.

The first use of the cable last week was to report the arrival of Liberace at Waterloo Station. There were no dinners, demonstrations, parades for the cable. What does it take to be a prodigy now? What has happened to hope? What dignity do we attach to the uses of our machines?

The *New York Times Book Review* one week last September carried a long account of an important new book written by a thoughtful physicist and reviewed by the dean of observers of scientific progress, Waldemar Kaempffert; in the generally favorable comment the reviewer paused to ponder the optimism of the physicist and was not altogether happy about the social effect of scientific advance which it seemed to him the scientist had characteristically ignored. He said:

> As science advances and its discoveries are applied by the engineer there is a need for more planning, more organization, more control. The world is rapidly undergoing a process of standardization. The Main Street of one city looks just like the Main Street of every other. Europeans are scarcely distinguishable from Americans; marked departures from the standard in behavior and in clothing are likely to invite the interference of the police. Is all this good? Should the individual man obliterate himself in favor of the average man?

This is at least part of what a physicist friend of mine meant when he made the jesting definition, "An engineer is a technologist who doesn't know when to stop."

Early in 1955 Professor David G. Moore and Mr. Richard Renck, of the University of Chicago, published an interesting paper entitled "The Professional Employee in Industry." Their findings were tentative and based on a sampling procedure, rather a small sample, but suppose we take the conclusions as at least worth pondering. They said:

> Because of the central position of technology in modern industry, it would seem that professional employees, including engineers and natural scientists, should be a satisfied, well-integrated group. Evidence . . . , however, indicated that these employees tend to be chronically frustrated and dissatisfied. Factors in the morale of professional employees revolve primarily around a fundamental conflict which exists between the expectations and values of professional employees and the opportunities which they have to realize their ambitions and interests as professionals in the industrial setting. "Successful" professional groups apparently have realized their status needs through recognition from and acceptance by higher levels of management.

The inference from this is that engineers and scientists do have status in their own opinion and in that of society but are somehow disappointed in the degree of its recognition in their industrial jobs. Besides the question as to whether this is a fair picture of the attitude of the employee, there are other questions. What are the ambitions and interests of the professionals? Where are they thwarted? Do they in fact have the status in the community accorded to the doctor, the lawyer, the minister, perhaps even to the successful businessman? Do parents of the highest sensitivity and with the greatest freedom of choice covet the engineering profession for their children? Or are we really talking at heart about a group who, as a whole, are perhaps more feared than admired, paid well because they are needed but wanted only for rather specific talents, expected to refrain from exercising other talents, paid well because they are scarce but otherwise still regarded as the worker-ants of society, the useful but not finally important or even interesting men; in effect, not accorded other symbols of status than the one indicated by high pay, chance for increase in pay, lots of equipment to work with, a decent community with or without a polo field, a job which has the interest of a puzzle but perhaps nothing higher? Will this status on the whole cause them to be invited to conferences on matters of vital concern to the society where their general talents and ethics are all they can contribute, and their specific expertise is not in demand? Have not science and even engineering a higher cultural significance than this implies?

All these do not seem to me to be insignificant questions. They have a good deal to say about how large the potential reservoir may be in which dredging for "creative talent" may effectively be done.

We need to look again at history to remind ourselves of the environments in which great engineering has been done and in which it has not; and of the attitude the engineer may have taken toward the consequences of his work.

The Greeks were very interested in speculating about the nature of the universe; they had aggressive and good minds and not all their speculations were crazy. But they were uninterested in most material considerations and had no desire to apply what they knew. Archimedes was a sport. They had no engineering.

The Romans as a whole were little interested in theory. Lucretius was more like a Greek, as Archimedes was more like a Roman. But they were good practical observers; they wanted viable roads for their legions and ample water for their fountains and baths; they were a great group of engineers. It may be significant that the words "civilization" and "urbane" both come from Latin roots. It may be significant, too, that people of our day tend to admire the Greeks more than the Romans, even to suggest that they resemble the Greeks more, a dubious suggestion.

The people of the Middle Ages are regarded by many as thoroughly benighted. They were not on the whole favorably disposed to scientific investigation, particularly of matters which related to the cosmos or might in any way challenge the superior statements of theology. But they were much greater engineers than they are usually credited with being. The application of power to the making of cloth, for instance, began with them; from it came the cloth trade, and the beginning of many forces which have been difficult to deal with ever since.

The marriage of scientific theory and engineering practice was a long time coming. It is generally recognized now by many people but resisted by others. Scientists understand it well enough and think a nation may not be secure which relies for its fundamentals on other people, no matter how skillfully these may be applied by the borrower nation. They have tried hard to explain this to the rest of the world; their statement has often been repeated by others. Whether action supports the statement may not always be evident. There are still many engineering schools which speak of a few others as too theoretical. Against this is the trend to make the undergraduate training in engineering continuously more fundamental and general, continuously less of immediate practical value. Who is right? Why?

On the other hand, the identification of engineering and engineers with aesthetics was a long time dying. It did not surprise the Renaissance that Leonardo had multiple interests and talents. Although the Beaux-Arts of France parted from the Polytechnique early, the Beaux-Arts continued to foster men like the brothers Garnier, like Auguste Perret. In Germany architecture was naturally taught in the Technischen Hochschulen. In our own land early chairs like the one at Michigan were often supposed to seat a Professor of Architecture and Engineering. Most, though not all, the subsequent departments of architecture were housed in institutes of engineering or in colleges of engineering in universities. William Le Baron Jenney, the first professor at Michigan, was more engineer than architect. Then engineering became more complex and architecture more aloof and architectural education separated itself from the knowledge of engineering on the one hand and the intuition of the painters and the sculptors on the other.

And questions of morality or aesthetics or even general social good in connection with the use of engineering works seem seldom to have been raised in the early days. Seneca declaimed against the promiscuous and vulgar conduct of the Romans at the Baths, but Seneca was not an engineer. The quantities of water which poured into Rome through the many aqueducts were much used for trivial purposes or worse. The mighty engineering of the Colosseum provided seats for the entertainment of the mob at depraved spectacles. Did the engineers like the spectacles too? Did they build the Colosseum despite their abhorrence of the events, on the ground that it was none of their business? We do not know.

Are we prepared to say whether or not it should have been any of their business? Was their only business to do as well as they could whatever society asked for that was at all within their competence? The questions of the Middle Ages when they were aimed at machines were questions relating to faith, and were not frequent; the monasteries were quite as assiduous in the cultivation of the machine as the incipient burghers; and the greatest achievement of medieval engineering appears in buildings for the worship and the glory of God.

But as the majority of engineering developments moved from static constructions to dynamic ones, the questions became more insistent. You could put a bridge in the wrong place, you could build an ugly bridge, but at most the only evil purpose it could serve was to carry troops across, and since it could be readily destroyed even this use was not implicit. When things began to move, another dimension came into effect. It was the dimension of time; and if there was implicit danger it was in the implications of the foreshortening of time. It was a dynamic phenomenon.

Serious protests really began only after the Industrial Revolution. At the outset they came mostly from poets or others, men like Wordsworth, for example, who had a picture of pastoral England, not always a true picture, and who saw the destruction of a peasantry they admired and of a physical countryside they loved. Men like Dickens could even relish the new innovations as some kind of magic in *The Pickwick Papers;* somewhat later and only after the Chartist riots did he begin his bitter attacks on the blight of the Midlands. There was uncertainty as to where to level these attacks. Should you level them at the machine itself? Some tried that. Should you level them at the managers? More tried that. Should you level them at the inventors who made the machines? The latter generally escaped the criticism; indeed, I know of no serious case where one of the inventors himself gazed upon his inventions with many feelings besides pride and ambition to do better, or paused to ponder the implications of what he had presented to society, save as they were benign. Should he have so pondered? Would society have been any the better therefore?

Gradually there was some amelioration of the effects of the "dark satanic mills," and the benefits of their produce began to seem to most people to outweigh their blight. It is this historical experience which gives many contemporaries confidence to believe that the same tempering of the wind may again occur in our century. The wind has, however, become a much stronger wind.

Revolutionary as were the machines that made things, as were the first engines that delivered unusual quantities of power, it was the devices that began to shorten space and therefore time that introduced the explosive change which has been threatening us for at least half a century, though at the beginning of the twentieth century only a few people such as Henry

Adams seem to have perceived the threat. There have been perhaps six large upsetting notions. The notion of relativity and our observations of the galaxies are most disturbing philosophically. They have forced the thoughtful to grave doubts about anthropocentric religions. This troubles theologians perhaps more than it does priests, but in any event it is likely to have a profound effect upon the way we think of man.

On the more pragmatic side, the four great innovations that seem to me to pose these problems with a gravity we have never felt before are those which have collapsed time so that world geography is hardly any consideration in deciding where a given individual shall be today and where tomorrow; those which have collapsed time in a very different way, the instruments of communication, which tempt and permit humans to express themselves on any topic to any one or indeed to every one at the very moment when they have a reaction about the topic, together with similar developments in video which will bring the facial as well as the oral expressions into this immediate and direct contact; the ability to transfer power from remote places or even to create it in any place and in such abundance as to make it possible for many humans, perhaps some day all humans, to put machines to work for them for any purpose whatever, any purpose however trivial or even evil; and finally the implications of the new electronic control mechanisms which begin to introduce the machine as a substitute for certain operations of the human brain, often performing these operations better, not portentous operations yet, possibly never portentous operations in any Frankensteinish sense, but nonetheless with no clearly foreseeable limits now.

All of these are explosive in their connotations even now, more explosive in their promise. Of course, they can serve many good ends, but in the actions they serve they are neutral; they can also serve bad ends. The great question is, can the men who make them profess the same neutrality as is implicit in their creations. At what point of their advocacy are they to stop? In matters of this sort and up to now, scientists have often worried about the future; not many engineers have displayed concern. Is the engineer indeed a technologist who does not know when to stop? If so, should he know?

Whether or not you believe in progress may be a matter of your upbringing and education. A humanist, as Howard Mumford Jones once remarked, may be doomed to pessimism because he is committed on the whole to the study of man's actions up to the present, and there is little if anything in these actions and how they come out to suggest that human beings have really improved much when their backs are against the wall.

A scientist may, and many scientists do, accept as an act of faith the idea that any increase in knowledge is a good. Since science is obviously consistently adding to knowledge, it is always reducing error and thus producing a good. Once the article of faith is accepted, then you have to believe in progress.

Either of these views has a certain logic in it once the basic premise is accepted. The scientist may regret the way his findings are being used by humans, but he knows there is more knowledge all the time and he can hope that less error may lead humans not to use the findings so badly. So scientists can be and usually are optimistic for the long pull; although it is only fair to say that they have been among the most trenchant and effective Cassandras of our day—Cassandras whom we have heeded far too little.

But where does this leave the engineer? Knowledge is for him something to be put to use. He is dedicated to the application of useful knowledge. If the knowledge is not useful, it may not be an absolute good. No more than the scientist can he always be happy with the use of his works. But he can avoid looking at the use. He can keep the television tube dark in his home, or even buy no set at all, while he works all day to improve the picture. He can make the planes fly faster and faster while he regrets that people see less and less on the way, as Winston Churchill reminded us in 1949. He may regret that the elimination of time as a factor of travel is destroying the indigenous, leveling everything to an average; he may be sensitive to the idea that while it is good to level things upward, it is not so good to level things downward. He may worry lest rapid travel around the world lead to superficiality. If it is easy and quick to get to a remote area so that we are more aware of the area, this may be good; if it is also easy and quick to get back, so that we do not stay very long, this may be bad; if scholars are always on the move it may be that they will stop thinking. This has happened sometimes. Is he aware of these consequences at all? Who ought to be more able to be aware and foresighted? Should he be aware? What should he do about it if he is aware? Is it enough just to make a still faster vehicle?

Is it enough to provide more and more skillful ways for people to talk to each other if it encourages careless and spontaneous and hateful reactions to stimuli which in another day, say in a week's journey from a colony to Washington, might have been pondered as the horse plodded along? Is it enough to provide everyone with more power and incipiently more leisure, four-day weeks, three-day weeks and longer life with still more idle days to spend, and be satisfied with the technical skill one has displayed in conquering the technical problem? What is a society to be like in which the time one works in theory is small but the time one works in practice is large because the world is filled with people laboring at manual hobbies, doing work the machine could do, seeking the primitive retreat, the peasant bread, the open sky on a no longer useful cow pony, doing all the things that used to have to be done but now calling it play because the work they actually have to do deprives them of any chance for self-satisfaction? And indeed what would be the outcome of this on the capacity of salesmen to purvey all the products of the silent machines running inexorably twenty-four hours a day and never being able to afford to halt; engineers in metal, technologists who did not know when to stop?

Is it enough to have a fast car, a superhighway, an elegant bridge, a beautiful building, when the whole city is a maze of used-car dumps, parking ramps, neon signs, visual disorder; when every city is like every other city and there is no particular human reason for living in any particular place; when the Sunset Strip is ubiquitous from Los Angeles to Passamaquoddy, from the Lake of the Woods to Lake Pontchartrain? This is the way we are going, is it not, faster and faster, more and more comfortably, from one ugly place to another one? Or is it?

The possible danger in an aloof point of view taken by the engineer is that it is reasonable to look on all these wonders—and they are wonders—as progress when looked on purely as exercises in engineering. The difficulty is that the world and human life are not just an exercise in engineering.

Here is where it may be dangerous to disregard the overwhelming protest of the painters, the sculptors, the poëts and the novelists which has been made in increasing volume over the last fifty years, perhaps over the last century. It is very easy to dismiss them as "screwballs" who know no science or engineering and hence are bound to be wrong. They might answer with as little justification that scientists and engineers are the "screwballs" since they choose to ignore all the inconvenient demonstrations of how their potential goods have turned bad.

This enormous evidence from the arts (it is probably present in music, too, but the abstraction of music helps to conceal it) can hardly be disregarded as trivial. It is not merely the conventional bellow of the technologically unemployed. It is more nearly the expression of hypersensitive people to surroundings and conditions of men which are sensed in some degree by any sensitive person. The city does not seem to them a better city; the words and the messages that go over the wires and appear on the tubes do not appear to them to be wiser and finer words and messages; the final result of the applications of the freer energy do not seem to them to have freed man in any valuable sense; they are not impressed by a future society in which no man or only a few men have to do any serious amount of physical labor but have found nothing else better worth doing. They have no conviction that this leads us anywhere. They are better mentors than the writers of science fiction.

They often find themselves in a world which, however real it may seem to the engineer, seems to them to have no reality; they do not sense personality or conscience in a computing machine; they are worried about the consequences of large capacities freed from personality and conscience; and so they sense themselves individually as lost souls; and then most of us, looking at their art, find ourselves disturbed, perplexed, sometimes angered; or we seek to accept it as part of our modern life without admitting the very broad premises upon which it is based, using it as a kind of decoration. But this is at least an effort to meet the messages; to consign them to the pit as meaningless is an act of folly.

When they suggest specific remedies such as a moratorium on science, or blame a machine failure for a few human deaths as Faulkner was recently unwisely moved to do, we have a right to wish they were more sophisticated on the other side; but to dismiss them as nonsensical is to be like the Temanite, Shuhite, and Naamathite, people with whom all wisdom is certain to die. The message they have is clear and real, despite the unrealities in which they couch it. The Brave New World is not all it ought to be; indeed, it may not be either very new or very brave; and anyway it is very frightening—less perhaps because of how one might now come quickly to die, than because of how one might now come quickly to have to live.

Out of this I draw the questions that disturb me. They can be summed up by asking what manner of men we want these creative people to be of whom we steadily say we want more and more. Are they merely to be more and more skillful in making every physical act smoother and faster and more accurate? Are they to be content with the beauties inherent in any job well done? Do you want them rather to be more than that? Do you want them to have a consciousness of the consequences of their acts? Shall they prevent the building of economic dams which destroy the natural beauties of a Snake Canyon; shall they decline to provide superhighways which lead only from chaos to chaos: shall they be among those who rebel against the ugliness of the city they have made possible and join forces of those who know that beauty is one of the things that are essential for the good life; shall they attempt to make not only fine television tubes but have more to say about the quality of what the tube presents; in other words, shall they have a full-fledged and active conscience?

More than that, how do you want them to exercise this conscience? Is all you want that they shall as individual citizens regret the misuses but like individual citizens be impotent? Or are you going to ask that because they should have more foresight they should act as an élite ought to act, act in concert on some issues? It is a very dangerous idea.

The answers to questions like this are difficult, and they are portentous, too. If you ask for the fuller concept of the engineer, you will without doubt attract many men of talent and character whom you do not now attract; men perfectly capable of carrying on the innovations and the calculations but uninterested if the target is not set high enough; for such men, of whom we have of course brilliant individual examples in our audience today, status is clearly attained. How many such brilliant men of character does society really want?

Do you want to open this Pandora's box? Such men are prone to think too much. They are troublesome. Some will have off-beat political ideas and may not be clearable in any given moment. All will be querulous of many human actions. Their work will have taught them that impoliteness is not always unvirtuous. They have the potentials of joint effort which could be dangerous.

I do not know what we want. But it is worth thinking about. It will affect both the kind of people who are selected for the engineering professions and the kind of education we try to provide them.

Let me reaffirm what I mean by all this, in closing. There are various qualities which go to make up a first-class man. Some of these, such as imagination, self-reliance, tenacity and comparable qualities, can be combined to produce first-class technical men who will manage whatever it is the society wants, provided the society is able to state pretty clearly what it does want. Such men may be what are really desired for the large army of technologists for which there is presently such a shortage. This may well be the kind of man the USSR is training.

If this is all you want, a good deal of our present engineering education may be somewhat of a waste of time. Education will not in itself produce sensitivity, conscience, speculation, but it can encourage or discourage those who have such instincts to develop them or to suppress them. People who do not suppress them will be more difficult to deal with, harder to manage, not always willing perhaps to produce what society thinks it wants; it is even conceivable that they might learn how to use the power incipient in them for human benefit. Does society dare risk the possible production of this kind of leaders, or would it rather have an extremely competent group of unquestioning technicians? At present we really have not said.

A personal view may not be worth much, but I expect you are entitled to it now. I believe there has been a modicum of human progress due to applications of science by engineers, but that this is far below what might have been achieved with the same amount of technology and that it has in particular been destructive of many human values that might have been and still can be retained. I believe that we have not found a way to establish status in our society for people who are content to be merely technicians in any line of endeavor, even though we may, like the Russians, give them many material advantages. That is not all there is to status. Since I believe in our kind of society, I believe this is a source of strength and not of weakness. I believe the Russians have an advantage over us in the production of quantities of unquestioning technicians on a crash basis because they are able to educate these people without encouraging them to consider whether the political system, the economic system, the social system, the ethical system is open to improvement. I have been apprehensive lest we be attracted to the Russian solution.

I believe we make our task more difficult when we do permit and even encourage such discussions in our education, but on the day when we discontinue such efforts I believe we shall have lost our primary advantage over our competitors. There would then be left nothing of spirit, only a matter of numbers, of discipline, and of aptitude. I think we cannot claim an advantage in aptitude, and if we were to discard this most important element, free inquiry into all questions, we should throw away the only thing which can in the long run preserve us against the mass man of the East.

DOUGLAS BUSH

The Humanities

Delivered at the thirty-seventh annual meeting of the American Council on Education in Chicago, Illinois, October 14, 1954.

Bush, a distinguished literary scholar, is professor of English at Harvard University.

No one would ever speak of "the plight of the natural sciences," or of "the plight of the social sciences," but it is always proper to speak of "the plight of the humanities," and in the hushed, melancholy tone of one present at a perpetual deathbed. For something like twenty-five hundred years the humanities have been in more or less of a plight, not because they are themselves weak, but because their war is not merely with ignorance but with original sin; and as civilization has advanced, the means of stultifying the head and the heart have greatly multiplied in variety and power. As a random sample of cultural leadership, or at any rate of a common attitude, I should like to read a declaration of faith delivered some years ago by the chairman of the department of humanities in a well-known technological institution. We will call him Professor X. This is most of the report, from the *New York Times,* of his speech to a convention of engineers.

> Professor X . . . asserted last night that it would be "morally wrong" for him to advise the reading of literary classics in this fast-moving age of television, radio and movies. . . .
>
> One should read for the purpose of doing something with what one reads, he asserted; not of polishing one's mind like a jewel, but of improving the world around.
>
> Take up a book because it will tell you something of the world. . . ; read what you want to read, not what you think you should read. "This is the frame of mind that makes reading worthwhile and often deeply rewarding.
>
> "For example, it would be morally wrong for me to urge you to take up a classic like 'David Copperfield' and to settle yourselves in easy chairs [sic] for winter evenings' reading. If you tried 'David Copperfield' you would grow restive; you would think of all the other things you might be doing more

consistent with your daily environment—looking at television, listening to the radio, going to the movies.

"Moreover, you would wonder why you should spend so much time laboriously reading 'David Copperfield' when you could see the book as a film, should it return some time to the neighborhood movie."

"The single prescription for adult reading," he added, "should be to read something different, something that will change your mind. Herein lies compensation for the loss of the purely reflective life."

Engineers are not, to be sure, in common repute the most cultivated branch of mankind, but did even they deserve such counsel, and from such a source? The humanities, as I said, have always had to contend with the crude urges of the natural man, with his resistance to higher values than his own, but the speech I just quoted from reminds us of the many new ways there are of escaping from active thought and feeling into a state of lazy collapse, of passive surrender to unthinking action or external sensation. Many people would endorse our oracle's view that one should not read to polish one's mind like a jewel but for the sake of improving the world around. The humanistic tradition has always stood for improvement of the world, but it has always insisted that a man must make himself worthy of such an enterprise; one of our perennial troubles is that improvement of the world is undertaken by so many unpolished minds. Then our touching faith in machinery is illustrated by the quaint assumption that a movie is the same thing as a great book. And that *Ersatz* doctrine extends down through television to the comics, which have now joined the march of mind by reducing literary classics to capsule form. That sort of thing, by the way, was done, and done much better, a dozen centuries ago, and has been commonly labeled a symptom of the Dark Ages. But this is only a reminder; there is no need of enlarging upon such powerful elements in our popular civilization. The opposition to such elements comes from the humanities.

Negative terms, however, are not enough. The "humanities," in the original meaning of this and kindred words, embraced chiefly history, philosophy, and literature. These were the studies worthy of a free man, that ministered to *homo sapiens,* man the intellectual and moral being, and not to *homo faber,* the professional and technical expert. And these, with divinity, completed the central circle of human knowledge and understanding. Divinity went overboard long ago; history, which once was literature, is now a social science; and philosophy, though still grouped with the humanities, has become a branch of mathematics. Thus in common usage the humanities mean literature and the fine arts. That is an unfortunate narrowing but we may take things as we find them and may concentrate on literature, which is central and representative.

One plain fact nowadays is that the study of literature, which in itself is comprehensive and complex, has had to take over the responsibilities that used to be discharged by philosophy and divinity. Most young people now get their only or their chief understanding of man's moral and religious quest through literature. Anyone who has been teaching literature for twenty-five or thirty years, as I have, can testify to the marked change there has been in the spiritual climate during that time. (A rigorously scientific colleague of mine, in psychology, will not permit the use of the word "spiritual," but I use it anyhow.) I am speaking mainly of the higher order of college students, but it would be hard to imagine even the better students of twenty-five or thirty years ago reading Dante and George Herbert and Milton and Hopkins and Eliot with the real sympathy that many now show. For the more intelligent and sensitive young people of today, and there are very many of that kind, are a serious and conservative lot. They not only live in our unlovely world, they have no personal experience of any other. They are aware of hollowness and confusion all around them, and what is still more real, of hollowness and confusion in themselves. They feel adrift in a cockboat on an uncharted sea, and they want a sense of direction, of order and integration. And in literature they find, as countless people have found before them, that their problems are not new, that earlier generations have been lost also. Most of the young people I see find in literature, literature of the remote past as well as of the present, what they cannot find in textbooks of psychology and sociology, the vision of human experience achieved by a great spirit and bodied forth by a great artist.

I apologize for elaborating what may be called clichés, but those familiar lists of courses in catalogues make one forget that the frigid label "English 10" or "French 20" may represent an illumination and rebirth for John or Betty Doe. Not that courses are the only or even the main road to enriched experience and sensitivity, but they are one road; and a teacher can help as a guide or catalyst. Josiah Royce is said to have complained that a philosopher was expected to spiritualize the community. The modern philosopher is expected only to semanticize the community; the other function, as I said, falls upon the teacher of literature. I do not of course mean inspirational gush. I mean that teachers, conducting a critical discussion of a piece of great literature, necessarily deal not only with the artistic use of words and materials but with the moral and spiritual experience that are its subject matter. That is why, as [Harvard] President Pusey has said, the humanities must be the cornerstone of a liberal education. Naturally teachers will have their methods under constant scrutiny, but their material, the world's great literature, can hardly be improved; all it needs is a chance to work upon responsive minds and characters.

While I cannot guess the temper of this gathering, and while all the administrators present may, for all I know, regard the humanities as a pearl of great price, that is not their general reputation. Administrators are commonly said to prize the solid and tangible virtues of the natural and social sciences and to look upon the humanities as a nice luxury for the carriage trade. How far that general reputation is true or false I wouldn't know, but, just in case it has a modicum of truth, I have been insisting that the humanities are not a luxury; they are the most practical of necessities if men and women are to become fully human. The humanities commonly suffer in esteem because they do not lend themselves to statistical reports of achievement. You cannot demonstrate with graphs and charts that John or Betty Doe, through reacting to a piece of literature, became a person of richer moral and imaginative insight, of finer wisdom and discrimination and stability. For the experience of literature is an individual experience, and nothing that is really important can be measured.

When we look at the American educational scene, the diversity of standards is so great that generalizations about this or that part of it may be violently contradictory. At any rate educational history of the past fifty years seems to furnish a pretty good forecast of the bad effects of the deluge to be expected in the next fifteen. In school, college, and university, the results of the huge increase in the student body suggest that the principle of education for all, however fine in theory, in practice leads ultimately to education for none. An editorial in the *New York Times* of September 13, 1954, takes the usual line of defense. The principle of education for all, it says, forces us "to accept the principle, also, that the function of education is primarily social and political rather than purely intellectual." "It cannot be denied," the *Times* proceeds, "that this means a down-grading of the learning process. We are adjusting to an 'average' that must be spread so widely that it comes down automatically. Education is no longer the intellectual privilege of the gifted few. It is held to be the democratic right of all." The *Times* does go a little beyond this orthodox assent to express uneasiness over the sacrifice, in elementary and secondary schools, of quality to quantity.

To mention one of the many results, there has been an appalling growth of illiteracy at all levels of education, even in the graduate school. (Somehow stenographers are still literate, even if their college-bred employers are not.) At every orgy of Commencements one wonders how many of the hordes of new bachelors of arts can speak and write their own language with elementary decency, or read it with understanding. After all, the polished mind is suspect, whether in a student, a professor, or a Presidential candidate. And illiteracy, and contentment with illiteracy, are only symptoms of general shoddiness.

Obviously one main cause of this state of things has been the sheer pressure of numbers, along with a deplorable shrinkage in the number of qualified teachers. But the situation would not be so bad as it has been if the downward pressure of numbers had not been powerfully strengthened by misguided doctrine and practice. The training of teachers and the control of school curricula have been in the hands of colleges of education and their products, and these have operated on principles extracted from John

Dewey's philosophy of barbarism. (If that phrase seems unduly harsh, I may say that I have in mind Dewey's hostility to what he regarded as leisure-class studies; his anti-historical attitude, his desire—intensified in his followers—to immerse students in the contemporary and immediate; and his denial of a hierarchy of studies, his doctrine that all kinds of experience are equally or uniquely valuable; and it would not be irrelevant to add his notoriously inept writing.) The lowest common denominator has been, not an evil, but an ideal. The substantial disciplines have been so denuded of content that multitudes of students, often taught by uneducated teachers, have been illiterate, uninformed, and thoroughly immature. There is no use in priding ourselves on the operation of the democratic principle if education loses much of its meaning in the process. When we think, for instance, of education for citizenship, which has been the cry of modern pedagogy, we may think also of the volume and violence of popular support given to the anti-intellectual demagoguery of the last few years. Mass education tends to reflect mass civilization, instead of opposing it. Even if education were everywhere working on the highest level, it would still face tremendous odds.

The great problem has been, and will be, first, the preservation of minority culture against the many and insidious pressures of mass civilization, and, secondly, the extension of that minority culture through wider and wider areas. The rising flood of students is very much like the barbarian invasions of the early Middle Ages, and then the process of education took a thousand years. We hope for something less overwhelming, and for a less protracted cure, but the principle is the same; Graeco-Roman-Christian culture not only survived but triumphed, and with enrichment. If we think of our problem in the light of that one, we shall not be disheartened but recognize both as phases of man's perennial growing pains.

Throughout history it has been a more or less small minority that has created and preserved what culture and enlightenment we have, and, if adverse forces are always growing, that minority is always growing too. In spite of the low standards that have commonly prevailed in public education during the last fifty years, I think the top layer of college students now are proportionately more numerous than they were thirty years ago and are more generally serious and critical. There is a growing nucleus of fine minds, and teachers are concerned with the enlargement of that all-important group. At the same time, without retreating from that position, one wonders what it is in our educational process or in our culture at large that often causes a liberal education to end on Commencement Day.

I have no novel and dramatic remedy for the evils that have shown themselves so clearly already and will become more formidable still. But I might mention a few things of varying importance which do not seem utopian. Of course I represent no one but myself, and I cannot even say, like a member of the House of Lords, that I enjoy the full confidence of my constituents.

In the first place, I see no reason why the flood of students should be allowed to pour into college, why automatic graduation from school should qualify anyone for admission. We ought to recognize, and make people in general recognize, that a desire for economic or social advantage, or for merely four years of idle diversion, is not enough. Under such pressure as is coming, surely the state universities have the strength to set up bars and select their student bodies, instead of admitting all who choose to walk in the front door and then, with much trouble and expense, trying to get rid of some through the back door. Doubtless such procedure would require a campaign of enlightenment and persuasion, but legislators always have an alert ear for the cry of economy, and the public must be convinced that higher education, or what passes for that, is neither a birthright nor a necessary badge of respectability, and that useful and happy lives can be led without a college degree. As things are, we have an army of misfits, who lower educational standards and increase expense, and no branch of a university staff has grown more rapidly of late years than the psychiatric squad.

Secondly, many people have grounds for the belief that the multiplying junior colleges can and will drain off a large number of the young who for various reasons are unfitted for a really strenuous four-year course.

Thirdly, I think the need for formal education beyond high school would be much lessened, and the quality of both secondary and higher education greatly improved, if the colleges and universities, getting the public behind them, made a concerted and effectual demand that the schools do their proper work and do it much better than a great many schools have been doing it. Quite commonly, a distressing proportion of a college course now consists of high school work. We have grown so accustomed to a battalion of instructors teaching elementary composition to freshmen that we take it as a normal part of college education, whereas it is a monstrosity. Imagine a European university teaching the rudiments of expression! If high school graduates are illiterate, they have no business in college. For a long time, and for a variety of reasons, we have had slackness all along the line; somehow, some time, strictness and discipline have got to begin.

Increased enrollments have almost inevitably led to increased reliance upon large lecture courses. There are administrators who assume that there is no limit to the effectiveness of a lecture course except the size of the auditorium, and there are also teachers who see positive virtues in lectures and can themselves display them. Perhaps because I never remember anything I hear in a lecture, I do not share that faith. I favor classes small enough to allow discussion, and that is expensive. But there are possible economies that would be highly desirable in themselves. We do not need to maintain the naive doctrine that there has to be a course in anything in which anyone ever has been or might be interested. Many catalogues list courses that can only be called fantastic, and I don't think I am guilty of partisan prejudice if I say that these are rarely found among the humanities. If we had fewer and less specialized courses, and if we did not have our armies of composition teachers, a considerable number of man-hours would be released for smaller classes.

One thing that has suffered grievously and conspicuously in this last generation has been the study of foreign languages. The usual reason given is again the pressure of numbers, the numbers who are not going beyond high school, but again a positive reason has been open or quiet hostility. Languages have been pretty well crowded out of the school curriculum, and of course there has been a corresponding decline in college study. Nothing has been commoner in recent decades than the applicant for admission to a graduate school who has had little or no acquaintance with any foreign language except possibly a year or two of Spanish. Serious study of a foreign language means work, and a first principle of modern pedagogy has been the elimination of work. Thus, during the years in which we have all become conscious of one small world, and in which this country has become the leader of that world, educational theory and practice have retreated into cultural parochialism. There is no need to argue how necessary for the ordinary citizen is some knowledge of a foreign language and a foreign people. In the last few years a good many parents have been aroused, and the Modern Language Association has been putting on a vigorous campaign, so that progress has been made; but there is a long way to go. It is encouraging that in some cities successful experiments have been made in the teaching of languages in elementary schools, where, for good psychological reasons, they ought to begin. I wish there were something encouraging to be said about the ancient languages, but we are concerned with actualities.

Finally, since I touched on the large number of young people who are in college and shouldn't be, I might mention those who are not and should be, and who may be lost in the oncoming flood. Educators and others are more conscious than they once were of our failure to recognize and foster promising students who cannot afford college, and increasing efforts are being made in that direction; but we are still very far behind England, where bright students are picked out at the age of ten or eleven and brought along on scholarships. If we spent on exceptional students a fraction of the time and money we have spent on nursing lame ducks, there would be a considerable change in the quality of education.

One last word on a different matter. Like everything else, the Ph.D. has been cheapened by quantitative pressure, and it might be earnestly wished that it were not a union card for the teaching profession. There are plenty of young men and women who would be good teachers without such a degree, and the degree itself ought to mean something more than it does.

Along with that may go another earnest wish, that both administrators and members of departments would abandon the principle of "publish or perish." Socrates would never have had a chance at an assistant professorship.

WAYNE MORSE

America's Educational Needs

This speech constituted the bulk of Senator Morse's testimony before the Committee on Labor and Public Welfare of the United States Senate on March 11, 1958.

After a career as a legal scholar and dean of the University of Oregon's School of Law, Morse was elected to the United States Senate in 1944. A peppery controversialist, he resigned from the Republican Party in 1952 and subsequently became affiliated with the Democratic Party. He was re-elected as a Democrat in 1956 after one of the bitterest campaigns in Oregon's history.

This hearing extends to all proposals for science and education for national defense now pending before the Senate Labor Committee and it is with that understanding that I wish to bring out a few points I feel have not yet been sufficiently emphasized.

Most of the testimony we have had so far has involved higher education and most of that has emphasized higher education aimed at improving our standing in science and technology vis-à-vis the Soviet Union.

I do not quarrel with the need to improve the use we make of our intellectual resources in these fields. But I would warn this committee against stopping there. We need a national scholarship program, and we also need grants to the States for education at the elementary and secondary levels. At all levels, aid must not be confined to any special fields of study, and that is true even if our sole purpose is to raise our standards in terms of the progress being made in Soviet Russia.

It is quite true that action by Congress in this field has been stimulated by the Russian sputniks.

But while Soviet achievement with satellites and missiles presents a challenge to us in these fields, we must not react so defensively that we meet only that one challenge. We know enough about communism to know that it menaces western civilization as a whole, not just our scientific and technical capacity. It will not confine its assaults upon us to these fields. It is a challenge to our entire culture, to our political, economic, and social systems, to our religions, and to our creative arts. The Communist system will seek by any avenue it can find to overthrow our own. Therefore, we must develop our intellectual resources in all fields of endeavor—in the humanities, the arts, and the social sciences, as well as in the physical sciences and mathematics.

For Communist advances are not made only via modern transportation. They are made through literature, through all kinds of propaganda, and through subversion. Its appeals are made to the sympathies and aspirations of mankind. It attacks any weakness that appears in a national society, and cannot be guarded against just by putting a rocket on the moon ahead of Russia, as important as that is.

We must remember that it is all the intellectual power and talent of our youth that must be mobilized, whatever their field of endeavor. I think this must be the framework of the legislation that is developed from these hearings.

That is why I said a few moments ago, Mr. Chairman, that we need to watch out that we do not waste brainpower in our country. I do not think we have any right to deny to a boy and girl a college education if he or she has the mental potential to do satisfactory college work. We need to follow various criteria for admission to college. A high school transcript is one, but it must not be made an exclusive one.

I would like to point out that in all my years of teaching I used to take the position that if a boy or girl of normal intelligence failed out of the law school it was my failure and my faculty's failure and not the boy's or girl's. It simply meant that we had failed some way, somehow, to find out where that particular student's best aptitudes lay. That is why I always sought to get a student transferred to some other academic discipline at which that boy or girl could be a success.

I recognize that there are those students who just have no intention of doing satisfactory work. They attend college primarily for recreational purposes. They, of course, should be flunked out. We also have a certain percentage of students that do not have the intellectual capacity to do college work.

But I want to point out that time and time again, so many times that I am not going to accept a high-school transcript as an exclusive criterion for admission to college, the high-school C student and low B student can make a satisfactory record in college. Frequently, greater maturity, the passage of time, a developing sense of values, a new-found ambition, and other similar factors cause a boy or girl to find himself or herself upon entrance to college. To deny such students admission to college, I think, is wrong from the standpoint of the Nation, and it is wrong, Mr. Chairman, from the standpoint of what it does to the individual student.

I am speculating and conjecturing about this but I am inclined to believe that a scientific study would prove my conjecture right. We are doing great psychological damage to a lot of young men and young women in this country by denying them admission to college because of the fact that they are C high-school students. I wish there were some way of measuring the cost of this human loss to the American society.

I am critical of college presidents about this only because I think that too many of them are not giving us the assistance that we need in trying to get legislators to see that there are other criteria for admission to college that must be followed. Many college presidents are harassed men. They are running institutions with inadequate funds. They see a flood of students pounding at the school gates. They understandably ask such questions as the following: Where are the classrooms? Where are the teachers? Where are the facilities? How are we going to educate all of them with our inadequate budget? Not being able to answer such questions they adopt shortcuts. They pick what they think are the upper 5 or 10 percent of the applicants and deny an education to the rest. This is inexcusable human waste.

It is an easy way out, but it is a wasteful way out. We in a legislative position have the duty and the obligation to these young people to see that the education facilities are available so that they can obtain the best education their abilities will permit.

The major premise on which I approach this problem is that I want to see the maximum education benefits given to every boy and girl who wants to go on and develop his or her mental potential. That means I want whatever facilities are necessary to save the brainpower of American youth.

The chairman has heard me say on the floor of the Senate and I repeat for the record this morning, "We are not going to keep ahead of Russia in manpower but we just better not fall behind Russia in brainpower." We are going to fall behind Russia in brainpower if we adopt any such rule of thumb that too many college presidents are adopting these days that only the upper 5 to 10 percent of high-school graduates should go to college. It is not a sound criterion that we should take this upper 5 to 10 percent of high-school graduates and let the others go ahead and do some other type of work. It is a waste, I repeat, of valuable brainpower.

I want every American boy and girl to have the opportunity for a maximum development of his brainpower potential.

I would be the first to admit the need for better high-school standards in many places. This is especially true in connection with high-school preparation for college. But my point is that we cannot justify penalizing an American boy or girl's chance to go on to college simply because of a C average in high school. We need to do a better job at the high-school level it is true. But we also need to develop a college orientation program during the first year of college that will save many high-school graduates from being denied a chance, with greater maturity that rapidly develops after high school, to go to college.

That is an underlying thesis of the remarks I make here this morning.

I think we must start meeting our national responsibility by providing financial assistance to the States for their elementary and secondary schools.

No American program that deals only with the final stages of our education system, as the Eisenhower administration's program does, is going to restore America to an equality with Russia, even in the fields of science and technology. In my judgment, any legislation that comes out of the 85th Congress on education that does not deal with this part of the education system will not meet the real need. We know from many estimates, including the White House Conference on Education and the President's Committee on Education Beyond the High School that educational expenditures must be increased at least 75 percent within the next 15 years just to stay where we are now. With half our public elementary and secondary school revenue tied to local property taxes, there is little hope, in my opinion, that local governments can double their contributions to education. And we should be improving our education system in that time, not just maintaining what we have now.

As a matter of fact, just what do we have now? First, we have 840,000 boys and girls attending classes only part time because of classroom and teacher shortages. I respectfully ask what good we can do these youngsters by offering them scholarships to attend colleges and universities? They are being penalized right now, and the penalty will be felt again when they compete with full-time students for financial assistance to go to college which so many of us think necessary and desirable.

Second, we have 87,391 emergency teachers. I do not intend at all to disparage these men and women by pointing out that they do not have the minimum requirements for teaching in their States. We can be thankful we have them at all in the teaching profession. But their continued employment means that our boys and girls are not getting the standard of instruction that each State has fixed for itself. Interestingly enough, the United States Office of Education does not seem to regard these emergency teachers as replaceable, but includes them in its figures for the entire teaching staff in American schools. The skill of our teaching staff as a whole will not rise to where we want it until salaries are raised to a level in keeping with what these men and women can earn outside the profession. That is one of the primary reasons why I believe Federal grants to the States are essential.

Third, we need more classrooms and other school facilities. As we cast about for construction projects to stimulate our sagging economy, I can think of no more useful and timely program than one of school construction. . . .

Just last year, the administration was agreeing with us about the classroom shortage to the extent of giving half-hearted support to a construction bill. Now it has abandoned that program, without, of course, giving any indication that Federal assistance is no longer needed. It did not because it cannot. At the opening of the school year, the Nation required about 200,000 new classrooms to meet new enrollments and replace obsolete buildings.

The States are building about 60,000 new classrooms a year, thereby keeping up with new enrollments but making only a small dent in the backlog of construction needs. . . .

To those who still cling to the old notion that Federal assistance would lead to Federal control, I remind them of the history of Federal school construction. A great many people have forgotten that school buildings were among the major projects built by the Federal Government during the depression of the 1930's. In the 1955 report on Federal Aid for School Construction by the Library of Congress, there is contained a summary of the activities of the Public Works Administration and the Works Projects Administration. PWA made its grants to the localities to use for the construction they needed most. From 1933 through 1942, PWA made allotments for 6,687 elementary and secondary schools costing over $979 million. Every State of the Union participated in this program. School buildings comprised 40 percent of all non-Federal projects for which PWA made allotments.

Every Senator, in other words, has schools in his State that were built with Federal grants in the 1930's. Can any one of them show where any Federal control of teaching methods or curricula has resulted? Can anyone point to a single school in this country built with PWA funds and say that it fell under Federal domination because Federal money helped build it?

Then we have WPA schools. The WPA did not make grants to the localities or States, but built its projects directly. Over a period of 8 years, more than 5,900 new schools were built, and more than 33,000 others were modernized under WPA, at a cost of $466,700,000. Can any Senator who is opposing Federal aid because of fear of Federal control point to any WPA-constructed school and say that it is now being run or dominated by the Federal Government?

The same record can be shown for Public Law 815, under which Federal money is provided to build schools in the so-called federally impacted areas.

I think the record already made on Federal funds for school construction puts to rest these fears of Federal control of the schools of America.

In fact, I digress to point out that millions of dollars have poured into the States over many, many years for the so-called land-grant colleges under the Morrell Act. I am going to have complete computations shortly on this. We are at work on it now.

Does any Senator want to tell me that any State college in his State is dominated by the Federal Government because it has been the recipient of great sums of money over the years?

Of course, the answer is that such a charge is nonsense. It is pure nonsense. It is a fear argument. It is a scarecrow that is being built up in the communities of America, with the result that timid politicians too frequently are following this propaganda line, and unwittingly, I am sure, but nevertheless effectively, denying to American boys and girls the educational opportunities that I think are their heritage.

I have said before, and I repeat this morning, we cannot let the educational opportunities of American boys and girls be dependent upon an act of God. The place of birth of an American boy and girl is an act of God.

I take the position that every American boy and girl, wherever born in this country, is deserving of an equal chance for the maximum development of his or her brain potential. That is basic in this whole philosophy that the chairman and I have been fighting for, along with other wonderful colleagues in the Senate, for decent Federal aid to education for many years past.

The committee already has before it the testimony of Dr. Edward Teller to the effect that there is no more important segment of our school system in developing scientists and engineers than the high-school level. I wish to reinforce that opinion with my own, based on twenty-one years of teaching at the college level. Every college professor and administrator knows that what is accomplished with a student in college depends in large measure upon what he brings with him, intellectually speaking, from high school. If the high-school training is deficient—and we have a lot of evidence that it is—then the colleges must make up the difference. They are doing it with special classes for freshmen, for example, in English, in mathematics, and other basic subjects that should have been learned in high school. This does not even take into account the number of boys and girls with good minds who were unable to meet college requirements at all. Money will not solve all this problem of our educational deficiencies. But it is a part of the problem where the Federal Government can and should help out. . . .

Now I would like to devote myself for a moment to the college aspect of education for defense. . . . Last November, I received from the chancellor of the Oregon State System of Higher Education a copy of the statement presented to the House Subcommittee on Special Education on behalf of the Oregon State Board of Higher Education. It presents a very convincing case, in my judgment, in showing that scholarships alone will be of little value without accompanying grants that will enable our colleges and universities to expand their facilities.

"Unless some way can be found to build classrooms, libraries, laboratories, dormitories, and other college buildings," says the Oregon State Board of Higher Education, "there will not be enough space available for students. Unless funds are available to pay adequate salaries to attract and retain added faculty, there will not be enough professors available to teach students who might be recruited by a scholarship program."

Oregon expects a fifty-eight percent increase in four years in the enrollment in our eight institutions in the State system of higher education. A scholarship program that would increase the number of boys and girls able financially to enroll in these schools would require the schools to raise their admission standards in order to cut down the total number admitted. Oregon has traditionally admitted all Oregon high-school graduates to its colleges. Recently, it has had to abandon that policy. I think it is most unfortunate that we had to do so in Oregon. I know that some schools do favor selective admissions and may welcome a greater degree of selectivity. But at the same time it is the objective of a Federal scholarship program to give college training to qualified young men and women presently unable to obtain it for financial reasons. It is surely not the objective of these scholarship programs . . . to raise admission standards only, and keep the number of students admitted at current levels or at levels only proportionate to the population. Yet that is the effect they well may have if we do not help the institutions expand their facilities. . . . I have come to the conclusion . . . that a direct grant, as a kind of matching sum for each student entering an institution under a Federal scholarship program, is essential if their facilities are not to be over-loaded. I urge the committee to add such a provision to any Federal scholarship bill it approves.

I also want to call attention to S. 714 and other bills like it that would re-establish education and training benefits for veterans. Hearings have been held on these bills by the veterans subcommittee, and I am very anxious that action be taken. The World War II and Korean GI bills were an investment in our intellectual resources that will continue to bring returns to the Nation for many years to come.

I wish to close by emphasizing that better facilities and teachers in the sciences at all levels of education are vital to our military defense. But meeting the needs of war is not enough; we must prepare our citizens to attack as well the problems that lead to war. To do that we must develop our brainpower in the social sciences and the humanities, in addition to developing our brainpower in nuclear physics and aerodynamics. It may well be that in today's world it will take more "brains" for us to live in peace than it would take to go to war.

In my judgment, the American people are far ahead of the administration and even ahead of Congress in their willingness to put forth effort and even money to improve our education system. We need to show them that we in Congress will also do our part and we must do it now.

I would like, Mr. Chairman, to also quote from that great educator and politician of Pennsylvania, Thaddeus Stevens, who once pointed out that we should "learn to dread ignorance more than taxation."

I also would like to emphasize, in closing, that great tenet of Thomas Jefferson, "The strength of a democracy can be no greater than the enlightenment of its people."

Who among us can deny the fact that if we fail to give the support to the

American school system that we should, we are selling short future generations of American boys and girls?

Lastly, I will close the record with a couple of rhetorical questions.

As I have said in debate in the Senate: "Give me that price tag, will you, on a nuclear physicist. What is he worth? What is a great biochemist worth? Price him for me."

But let us move out of the natural sciences into the social sciences. What is the value of a great theologian? What is a great historian worth? What is a great linguist worth? . . .

What is a great teacher worth? What is any trained mind worth? You cannot price trained minds because in fact they are priceless.

To the American people I say from this witness chair this morning, as a people we are guilty of a great waste of a great natural resource in America, the greatest natural resource we have, the brainpower of millions of our boys and girls. They are God's gift to America.

I want to plead that the politicians in the Congress . . . do a little rethinking about this whole matter of training brainpower, because the real source of fear of Russia, the real cause of fear of Russia, in my judgment, is the fear that she may outstrip us in brainpower. I urge the passage of a broad Federal aid to education bill.

ERNEST EARNEST

Even A.B.'s Must Eat

This essay was first published in The American Scholar for Autumn 1944.

Earnest is professor of English at Temple University.

There is considerable current alarm about the future of the Liberal Arts College. Naturally this emotion is felt most keenly by persons whose livelihood depends upon the continued existence of that type of institution. They usually defend their bread and butter by eloquent pleas for non-material values. Thus the many articles in academic journals are likely to be labeled "A Defense of Humanism," or "The Humanities and the Opportunity of Peace." And the discussions are filled with phrases like: "stimulating . . . a critical and aesthetic taste"; "an appreciative love for what is truly and enduringly beautiful"; "teach hope, love, and courage"; "recognize or retrieve those eternal truths which are above the stream of evolution and change"; ". . . true education is but a continuous process of re-examining, re-appraising, and re-vitalizing the interrelationships of existence." And of course there is always the old stand-by: education for democracy.

Now I have no quarrel with any or all of these objectives except, perhaps, with their vagueness. There is always the suspicion that when a use cannot be found for something, it will be asserted to have "higher value"—like an impractical coffee urn kept in the china closet as an *objet d'art.* Our Victorian ancestors were more prone to that sort of thing than we are—though the whatnot has come back in decorator-designed interiors. The magazines are beginning to speak of "the revival of the style of a more leisurely and comfortable age." There is a suspicious parallel between the advertising of Victorian reproductions of furniture and the arguments of the humanists. Please don't ask for a definition of humanist or humanity; there seems to be no agreement on that point. A working definition might be *humanist:* a person who teaches some subject other than science or a vocation; and *humanity:* a subject that students must be *required* to take along with the ones they really want.

Now I, for one, do not believe that a college course in Lunchroom Management or Clothing Selection is preferable to one in aesthetics or Greek history. I am not at all sure that the first two are the more practical. But I do not believe that any number of eloquent pleas for recapturing the "lost soul" of society is going to entice students into the College of Liberal Arts. In fact any students who are attracted by the grandiloquent phrases are likely to be aesthetes, impractical idealists, or potential school teachers. Boys and girls from wealthy homes may come also, but they come for very practical reasons: four years of pleasant life, social polish, and a certificate of culture useful in certain social circles. As a rule the Liberal Arts College is very efficient in supplying these requirements. Certainly more efficient than a school offering training in lunchroom management or methods of teaching shorthand.

It is quite another matter to educate one to appreciate "what is truly and enduringly beautiful" or to "recognize or retrieve . . . eternal truths." Too often it is assumed that these things can be taught as entities unrelated to other considerations—that there is a world in which morality, truth, and beauty exist apart from the ethics of business, or the truth of a scientific or social theory, or the beauty of a particular poem or office building.

The advocates of liberal arts training will deny this. They will argue that a knowledge of philosophy helps one to understand the values of contemporary life (or more often the alleged lack of values); that mathematics trains the accurate use of the reason (an idea long since exploded by psychologists); that history helps in an understanding of today's politics; and that literature and art give one standards of judgment to apply to contemporary literature or art, or that they do something or other for one's personality—something very fine, of course.

Students often pay lip service to these doctrines: they say that they want college to give them "culture." But that is almost always a secondary aim. The vast majority of students are in college to become engineers, accountants, physicians, social workers, teachers—or even chiropodists and undertakers. If at the same time they can acquire the mystic quality called culture by taking a few courses in language, history, and literature, they are willing to spare a little time from their real purpose. But few pre-meds will elect Fine Arts I if it conflicts with Biology 127; and fewer civil engineers will study Chaucer when they can get Strength of Materials instead.

All this may be simply an indication of mistaken values, the symptoms of a materialistic national culture, the worship of false gods. I believe that it is rather an indication of faulty methods. Two deeply religious men may both desire the kingdom of heaven; one may try to reach it by praying continually, wearing a hair shirt, and refusing to bathe; the other by ministering to the sick. It is quite possible that the second man will find very little time to examine his soul or clarify points of theology. He therefore spends less time on his "specialty" than does the ascetic, but he may be more fully obtaining his objective.

The analogy may apply to a liberal education. It is quite possible that extreme specialization is not the best preparation for most professionals or intellectual occupations. It is impossible in a paper of this sort to support this point of view in detail. But it is a point of view almost universal among believers in a liberal education.

However, I venture upon two assertions: one, that the liberal arts colleges fail to implement this point of view; and two, that they fail to demonstrate its validity. To put the case more specifically: I believe that the liberal arts college fails to relate its work to the world the students must face, and that it fails to make the student understand its aims. In colloquial phraseology, the liberal arts college high-hats the vocational phases of education, and it fails to sell itself to its customers.

Almost all the defenders of a liberal education use a tone of moral superiority. The phrases quoted at the beginning of this essay suggest an out-of-this-world point of view. Yet if the liberal arts college is to survive, it must function in this world and must make that function clear. In a democratic society, the primary function demanded of a college or university is that it prepare its students to earn a living. The point of view stated by Jacques Barzun, "Vocational training has nothing to do with education," implies that education is only for a leisure class or a scholarly elite. Only at their peril can liberal arts colleges cater to a Brahmin caste. Most students and parents are certainly not going to be less materialistic about their bread and butter than are the defenders of a liberal education.

It may seem that this premise denies any possibility of preserving the liberal arts. Not at all. I have already pointed out that the arts colleges insist on the superior value of their training as preparation for an intellectual vocation or profession. I agree with this point of view. In the rapidly changing world of business, technology, and social order, a narrowly specialized training is often obsolete before the student graduates. Many of my former college mates are in fields of activity which did not exist twenty years ago. No vocational training then offered could have helped them. A contemporary radio news analyst would certainly find his college work in European history more valuable than his course in News Story Write-Up. History, language, literature, philosophy have vocational value. More obvious is the vocational aspect of social science and psychology. All these are elements in a liberal arts program.

Specifically I suggest that the liberal arts colleges integrate their programs with vocational fields. For instance: what courses should be elected by a student interested in entering the diplomatic field, or social security, or a host of other governmental activities for which the A.B. course is the best preparation? Few faculty advisers have this information. Students themselves are often unaware that certain of these fields exist; more have no idea how to prepare for them. So, instead, they take a degree in marketing or dentistry or advertising—anything with a label indicating possible usefulness. Students are often amazed to find that they can enter law school with an A.B. in history and literature instead of a B.S. in "pre-law."

This brings us to my second recommendation: a better publicizing of the vocational usefulness of a liberal arts education. Bulletins and catalogs of vocational schools often have much to say about opportunities in the fields they train for; those of liberal arts colleges are extremely reticent on this point. Except for occasional listings of requirements for medical school or teaching, there is almost no discussion of so crass a topic as preparing for a job. For instance, in a recent study of training for the field of social security, Karl de Schweinitz states that the best possible background is the academic discipline and a cultural education. It is significant that this study was made for the Social Security Board and not under the auspices of the colleges.

All this may seem to imply that the liberal arts colleges should turn themselves into vocational schools. The answer is that they are vocational schools and always have been. Harvard College was founded specifically to train ministers of the gospel. The classical education of the nineteenth century was regarded as the best possible training for the law and the church. Today students in liberal arts colleges are preparing to become biologists, psychologists, sociologists, teachers, and lawyers.

What I suggest, then, is not a revision of the curriculum: no addition of gadget courses to attract uncritical customers. It is simply that the colleges accept the fact that they have a vocational function and that they exercise that function intelligently. That means vocational guidance for students, not in a haphazard way, but by trained counselors with adequate budgets for research; it means well run placement bureaus; it means making vocational information readily available to students; and it means a constant and intelligent study of the changing needs of the community. It is shortsighted if not unethical to turn out thousands more pre-meds than the medical schools will accept; to produce English teachers far in excess of demand, and at the same time to ignore fields where educated persons are desperately needed.

But what happens to "culture" in all this? Does it mean that we forget all about the permanently true and beautiful? My answer is that "culture" is always a by-product of something else. Shakespeare's plays are now studied chiefly for their cultural value; they were written to attract patrons to the box office. Architects have always designed their buildings for specific utilitarian purposes. Stiegel produced his famous glass for a market; he went bankrupt when he overestimated the market. The arts have always been closely linked with the business of living. It is only when they become art for art's sake that they wither. Similarly, culture for culture's sake becomes exotic and unreal. If literature and history and philosophy cannot be related to the life of the community, they have no very important values. In other words, if a psychologist is not a better psychologist because he knows something about the development of human thought and the expression of human nature through art, then there is little hope for philosophy, history, and literature.

Many of the defenders of a liberal education emphasize its broader social values: the making of intelligent citizens; the training for life rather than making a living; the understanding of ethical and moral values. But a member of a democratic society functions in that society chiefly through his occupation. A man's contribution to his age is above all his contribution as a physician, a manufacturer, a chemist, a writer, a publisher. A physician's knowledge or lack of knowledge of sociology will appear during dinner table conversations and at the polls. But it is vastly more important in his work as a physician and member of a medical association. It is there that his knowledge or lack of knowledge chiefly affects society.

Culture does not function in a vacuum. The "lost soul" of society will be found not in college courses, but in the market place and the laboratory and the court of law. The liberal arts college cannot educate some sort of mythical men of vision; it must educate chemists and sociologists and journalists with vision. When it fully accepts this function, it will no longer be troubled by falling enrollments. The professors can cease to worry about their own bread and butter when they recognize that even an A.B. must eat.

Critical Note on Earnest

Earnest's essay is especially interesting as a study in audience adaptation. Some of its more specific rhetorical characteristics could be singled out for praise, such as the clarity and sprightliness of its style, or its use of synecdoche (the substitution of a part for the whole, as when Earnest refers to "training in lunchroom management" instead of the more general "vocational training"). Other characteristics are less commendable, such as its unsupported and irresponsible generalizations; for example, "Almost all defenders of a liberal education use a tone of moral superiority." But the most striking feature of this essay is its mode of adapting to its audience.

The original audience consisted of readers of *The American Scholar*, the journal of Phi Beta Kappa. Its readers are college and university alumni and faculty members who, usually as undergraduates, have been admitted to Phi Beta Kappa. Because of these facts, we are able to draw two inferences concerning Earnest's initial audience: 1) it is an unusually intelligent audience; 2) it is an audience consisting almost entirely of former students of the liberal arts and sciences (only students of these disciplines are eligible for Phi Beta Kappa). When, in this essay, Earnest *assumes* that his audience *will* be interested in the prestige and welfare of liberal arts, instead of *arguing* that they *should* be interested, he is probably proceeding on a safe assumption. It is likely that this audience would have a lively interest in Earnest's subject and a great deal of sympathy for his general objective of elevating the prestige of the liberal arts. So, there are some assumptions which Earnest makes about his audience that seem to be well founded.

When we examine Earnest's essay with care, we find that there are actually two audiences involved in it. There is the audience of readers of *The American Scholar:* the audience that Earnest is addressing. There is also a vaguer audience, one that we might call "the general public," before whom the liberal arts are to be justified: the audience that Earnest is discussing. The essayist is telling this first audience—his readers—how liberal arts must be justified to this second audience—the general public. More specifically, he is saying that the liberal arts must be justified to the general public in terms of practical utility. And it is a definite sort of "practical utility" that Earnest is endorsing. He illuminates the term in his charge that the liberal arts college "fails to sell itself to its customers" and that it must "prepare its students to earn a living." In sum, Earnest is recommending the practical utility of the marketplace, the utility of business enterprise and money-making. He is assuming that the general public, the audience he is discussing, will not be sensitive to moral or aesthetic defenses of the liberal arts, but would respond to practical and "business-like" defenses.

Are Earnest's assumptions concerning this general public well founded? There is much evidence that they are. Students of American society from de Tocqueville to Riesman have repeatedly noted the high respect which Americans have for practicality and prudence. We have been called a pragmatic people, meaning that we are often more concerned with the material rewards of an enterprise than with its moral or aesthetic qualities. So when Earnest assumes that liberal arts will be "sold" to the general public only in terms of material benefit, he seems to stand on firm ground. At the very least, he could cite an impressive number of social critics who would agree with him in this assumption.

However, when we have examined only the techniques of audience adaptation in relation to audiences, we have not yet exhausted our subject. It remains for us to examine the relationship between these techniques and the subject and substance of the discourse. It is in this third area of examination that we begin to see a serious weakness in Earnest's essay.

One curious consequence of persuasive argument is that the techniques of persuasion can sometimes have an effect independent of the substance of persuasion. A way of arguing, if it is repeated often enough and attractively enough, can eventually not only gain belief in the idea being argued but can also accustom an audience to certain means of persuasion. For example, there is a tendency in current public discussion to justify increased appropriations for education on the grounds that education serves our country in struggling against communism. Now if this argument takes hold, it will result not only in a widespread belief in increasing appropriations for education; it may also result in the widespread belief that any proposal must be justified in the same way. In being persuaded to believe in increased appropriations for education, an audience will also be conditioned to believe in a certain way of arguing. Here we can see how the manner of argument can have an effect independent of the matter of argument. This is not an invariable law of persuasion—human behavior is much too complex for very many invariable laws—but it is a distinct tendency.

With this tendency in mind, we can see that Earnest, in defending the liberal arts by their practical utility, is actually helping to reinforce "practical utility" as an important criterion of judgment. When Earnest insists that arguments from practical utility are superior to moral or aesthetic arguments, he is inducing an audience to share this belief. A monumental irony arises from this situation: one of the primary objectives of the liberal arts education which Earnest is concerned to justify is to encourage the application of standards *other than* "practical utility." In a sense, then, Earnest's techniques of argument defeat his persuasive aim. By the very means which he suggests for justifying liberal arts education to the general public, one of the most important effects of liberal arts education would be nullified. Training in the liberal arts encourages us to apply moral and aesthetic standards of judgment; Earnest encourages us to judge the liberal arts themselves unmorally and unaesthetically. His rhetorical techniques, then, are incompatible with his subject.

We are left with both a moral and a question. The moral is: The means of persuasion employed by a speaker or essayist can have great, not easily foreseen effects on the ideas he is trying to communicate. It is, therefore, never enough to select techniques of persuasion according to what the audience wants or expects. The speaker must also be certain that his persuasive techniques are compatible with his subject.

The question is: How can liberal arts education be justified to those who do not already believe in it?

Questions

What shortcomings of contemporary higher education are analogous to those which troubled Wilson in 1909? To what extent should students be permitted to choose their own courses of study? Are students as well qualified to make these choices as faculty members? Should faculty members prescribe students' courses? What, if any, are the responsibilities of the college outside the classroom? Should the college provide its students with more than instruction?

Should liberal arts studies be required of engineering students? Should engineering be made an exclusively graduate program? Are engineers too narrowly specialized? Is any increase in knowledge a good? Why? How important is the role of scientists and engineers in governing society? Burchard said in 1956 that we had not yet indicated whether we wanted scientists to be responsible leaders or unquestioning technicians. To what extent is the role of the scientist in society defined today?

How can elementary and secondary schools be improved? Should Driver Training, Home Economics, and Wood Working be eliminated from secondary schools? What courses are essential and what courses are superfluous?

Should higher education be restricted to the highly intelligent, or should every high school graduate have the chance of entering college?

What role may the federal government properly play in education? Should the federal government help raise teachers' salaries? Would federal appropriations for education be accompanied by federal control of education? Would there be any advantages to some federal control of education? Any disadvantages?

What is the proper purpose of higher education? Should colleges aim to equip their students with the techniques of earning money? Is the ability to earn a living the same as being educated?

What is "education"? In what respects does Wilson's conception of education differ from Burchard's? From Bush's? From Earnest's? Do Burchard and Bush differ? Do you prefer Bush's or Earnest's defense of liberal education?

Suggestions for Further Reading

Barzun, Jacques. *Teacher in America.* New York: Harcourt, Brace, 1945.
Bowles, Frank H. *Admission to College; A Perspective for the 1960's, 57th Report of the President, College Entrance Examination Board.* Princeton, New Jersey: College Educational Testing Service, 1960.
Bundy, McGeorge. "Blueprint For An Ideal College," New York *Times Magazine,* Dec. 11, 1960, p. 13.
Conant, James B. *The American High School Today.* New York: McGraw-Hill, 1959.
Education in the USSR. U.S. Department of Health, Education and Welfare. Washington, D.C.: Government Printing Office, 1957.
General Education in Engineering. American Society for Engineering Education pamphlet, 1956.
Griswold, A. Whitney. *In the University Tradition.* New Haven: Yale University Press, 1957.
———. " 'Loyalty': An Issue of Academic Freedom," New York *Times Magazine,* Dec. 20, 1959, p. 18.
Hechinger, Grace, and Fred M. Hechinger, "What the Tests Do Not Test," New York *Times Magazine,* Oct. 2, 1960, p. 14.
Hirsch, Werner Z. *Analysis of the Rising Costs of Public Education.* (A Report to the Joint Congressional Economic Committee. 86th Congress, 1st Session, Joint Committee Print.) Washington, D.C.: Government Printing Office, 1959.
Life Adjustment Education for Every Youth. U.S. Department of Health, Education and Welfare, Bulletin 1951, No. 22. Washington, D.C.: Government Printing Office, 1953.
Millett, Fred B. *The Rebirth of Liberal Education.* New York: Harcourt, Brace, 1945.
Paying for Better Public Schools. Committee for Economic Development pamphlet, 1959.
Rickover, Hyman G. *Education and Freedom.* New York: E. P. Dutton, 1959.
Schutter, Charles H., and Richard L Spreckelmeyer. *Teaching the Third R; A Comparative Study of American and European Textbooks in Arithmetic.* Council for Basic Education pamphlet, 1959.
Solow, Herbert, "Colleges Are Too Cheap," *Fortune,* September, 1957.
Whitehead, Alfred North. *The Aims of Education.* New York: Mentor, 1949.

5. Censorship

Introduction

In principle, freedom of expression is widely believed to be essential to the continued vitality of democracy. Leslie Moeller shows in the first speech in this section, however, that Americans are quick to censor moral or political ideas of which they do not approve. Few problems have plagued us so persistently. Religious persecution in the Massachusetts Bay Colony, the Alien and Sedition laws, the Know-Nothing Party, and the McCarthy era are well-known instances of a lack of tolerance for the views of others, a phenomenon which is evident at every twist and turn of American history.

The problem arises because absolute freedom is not feasible. We cannot permit demagogues to incite armed insurrection. We cannot permit publishers and broadcasters completely to disregard accepted standards of public morality. Lacking a clear-cut standard, we are forced to adjudicate each case on its merits, to find in each case a desirable compromise between freedom of expression and the public welfare. The issue depends on value judgments and individual beliefs, and these vary greatly from group to group and time to time. Before his election, President Kennedy was very critical of the Eisenhower administration for suppressing information. Soon after entering office, however, the new president indicated that his administration's policies probably would not differ greatly from those of his predecessor's. Fred Millett, in the third selection in this section, rejects condemnation by laymen of literary works on moral grounds, but accepts the moral evaluation of a professional critic.

There is no one grand solution to the problems associated with censorship, but certainly there are better and worse ways of protecting individual and group rights in any given case. Moeller, Mollenhoff, Millett, Fischer, and Murray here demonstrate how difficult it is for reasonable, intelligent men to agree on which ways are better, which ways are worse. The sad history of past and present totalitarian regimes demonstrates the importance of finding the better ways.

LESLIE G. MOELLER

Do the People Care?

This speech was delivered at the Rochester Photo Conference sponsored by George Eastman House and by the National Press Photographers Association, Rochester, New York, September 9, 1957.

Leslie G. Moeller has been director of the School of Journalism at the State University of Iowa since 1947.

We are accustomed to think of the United States as a land of freedom, and it is indeed a land of freedom, but it is a land in which that freedom is under constant challenge. This challenge is greater than in many years past, and perhaps greater than it has ever been. The challenge has been more than a challenge; certain freedoms have been lost, and the fight to regain them is not going well.

In such a situation, what is the attitude of the average citizen toward freedom? How could we today describe the climate of freedom in the United States? How does the conduct of the mass media contribute to this atmosphere?

How might we describe the average citizen's attitude toward freedom of the press for both the electronic and the printed media? How much does he know about this basic right? Does he tie it to his own freedoms? And does he have a boiling point, a point at which he will take action in behalf of freedom of the press?

What is his degree of concern with the first and possibly the most basic element in freedom of the press, "the right of access," which in our own time has come to be called "freedom of information"? This right is elemental. Without access, there can be no news, there can be no picture. In today's nongovernmental world, access is no worse than before, and in certain areas, notably business, it is better. But in government access has worsened. Many legislatures hold closed committee meetings. Many public records are secret. Administrators have learned that the handout, and a close rein on subordinates, will often control the flow of information. Congress holds one third of its committee meetings in executive session. The military cloud of scientific secrecy is one of the great problems of our time. The Atomic Energy Commission is highly reticent in giving information about a life-and-death question: how extensive is atomic fall-out, and how dangerous is it for the citizen of today and for the citizen-to-be of tomorrow? The federal government has now for the first time in its history begun to espouse formally the theme that "the public does not have a right to know," and the Congress passed versions of a civil rights bill which specifically penalize the giving out of information on, of all subjects, civil liberties!

"Right of access" is then the great problem area today in freedom of the press, but the other elements are, however, equally important. Two of them, the "right of access to printing materials," and the "right to print without prior restraint," are not at the moment under extensive challenge. Two others, "the right to print without fear of reprisal when content is not unlawful and is not harmful," and "the right to distribute" are somewhat more in contention, but not so much as "freedom to know." The fact that these four elements are but briefly mentioned does not mean that they are not important—they are indeed very important—but merely that it seems more urgent to emphasize the current fight on freedom of information.

What makes up the existing "climate of freedom"? What elements help to determine it?

This climate can be examined from the standpoint of three overlapping groups which make policy or use it, or which are unavoidably affected by it. These groups are (1) the Policy-Definers, or Policy-Initiators, or the Access-Controllers, almost all of them in the area of government; (2) the Active Defenders of Freedom in General, who in most cases are also the Active Users of Freedom, although some are defenders in the abstract, without direct concern for their own immediate use of freedom, and (3) the Usually Passive Beneficiaries, who for the most part are everyday citizens not directly in the news-making or news-handling process.

The Policy-Definers and -Initiators in government (and it is possible here to discuss only this area) are under many stresses and strains. They usually operate in a "big" government. It is probable that bigness alone militates against freedom. More control and less freedom seem an attractive method for smoothing operations in a large activity. It is also true that a great many persons tend to think that men in public office should never make mistakes. This is a non-sensible attitude, but it exists, and accordingly a man who makes mistakes prefers to have them invisible. He then finds a policy of "news control" very attractive. Freedom of information means that the administrator must explain, and he must justify. For various reasons this is often difficult; for example, the situation may be very complex, and the public is not noted for its ability to understand complex situations. Explanation may also be merely undesirable; it requires time he'd rather use for some other effort which he may very logically feel is deeply in the public interest.

Another problem for the top-level federal Policy-Initiator is the basic conflict between the urgency for national security, especially in the face of communism, and the need to protect the rights and liberty of the individual. This contrast at times produces decisions which may protect national security but only at the direct cost of individual rights. For example, the Attorney-General prepares a list of so-called subversive organizations, but the organizations are not necessarily notified that they will be on the list, and they are not given the opportunity of a hearing before the issuance of the list. Membership in the organization, whether active or casual, intended or unintended, is then too often taken as evidence of subversive activity or tendencies, without further investigation.

The Active Defenders of Freedom in General include some Policy-Initiators, but for the most part the Defenders are from the press, or some segment of the law, or from education, or from that very wonderful group, the American Civil Liberties Union, or, less often, from the church. For the most part the Active Defenders have a concern with freedom as a phase of their professional duties, or because it directly affects their performance of duty, but many times they have also a disinterested view not directly tied to their immediate work. Other persons may at times fight for the "immediate" types of freedom which at the instant affect their own actions, but these defenders are not continuing advocates of "freedom in general."

The third group, the Usually Passive Beneficiaries, Mr. and Mrs. Everyday Citizen, give the strong impression of not bothering much with this sort of thing. It is true that American citizens told Dr. George Gallup's American Institute of Public Opinion that the one best thing about being an American citizen is "freedom"—but, in general, Mr. Average Citizen seems to feel that, as long as things go moderately well, freedom in the abstract is somebody else's business. Let the other fellow do it. In the fight for freedom of information in these past few years, what has the Average Citizen done? Where has he been? Certainly he has not been on the battle line.

What is more, his expressed record of attitude on freedom or on freedom of the press has not been cheering.

In a survey at the State University of Iowa, Prof. Charles E. Swanson found that 94.9 per cent of a sample of 373 citizens in a city of some 50,000 believe the newspaper should "print all ideas and opinions." However, the percentages change sharply when the points become specific. Only 82.3 per cent think the newspaper should be allowed to criticize a book or movie; only 75.9 per cent would allow the paper to attack the mayor; only 64.8 per cent would permit the paper to attack the president; only 58.2 per cent would permit criticizing the labor policy of an employer; only 56.0 per cent would allow the paper to attack local labor unions; only 54.2 per cent would print divorce hearings; only 53.3 per cent would print pictures of bodies of dead people; only 50.7 per cent would permit the paper to criticize the quality of gasoline, and only 35.9 per cent would allow reproduction of a painting of a nude.

The attitudes of the young people are also disturbing. Not long ago the Purdue University Public Opinion Poll asked high school students several questions in the area of freedom and civil liberty. These three thousand students were presented with the statement, "Newspapers and magazines should be allowed to print anything they want except military secrets." Only 45 per cent gave the answer "yes." 41 per cent give the answer "no."

The remaining 14 per cent are uncertain. 34 per cent say that the government should prohibit some people from making public speeches; only 53 per cent disagree and support the principle of free speech, while 13 per cent are uncertain. 26 per cent believe the police should be allowed to search a person or his home without a warrant. 25 per cent would prohibit the right of the people to assemble peaceably; these young people say that some groups should not be allowed to hold public meetings. 17 per cent say that local police may be right in holding persons in jail without telling them of any formal charge against them. 58 per cent agree that police may be justified in giving a man the "third degree" to make him talk. 33 per cent say that persons who refuse to testify against themselves should either be made to talk or should be severely punished; 20 per cent are uncertain on this point. 34 per cent would deny citizens the right to circulate petitions in some cases, and 32 per cent are uncertain on this point. 60 per cent say that police and other groups should have the right to censor or ban books and movies when they see fit. 49 per cent believe that large masses of the people are incapable of determining what is and what is not good for them—which is a rather vigorous rejection of the principle of democratic government.

It is obvious that these young people do not believe very wholeheartedly in the Bill of Rights—or at least they do not think of the Bill of Rights as something that applies in everyday life.

It is disturbing also to find that many Americans are afraid to talk. Radio Station KSL in Salt Lake City made a tape-recorder survey of "man in the street" opinion on the discharge of General MacArthur. 40 per cent of those interviewed had an opinion, but said that they were afraid to express their opinion publicly. What were their reasons? "You can't be too careful what you say." "I don't want to say anything until I find out how the 'others' feel." "Somebody might hold this against me later on." "I don't want the FBI investigating me."

The Rochester (N.Y.) *Times-Union* found many people would not talk in a survey on "Whether Rochester residents thought they were getting their money's worth out of increased taxes." One correspondent reported that she had to ask this question of "dozens of people to get one reply for publication."

The same situation has been described by Hans Knight of the Harrisburg (Pa.) *Patriot-News.* In a two-column letter in *Editor & Publisher* of July 13, 1957, Mr. Knight expressed some worries about freedom of speech, based on interviews with two thousand persons over a two-year period in gathering material for a Sunday column called, rather ironically, "The People Speak." He is concerned about their "fear of being on the record." He is referring to "people who should have something to say—people in responsible positions—but won't say it." He says these are "normal, articulate people with live minds who obviously could contribute something of value to the democratic process, but, by their own admission, are afraid to be quoted because of what they imagine might happen." He goes on to say that "What bothers me is the almost universal reluctance to exercise the freedom of speech on anything touching on the controversial. If controversy is the lifeblood of democracy, the flow of blood is sluggish."

Dr. George Gallup has asked Americans about the use of the right of free speech. He found that 92 per cent of those questioned had a more or less clear understanding of the expression. Of this group, only 50 per cent were in favor of "freedom of speech for everybody—that is, for example, permitting anyone to say anything at any time about our government or our country." 45 per cent would limit or qualify this right; 5 per cent are undecided.

So it appears that many, many Americans would deny or limit many of the freedoms, and that they are too often afraid to speak up and to speak out. It appears too that they are not very concerned about maintaining true freedom of the press, and that a great many of them are indeed willing to restrict it sharply.

At the very least, these Usually Passive Beneficiaries are unaware. They are not awake. They have not thought things through. They do not realize the full meaning of the words of William Allen White—that freedom is important only when it's lost. . . .

Freedom does not grow automatically. Freedom is a natural right of man, but man born in non-freedom often tolerates this condition for thousands of years. Freedom, once gained, lives on in an atmosphere of understanding and awareness.

"The man of freedom" needs to have a sense of the process of freedom —to realize that freedom has not come by magic, but through the musket at the shoulder, and the battle at the barricade, and the struggle in the legislative assembly and in the courts. . . .

An awareness of the endless nature of this struggle, and of the current state of freedom, is an essential part of the freedom climate. The citizen must be watchful, and knowing. He might, for example, ask the question, "What is happening to the right to travel abroad?" Such travel is an important freedom; it is the ultimate way of really knowing the rest of the world. In an earlier day, a United States citizen going abroad did not need a passport. Such a document did not exist. The citizen simply decided to go, and he went. Then came the passport. It was introduced as a statement of identification and its issuance was a formality.

Today the situation is different. The individual citizen has become an instrument of the policy of the national government. Can *you* get a passport? Will your trip be "in the best interest of the United States"? Let us suppose that some anonymous, faceless person in the State Department decides that your trip is *not* in the best interest of the nation. What happens then? What do you do? Can you prove that your going is indeed "in the best interest of the United States"? Even if you can provide such proof, is that freedom?

The wide spreading of information about these situations is important; information may not always be the foundation for attitude, but often it is basic. The citizen must know what's happening, and for this reason he must realize that freedom of the press in a modern mass society is the basis for all other freedoms. Freedom of the press is the amplification of freedom of speech, and these together represent the greatest and most basic of the freedoms, which is intellectual freedom, freedom of the mind. Economic freedom, and political freedom, and spiritual freedom are all important, but these rest essentially and finally upon intellectual freedom, and they cannot endure without it. . . .

CLARK MOLLENHOFF

Access to Information

This speech was delivered at the annual Lovejoy Convocation of Colby College on December 3, 1959.

Clark Mollenhoff, a lawyer and Pulitzer prize-winning reporter for the Washington Bureau of Cowles Publications, was designated Colby's 1959 Lovejoy Fellow as "a member of the newspaper profession who has made significant contribution to American journalism." He received an honorary LL.D. degree.

As you read the speech, notice that Mollenhoff encourages you to accept his assertions by supporting them with a large number of illustrations and that he holds audience interest by shifting rapidly from one idea to another. Contrast this technique with Thomas R. Waring's (pp. 93-97) use of fewer but more vivid images. Notice also the Mollenhoff's main ideas are not entirely discrete. Some ideas overlap others, and the thread of the argument loops back at several points to ideas previously introduced. Can you tell when the speaker passes from one idea to another? Do you achieve a clear grasp of his argument from a single reading? Try outlining the speech and then improving the organization.

On the surface it would appear there are few threats to the free press today. Those who are critical of governmental officials or of the great institutions of our nation do not have their presses smashed, nor are they likely to be subjected to the continuous personal harassment that resulted in the death of Elijah Parish Lovejoy.

Today there is the tendency in America to take our freedoms for granted. We assume that freedom of the press is so well established that it will always be with us. Our daily newspapers are filled with columns of print exposing wrong doing, and criticizing the mistakes of judgment by our public officials, our labor leaders, our television performers and television executives. Many newspapers pride themselves on finding room for all points of view, and have demonstrated it by carrying columnists who are as far apart as the conservative David Lawrence and such a liberal as Marquis Childs.

Members of the public and many newspapermen are inclined to accept the idea that the American people are so steeped in the traditions of a free press and its part in a democracy that no public official would dare to attack our idealistic concept of an uncensored and independent press. There is the view that Americans, born and reared in this tradition, would rise in fury to strike down the government officials who would seek to control or suppress the nation's newspapers. We often hear it said that Americans, reared in an atmosphere of freedom, would not put up with the encroachments on liberty that have been forced on people behind the Iron Curtain. We are told that they would not put up with the kind of conditions that have stifled many freedoms in our own hemisphere.

It seems to me that this philosophy of the indomitable American presupposes that Americans are somehow braver, stronger, wiser, and more valiant than people living in other parts of the world. I would think that the present stage in the space race would teach us that Americans have no monopoly on wisdom, enterprise, strength, or know-how. For years we kidded ourselves into thinking that simply because we are Americans, with many advantages over the Russians, we were guaranteed a long lead in the fields of nuclear weapons, aircraft, and space exploration. In recent years we have seen our lead dwindle and vanish while many of our leading scientists have complained that nonsensical security on many matters interfered with our scientific progress.

Now, many realists are willing to admit that we Americans have no guaranteed superiority in scientific areas. We have been forced to learn the hard way that the rate of accomplishment in scientific areas is tied pretty closely to our willingness to work, to study, and to make sacrifices.

There is little in our lazy, well-fed, luxury-loving attitudes of the present to make me believe that any great number of Americans have awakened to the recognition that we are not a super race. There is little to indicate that any large segment of the American people recognize that we must work and study to recognize when there are encroachments on our freedoms, or risk seeing these freedoms go down the drain as has our lead in the scientific field.

My concern today is over the apathy where there are serious encroachments on the right of access to information. It is an apathy that covers not only the general public but a good many representatives of the press. This lack of concern is either the result of a lack of knowledge of what a free press means to a democracy, lack of enough interest to dig in and learn where some arbitrary governmental secrecy policies can take us, or lack of guts to speak out.

It is time that more Americans recognize that we are no brighter, stronger, or more courageous than many people who have been crushed by totalitarian governments. We are only luckier—luckier because we are fortunate enough to be living in a free nation.

We are fortunate that the slogans of a free press are deeply enough rooted in our history that few American political figures would take the risk of any direct attack on the institution of the free press. I have no doubt that a direct attack on the free press would result in a loud outcry from the press itself, and from a few citizens. There is a recognition of the possibility of political repercussions from a direct assault on the press, and public officials are almost unanimous in giving at least lip service to the concept of an uncensored press. But, many of these same public officials find indirect ways to control the information available to the press.

They also find subtle ways to influence or coerce reporters or columnists who are too aggressive and too critical.

What are the subtle methods used to influence the press?

There are the smooth public relations operators who are helpful to the point where some newsmen lean on them too much, and forget how to do their own digging and thinking.

There is the misuse of security classifications—top secret, secret, and confidential—to withhold information that should not be classified. This is a particularly effective means for officials in the Pentagon to cover up mistakes as well as improprieties. This overclassification is expensive from a standpoint of storage of records, as well as from a standpoint of the extra cost to the government where there is misuse of government property or the rigging of government contracts.

There are efforts to give the impression that material is being withheld for security purposes, when it is actually being withheld for political purposes.

There is the practice of officials being unavailable or slow at responding to calls from reporters who are regarded as critical of the administration in power.

There is the practice of granting special interviews or other privileges (such as invitations to the White House dinners) to reporters who are regarded as basically friendly.

Most important, there are the efforts to arbitrarily hide the records of executive agencies on grounds that some vague "national interest" unconnected with security is involved in refusing to divulge "confidential executive communications."

We of the press must accept the fact that an aggressive press will always be faced with some obstructions or harrassment. Regardless of which political party is in power, there will always be some men in the administration who will adopt the attitude that public business is not the public's business. . . .

A few of these secrecy-minded officials are malicious and tyrannical despots with no real concept of the responsibility to the public that is inherent in the operation of a true democracy. Such figures can grow even in a democracy.

But, I would say that a majority of those who erect secrecy barriers are only well-meaning, but misguided and shortsighted.

These secrecy fanatics include men who believe a near totalitarian type of censorship is needed to protect U.S. secrets from the Kremlin. Read the testimony before the congressional committees and you will see who they are.

There are other secrecy fiends who rationalize the hiding of matters that have no connection with military secrecy on grounds that information released by the government will be slanted or twisted by political enemies. They rationalize their own slanting of government press releases on grounds it is really "in the national interest."

There is also the secrecy group that argues that secret discussions of governmental problems result in greater efficiency, and more frank discussions of different viewpoints.

Each of these groups overlooks the long documented record of how secrecy has been used to cover up corruption in government. They disregard the basic right of the public to know the arguments involved in a decision to award contracts or dispense other rights unless some real military security problem is involved.

There are some reporters and editors who will tell you that there is no real problem in obtaining information in Washington.

It may be true that some reporters and editors have run into no secrecy barriers. There is no problem of obtaining information that is favorable to an administration that is in power. There is usually no problem of obtaining access even to the busiest individuals if they are reasonably sure they are to be the subject of articles puffing their importance.

The problem of access to information arises when officials know (or suspect) that the inquiring reporter may unearth facts that are not wholly complimentary to the administration, or when the reporter is known to have been critical of the administration.

Point out the newsman who says he has no trouble obtaining information, and it is likely the subject will fit one of these patterns:

1. A reporter or editor who has been largely a patsy for the administration.

2. A reporter or editor who lacks either the imagination or the energy to go behind the self-serving declarations of agency press releases.

Reporters who are considered "friends" of the administration in power may have a few exclusive stories dropped in their laps in return for understanding and uncritical treatment.

By contrast, there are often efforts at retaliation against those who are critical of the administration in power. President Franklin Delano Roosevelt went so far as to summon Lyle Wilson, United Press Bureau chief, to the White House in a direct effort to kill a story. Roosevelt also threatened reprisal against the United Press if Wilson did not give in to his demands, but Wilson refused. Occasionally, presidents since then have been equally blunt.

But, it is seldom that a president will take such direct action as to summon a reporter or editor to the White House. More common are the subtle efforts of lesser officials to interfere with the reporter, to ridicule or undermine his work, to erect barriers that interfere with him on even routine assignments.

The New York Times occupies a unique position that makes its reporters less susceptible to the pressures of federal officials than other newspapers. It is a paper read in Washington and in the embassies all over the world. It has a voice that is loud as well as respected and feared by official Washington.

Yet, some reporters for this mighty newspaper find themselves subjected to subtle pressures when they are critical of the Administration. Bureau Chief James (Scotty) Reston. . . . was highly critical of the foreign policy of the late John Foster Dulles, [but] *The New York Times* bureau chief praises Dulles for "never taking any step to cut off my sources of information."

However, there were others in the administration who were not so understanding of the role of a critical press in a democracy. Reston's critical comments were met with hostility in some quarters and with subtle harassment by officials who were unavailable for interviews and dilatory or unavailable on telephone calls.

Columnist Walter Lippmann, speaking from the experience of his 70 years, commented before the National Press Club this fall on the tendency of government "insiders" to ridicule criticism from outside government as coming from ignoramuses—persons who don't have access to the conferences and secret files of the government.

Lippmann declares that formidable as this criticism is, he has no trouble getting the better of it:

> I tell the critic, you be careful. You will be denouncing the principle of democracy itself, which asserts that the outsiders shall be sovereign over the insiders. For you will be showing that the people themselves, since they are ignoramuses because they are outsiders, are therefore incapable of governing themselves.

Furthermore, Lippmann declared that as far as the affairs of the world are concerned those who regard themselves as insiders are actually outsiders since none of them read all of the U.S. papers and attend all the meetings dealing with foreign policy, and they have no access to the records of foreign governments that are equally important if one is to have the total wisdom the insiders indicate they have.

Columnists Drew Pearson and Joseph Alsop report that when they were critical of government policies and personalities, they found themselves subjected to investigations by agents of the F.B.I. and other government bureaus. They contended that no breach of security was involved but that they were subjected to probes to dry up their sources of information.

On the local level, the *Arkansas Gazette* found itself the target of the barbs of Governor Orval Faubus for aggressive opposition to Faubus on the explosive issue of the Little Rock schools. Despite the fact that the paper found its circulation cut and its advertising revenue off sharply, the publisher and editor stuck with their position to win an expensive victory.

Executive Editor Harry Ashmore left the *Gazette* this fall. He had won his battle, but he was aware that the bitterness of the integration fight had left scars that would remain as long as he directed the editorial policy of the newspaper.

Wally Turner and Bill Lambert, reporters for the *Portland Oregonian*, tackled the corruption in local politics and the mighty Teamsters Union. They found themselves and their newspaper subject to immediate attacks and a series of libel actions that might have terrorized a less courageous editorial department.

Vance Trimble, reporter for the Scripps-Howard syndicate, had no more than started his series on the nepotism on Congressional payrolls when he was subjected to vicious attacks from Congress. Fortunately, many newspaper groups rallied behind Trimble's effort, and an atmosphere was created that forced many members of Congress to drop relatives from the payroll or to cut their salaries. The force of public opinion also forced the Senate to adopt new rules opening Senate office payrolls for public inspection.

As head of the Sigma Delta Chi Freedom of Information committee, V. M. (Red) Newton, managing editor of the *Tampa Tribune*, lashed out at the secrecy that covered spending of counterpart funds. He was immediately subjected to a personal attack by members of the House Administration Committee. That crusade to open these spending records has been unsuccessful so far, but Newton and others are still pushing for open records on this congressional spending.

The term "managing the news" was used by Scotty Reston in explaining to the Moss subcommittee his complaint about government information practices. Reston, whose work has been largely in the foreign affairs field, was objecting to the practice of releasing selective facts to present the favorable picture the administration wanted to get across to the public. He complained that barriers were erected to block those who sought further facts that were inconsistent with the picture presented in the "managed news."

In the foreign affairs field and in some other areas, the "managing of the news" can be accomplished by misusing security classifications to cover part of the facts.

In fields where national security cannot be used to hide the facts, a new device has come into wide use for "managing the news." It is the claim by the executive branch of government that it has some inherent right to arbitrarily refuse to produce any records or give any testimony that includes advice or recommendations in the executive agencies.

The Eisenhower administration has pressed this broad secrecy doctrine with the argument that all communications containing advice or recommendations are "confidential executive business." The Administration claims some inherent "executive privilege" to hide such communications from the press, the public, committees of Congress, and even from auditors of the General Accounting Office.

Leonard J. Saccio, acting I.C.A. Director, testified before the Hennings Subcommittee that he believed this so-called "executive privilege" gave the I.C.A. the authority to withhold practically every document in the agency from the G.A.O. auditors.

"If I.C.A. wanted to apply the executive privilege, G.A.O. would not see one thing because practically every document in our agency has an opinion or a piece of advice . . . ," Saccio testified.

No agency in the executive branch has carried this arbitrary executive secrecy to the extreme point Saccio says it could be carried. However, the testimony by Saccio was an admission from within the executive department of the danger inherent in a doctrine that any executive department official can withhold any document that includes advice or recommendations.

It may be that some of you have such faith in the present administration that you feel quite contented to have that administration exercising an arbitrary power to refuse to produce records for the Congress, the G.A.O., the press and the public. However, it would be well to question whether you want such unchecked power to conceal records lodged in the hands of some other administration. . . .

It is only by viewing the power of arbitrary executive secrecy in the hands of the other political party that many can test their true reaction to such a broad claim of a right to refuse to produce records.

Apply the doctrine of arbitrary executive secrecy to the Teapot Dome scandals of the Harding administration. Then you will see how the claim of arbitrary executive secrecy could have been used to conceal these notorious scandals. The oil scandals of the Harding administration involved communications between Secretary of Navy Denby and Secretary of Interior Fall. Had a claim of arbitrary executive secrecy been invoked, it would have been impossible for Senator Thomas Walsh, the Montana Democrat, to establish the fact that eventually sent Secretary of Interior Fall to prison.

Assume that the Truman administration officials had claimed a precedent of executive privilege and refused to give testimony or produce records on the tax scandals. The communications between top officials in the White House, Justice Department, and Treasury would have remained buried, along with the crimes involving some of the highest officials of the huge tax collecting agency.

In 1948 there were some restricted efforts by the Truman administration to bar congressional investigators from some executive department records. The personnel records of William Remington were withheld under a general executive order placing loyalty files outside of the reach of congressional committees. William P. Rogers, [later] Attorney General, was then the chief counsel for the Senate committee investigating Remington. Rogers presided over the preparation of a report that was highly critical of this executive secrecy.

Richard M. Nixon, then a young congressman from California, had some sharp comments to make about this limited withholding of records by the Truman administration. Nixon said:

> The point has been made that the President of the United States has issued an order that none of this information (on Remington) can be released and therefore the Congress has no right to question the judgment of the President. I say that that proposition cannot stand from a constitutional standpoint or on the basis of the merit for this very good reason. That would mean that the President could have arbitrarily issued an executive order in the Meyers case, the Teapot Dome case, or in any other case denying the Congress information it needed to conduct an investigation of the executive department and the Congress would have no right to question his decision.

Nixon was only one of the many prominent Republicans who attacked this executive secrecy at the time. By contrast, a good many high ranking Democrats—including House Speaker Sam Rayburn of Texas—were defending the secrecy of the Truman administration. Many Democrats who were inclined to defend the secrecy in the Truman administration [were later] highly critical of the Eisenhower administration for merely extending the same basic principle. It demonstrates that political expediency has a tendency to encroach on the views of our elected representatives and to color their thinking. The press and the public cannot depend on either political party to be the beacon of right where their freedoms are involved.

After the Truman administration was so severely criticized by Republicans for imposing unjustified secrecy, it was amazing to see a Republican administration lay down a claim to a right of arbitrary executive secrecy that is broader than any similar claim in our history.

The new secrecy doctrine was made public in connection with the Army-McCarthy hearings on May 17, 1954—the same day the United States Supreme Court pronounced its historic ruling against racial segregation in public schools. The fact that the Supreme Court ruled on segregation on that day did not bury the colorful Army-McCarthy hearings or the fact that officials of the executive branch were refusing to give testimony before a committee of Congress.

President Eisenhower, in a letter to Defense Secretary Charles E. Wilson, authorized Army Counsel John Adams to refuse to relate conversations with Presidential Assistant Sherman Adams and William P. Rogers, then the Deputy Attorney General. The President wrote that in his view members of the executive branch should not be required to testify on conversations and communications with other members of the executive branch where recommendations and advice were involved.

Many large newspapers—still hysterical with the fear of the McCarthy era—saw this letter as only a blow at Senator Joseph McCarthy. If McCarthy wanted the testimony, then these newspapers were opposed to it. Unthinking editorial writers praised the Eisenhower letter as some new and brilliant statement of the separation of powers doctrine. Only a few looked behind the minor inconvenience it presented to McCarthy in his television battle with the Army and saw the full claim of arbitrary executive secrecy it embodied. Since then, many have changed their views.

The full threat inherent in Eisenhower's May 17, 1954, letter did not become apparent immediately. It took months and even years before it became clear that the administration would use that letter as a precedent for refusing a wide variety of information to the press, to a dozen congressional committees, and to the General Accounting Office.

Sherman Adams refused to testify in a congressional hearing on the Dixon-Yates case on grounds that his activities were all confidential executive business. His action was to set the pattern for officials of more than a dozen agencies of government to inform Congress and the G.A.O. that important records and testimony would not be produced. A half dozen committees of Congress prepared reports castigating this arbitrary withholding of testimony and documents.

The refusal of the executive branch to make certain evaluation reports and inspectors general reports available to the G.A.O. and committees of Congress has become a major barrier to investigations of the Defense Department and foreign aid spending.

Comptroller General Joseph Campbell, an appointee of the Eisenhower administration, has declared that the withholding of documents was hindering the G.A.O. in the performance of its statutory duties and "could be almost fatal" to the G.A.O.'s effectiveness.

The Moss Government Operations Subcommittee on government information has lashed out at the withholding from G.A.O. as being a violation of the law since the Budget and Accounting Act of 1921 provides that all agencies must turn over all records requested by the G.A.O. auditors. . . .

The concern of Congress is not so much over what has been withheld as it is worry over where this broad claim of a right to withhold records may lead at some future time. Members of Congress recognize that in the wrong hands the precedent could become a major tool in forming an executive dictatorship.

They know that it has been necessary to keep a constant surveillance over military spending—now 60 per cent of our budget—to expose corruption and force action against officials involved in the corruption.

As we have greater expenditures and more complex operations of our government we need more congressional investigations to constantly burrow into the activities of our public officials. The press needs the skill and the power of congressional committees to spotlight the big problem areas in our society.

Congress and the G.A.O. need the power to obtain records and testimony from those public officials in the executive departments who are responsible for administration and enforcement of laws.

This is a great issue of freedom in our time. It goes to the question of the right of Congress to serve as a check on the Executive department's activities. It goes to the question of whether a free people are entitled to information on the activities of government when no question of national security is involved.

This year, in this administration, it may represent only an inconvenience to the press, an irritant to congressional investigators, and an impediment to efficient work by the G.A.O. auditors.

But, what could such a precedent of arbitrary executive secrecy do under some later administration that may be less kindly in its basic outlook?

This problem may pass quickly. I hope it does. But it is the type of problem you, as citizens, will be asked to face many times in the years ahead. As graduates of a fine liberal arts college, you will be expected to give some leadership when arguments arise over whether projected government activity is a threat to freedom and the operation of a democracy. Some of you may be reporters, editors, or public officials deeply involved in grappling with the problem of whether certain practices are good for the nation in the long run.

Or you may be the voters—the great American jury that must ultimately decide whether officials will be allowed to appropriate certain powers to themselves.

You may not be asked to defend your printing presses or your life, but in many ways you will undergo tests that will determine whether you have what it takes to carry on in the Spirit of Elijah Parish Lovejoy.

After college, will you have the perseverance and the industry to continue to work at the job of knowing about public affairs? Or will you follow the mass that takes the position that this responsibility belongs to others?

Will you have the interest and moral indignation to fight against injustice or encroachment on freedom?

Will you have the integrity to disregard partisan politics and measure an issue or a man on things that are in keeping with his true worth?

Will you have the courage—the pure guts—to fly in the face of the currently popular view to do battle for what solid and serious study leads you to believe is right?

I am sure a certain percentage of this group will have the industry, the integrity, and the courage to face the large issues. But the real test of whether the Spirit of Elijah Parish Lovejoy lives—at Colby College and in the United States—will be based on how large a percentage learn that democracy is not something that can be taken for granted.

FRED B. MILLETT

The Vigilantes

This presidential address was delivered at the fortieth annual meeting of the American Association of University Professors at Buffalo, New York, on April 2, 1954. The following abridgment is from the text published in the AAUP Bulletin, Spring 1954.

Fred B. Millett is professor emeritus of English literature at Wesleyan University, Connecticut, and a past president of the AAUP.

Millett constructed the introductory paragraph of this speech with considerable skill. The swift pace of the thought and the wealth of concrete detail compel attention. At the same time, everything in the paragraph is so closely relevant to the statement of his theme which appears at the end, that it both prepares the listener for and helps him to understand the central idea.

On the evening of December 21, 1953, in the course of a C.B.S. television program, "This is Show Business," the well-known American playwright, Mr. George S. Kaufman, made the *ad lib.* remark, "Let's make this *one* program on which no one sings 'Silent Night.'" Before the show had ended, the switchboard of the Columbia Broadcasting System began receiving calls objecting to Mr. Kaufman's remark on the grounds that it was "anti-religious." During the next few days, between 200 and 500 letters protesting the remark were received by either the Columbia Broadcasting System or the show's sponsor, The American Tobacco Company. As a result, Mr. Kaufman was dropped from the show until calmer counsels prevailed and he was permitted to rejoin it. In the preceding May, an amateur production of *Mr. Roberts* closed after one performance at the Mitchell Air Force Base, Long Island, because several unidentified persons objected to Air Force personnel's being allowed to hear the salty language which had been tolerated by all and sundry members of its audience during the play's three-year run on Broadway. Last November, the Motion Picture Production Code Administration denied the appeal of Paramount Pictures to be permitted to retain in the dialogue of a picture depicting actual battle conditions in Korea three uses of the word "hell" and one use of the word "damn." A month or so ago, a most distinguished audience assembled for the private showing of a double-bill of moving pictures. The audience consisted of the Justices of the Supreme Court of the United States. The pictures were an old German movie entitled "M," and a French movie, entitled "La Ronde," which had played for two years in the most exclusive cinema in London's West End. In assembling to view these pictures, the Justices were not moved by a common interest in either abnormal psychology or licentious behavior. They were assembled to decide whether or not the sovereign state of Ohio had acted legally in banning "M," and whether the New York State Board of Censors had acted legally in banning "La Ronde" on the grounds that it "would tend to corrupt public morals." In that stronghold of public morality, Jersey City, the police recently advised booksellers to remove from prominent display all copies of James Jones's novel, *From Here to Eternity*. In Detroit, booksellers were discouraged from offering for sale pocket-sized editions of certain of the works of Hemingway, although they were permitted to sell the books in hard covers. In Cleveland, a dealer was told that he could sell a portfolio of reproductions of Renoir's paintings but that he should not display it. . . . These instances involving censorship are only a few of many examples that might be cited of the wave of suppression that has swept over this free land of ours during the past two or three years. . . .

Censorship, generally, falls into two significantly distinct classes, hidden and public. Of the two classes, the first is, of course, the more insidious because it is uncontrollable. Such hidden censorship is part and parcel of the system in accordance with which motion pictures are produced in the United States. All pictures that are to receive the approval of the Motion Picture Producers Code Administration must secure the approval *before* the pictures can be released. There is plenty of evidence that many of the specific stipulations of the Code are hopelessly outmoded. A specific ruling of the Code bans "pointed profanity and every other profane or vulgar expression, however used." It was this specific ruling that brought about the enforced elimination of three "hell's" and one "damn" from the picture showing actual battle conditions in Korea. Public censorship is that exercised by a legally constituted body such as the New York State Board of Regents, which may refuse to permit the showing of a picture anywhere within the limits of the sovereign state of New York. A more dangerous form of public censorship, however, occurs when private individuals or pressure-groups exert their influence to prevent the public sale of books or the public showing of moving pictures.

Three recent instances of attempted censorship deserve somewhat more detailed comment. "La Ronde," a French moving picture, based on Arthur

Schnitzler's classic dialogues, *Reigen*, directed by Max Ophuls, and acted by a distinguished French cast, had been shown legally not only in fifteen of the states but also in the District of Columbia. The Motion Picture Division of the New York State Board of Regents, however, refused, as I have said, to permit the showing of the picture within the state, and the ruling of the Board was sustained by the Court of Appeals by a three-to-two decision. The case was carried to the Supreme Court of the United States, and recently that court ruled that the New York State Board of Regents had no legal right to prevent the showing of the picture and that, in its judgement, the showing of it would not "tend to corrupt public morals." Thus, at long last, the innocent denizens of New York City were allowed to witness, if they so chose, a public showing of this famous film. Of "La Ronde," Mr. Bosley Crowther, the *New York Times* moving-picture critic, wrote, it "is a philosophical exploration of the delusions of illicit love. Some of it is obvious, some of it subtle and vague. . . . It is hard to imagine anyone without a good bit of sophistication understanding very well what's going on. It is ridiculous to think of this picture having been banned for being "immoral." Yet the only reason we're seeing it in this state is because the Supreme Court found the term 'immoral' inadequate as a standard for condemning a film."

The case of the motion picture, "The Moon Is Blue," is even more preposterous. As a play, F. Hugh Herbert's little comedy had played for months in a New York theatre without arousing any great enthusiasm or attracting adverse comment. Then, a film, made from the play, failed to receive the approval of the Motion Picture Producers Code Administration but was passed by the New York Board of Censors. As the time came for the showing of the film, protests against it appeared in various places. In Chicago, the police allowed the film to be shown but only to adult audiences. In Kansas City, Missouri, the police censors asked for five elisions. The Motion Picture Censorship Board of the State of Kansas demanded sixty-six elisions. In New York, the picture was attacked as containing serious violations of morality and decency. A showing of the picture in Jersey City was raided by the police, led by the Director of Public Safety, and the theatre manager was haled into court. The description of the cause of all this to-do may be entrusted to the judicious Mr. Crowther. The movie, he wrote, is "a skimpy little story of a girl who is frank about sex but wonderously deft in deflecting the passes of predatory wolves." What apparently upset the guardians of the Motion Picture Production Code was not only the frequent use in dialogue of such tabooed words as "virgin," "mistress," and "pregnant," but also a dissipated father's indifference to his daughter's sexual behavior. But, Mr. Crowther concludes, "the theme of this confection is as moral as a Sunday school book. . . . It is virtue that triumphs. The good little girl gets the man."

Certainly the most momentous attempt to prevent the exhibition of a moving picture involved the film called "The Miracle." Directed by Roberto Rossellini, the picture tells the story of a half-witted Italian peasant girl who is seduced by a stranger whom she believes to be a vision of St. Joseph. Proud of what seems to her a miraculous pregnancy, she is tormented by the villagers, who stage a mock-procession in her honor. In the end, she crawls away to bear her child in the shadow of an empty church. The New York Film Critics voted "Three Ways of Love," of which "The Miracle" was a part, the "best foreign movie of the year," but, under pressure, they made their award in the Rainbow Room of the R.C.A. Building at Rockefeller Center, and not in a public theatre. The attack on this picture was violent and inflammatory; it was accused of being both blasphemous and sacrilegious. Angry picket-lines marched and counter-marched before the theatre; there were threats that the theatre would be bombed. Although its showing had been licensed by the Motion Picture Division of the New York State Board of Regents, the License Commissioner of New York City immediately imposed a temporary ban on the showing of the film, and when he was enjoined from imposing this ban, the Board of Regents, after its special sub-committee had voted unanimously that the picture was sacrilegious, reversed the decision of its Motion Picture Division and banned the film. Legal recourse to the New York Court of Appeals resulted in a unanimous decision to sustain the Regents' ban. But Joseph Burstyn, the distributor of the picture, carried the case to the Supreme Court of the United States, and, finally, the Justices rendered a unanimous decision that the State of New York's banning of the film was unconstitutional. "New York requires," Mr. Justice Clark wrote, "that permission to communicate ideas be obtained in advance from state officials who judge the works and pictures sought to be communicated. . . . Such a previous restraint is a form of infringement upon freedom of expression to be especially condemned." On the issue of sacrilege, he wrote, "In seeking to apply the definition of 'sacrilegious,' the censor is set adrift upon a boundless sea amid myriad currents of religious views, with no charts but those provided by the most vocal and powerful orthodoxies. . . . Under such a standard the most careful and tolerant censor would find it virtually impossible to avoid favoring one religion over another." . . .

[Dr. Millett next discusses possible causes for the recent prevalence of the type of censorship he has delineated. He points out that the proportion of the American people obtaining a secondary-school education today is much larger than it was fifty years ago and suggests that the wave of censorship is due in part "to the concern of the half-educated for the well-being of the quarter-educated." Noting the "general atmosphere of hysteria and fear of communism that is being systematically engendered in America . . . ," Dr. Millett further suggests that the rise of censorship stems in part from the transfer of distrust, hostility, and fear of communism to "any other product of contemporary culture that for some reason seems strange or baffling or threatening to the half-educated mind."]

I should like to conclude by commenting on three propositions concerning censorship which it seems to me follow logically from the evidence I have submitted and mountains of evidence that have accumulated through the centuries: (1) Censorship in the field of literature and the other arts is usually stupid, and always unintelligent. (2) The censorship of literature is almost invariably self-defeating. (3) The censorship of literature is anti-democratic; in other words, it is fundamentally opposed to the philosophy of democracy.

(1) Censorship in the field of literature and the other arts is usually stupid and always unintelligent, because the critical assumptions that underlie censorship are aesthetically indefensible. The censor of literature does not condemn a literary work because it is a bad literary work; by his very nature, he is usually incapable of distinguishing between a good and a bad literary work, even if he thought it important to make such a judgment. The censor condemns a literary work and would prevent its circulation because it contains or implies ideas or attitudes that he regards as erotically, ethically, politically, religiously, or philosophically reprehensible, ideas and attitudes that he thinks would do damage, not to himself, mind you, but to other persons who might be exposed to them. Now, a literary work is not a good work because it contains ideas, of whatever sort, of which the censor would approve, nor is it a bad work because it contains ideas, of whatever sort, of which the censor would disapprove. If this were the case, a hymn embodying the soundest theology in the most banal style would be a good hymn, and a hymn expressing heretical ideas in a superb poetic style would be a bad hymn. Persons who are interested in rooting out heresies might condemn the second hymn as heretical; critics could hardly condemn it as being a bad hymn.

The relationship between the idea and the form of a literary work, and the relative significance of these elements in the evaluation of literary works are not, I admit, elementary problems. . . . The excellence of a poem does does not depend on the validity of the doctrine it expresses. The excellence of a poem depends finally on what is said, the manner in which it is said and, I should add, the relationship between the matter and the manner. If an artist is serious, he attempts in a work of art to express something that he regards as true and something that he considers it important to say. He also endeavors to give the most appropriate and appealing form possible to what he is trying to say. On both reader and critic, it is the form that makes the most immediate impression, but, if he is a good reader and a good critic, he will be able to grasp accurately not only the idea embodied in the form but the author's attitude toward that idea, his feeling about it. He is then, as either reader or critic, quite free to indicate that what the artist thought it important to say does not seem to him to be important or illuminating or weighty. But, so long as he is acting as a literary critic, he cannot condemn the work *merely* because its content seems dubious or dangerous. In the last analysis, the excellence of a literary work depends on a very subtle analysis and weighing of the content, the form, and the relationship between the content and the form.

(2) That the censorship of literature is usually self-defeating is so obvious as hardly to need explication. The very fact that a censor openly designates a work as dubious or dangerous is enough to draw the attention of at least a considerable segment of the public to a work that might otherwise have gone unnoticed. When the official custodians of the public morals of Boston were more active, it used to be said that some publishers looked forward eagerly to having their books banned there so that a considerable sale would be assured elsewhere. . . . The unintentional effect of censorship may also be suggested by the fact that the touring company of *The Moon Is Blue* now uses as advertising slogans, "SEE what the film couldn't show! *Hear* what the movie couldn't say!" . . .

(3) Finally, the censorship of literature is in basic opposition to the principle of freedom of thought and expression that is one of the basic tenets of a philosophy of democracy. Since I am not a political philosopher, I may perhaps be permitted to use as my authority a distinguished member of the Council of the Association, Professor Ralph Barton Perry. In his essay, "What Does It Mean to be Free?" he writes, "Freedom means *effective choice.* Man is free, in other words, in proportion as *he does or thinks what he chooses.* . . . It is choice that imposes on human life what is perhaps its greatest burden: for it is very hard to choose. It is because he has the capacity for choice that man is a moral being." Later, he says, "It is surprising how many who consider themselves good Americans, after three centuries during which this creed has been proclaimed, embodied in our state and federal constitutions, and consecrated in our tradition, still do not understand what the principle means. They still tend to lapse into the primitive view that it means freedom to think and communicate *true* or *safe* opinions."

The relevance of these principles to the problem of the censorship of literature requires no demonstration. An essential condition of freedom of thought and expression is the freedom of the artist to say what he believes to be true and important and the freedom of the reader to choose whatever expressions arouse his interest, satisfy his curiosity, or add to his understanding of the human plight. As Professor Perry says, "Whoever determines what alternatives shall be made known to man controls what that man shall choose *from.* He is deprived of freedom in proportion as he is denied access to *any* ideas, or is confined to any range of ideas short of the totality of relevant possibilities."

The urge to censor literature has countless and tangled roots. But one of the major roots is a view of human nature that is in basic opposition to that implied in the philosophy of democracy. The view of human nature that is held by most censors is that expressed with terrifying eloquence by Dostoievski's Grand Inquisitor in the apologue Ivan recites in *The Brothers Karamazov.* The Grand Inquisitor, the anti-Christ of Dostoievski's apologue, holds the view that man is "weak, vicious, worthless, and rebellious." Man "is tormented by no greater anxiety than to find some one quickly to whom he can hand over that gift of freedom with which the ill-fated creature is born." Opposed to this view is the Christian view, the view of Christ, whose view of man's capacity to choose, the Grand Inquisitor denounces. "Instead of taking men's freedom from them, Thou didst make it greater than ever! Didst Thou forget that man prefers peace, and even death, to freedom of choice in the knowledge of good and evil? . . . Instead of giving a firm foundation for setting the conscience of man at rest forever, Thou didst choose what was utterly beyond the strength of men. . . . In place of the rigid ancient law, man must hereafter with free heart decide for himself what is good and what is evil."

The burden of choice is heavy, but, within the framework of democracy—I should even go so far as to say within the Christian framework—the burden is inescapable. In these contexts, not only must man be entrusted with the responsibility of choosing between what is good and what is evil, but he must have access to all kinds and varieties of literature in order that his choices may be as meaningful as possible. Within the increasingly complicated structure of the modern state, in the face of the confusing chaos of creeds, doctrines, and dogmas, man may, to be sure, shift the responsibility of choice to whatever official or unofficial shoulders he may select, but in so far as he abnegates his own responsibility for choice, he becomes less than a mature and responsible moral or aesthetic being.

JOHN FISCHER

The Harm Good People Do

This article appeared in Harper's magazine for October 1956, and was reprinted, together with the rejoinder by John C. Murray, S.J., which follows it here, in Harold C. Gardiner, S.J., Catholic Viewpoint on Censorship (Garden City, N.Y.: Hanover House, 1958).

John Fischer presides over "The Easy Chair" column of Harper's.

A little band of Catholics is now conducting a shocking attack on the rights of their fellow citizens. They are engaged in an un-American activity which is as flagrant as anything the Communist party ever attempted—and which is, in fact, very similar to Communist tactics. They are harming their country, their Church, and the cause of freedom.

Their campaign is particularly dangerous because few people realize what they are up to. It can hurt you—indeed, it already has—without your knowing it. It is spreading rapidly but quietly; and so far no effective steps have been taken to halt it.

Even the members of this organization probably do not recognize the damage they are doing. They are well-meaning people, acting from deeply moral impulses. They are trying, in a misguided way, to cope with a real national problem, and presumably they think of themselves as patriots and servants of the Lord. Perhaps a majority of Americans, of all faiths, would sympathize with their motives—though not with their methods.

They do not, of course, speak for all Catholics. On the contrary, they are defying the warnings of some of their Church's most respected teachers and theologians. The Catholic Church as a whole certainly cannot be blamed for their actions, any more than it could be held responsible a generation ago for the political operations of Father Coughlin.

This group calls itself the National Organization for Decent Literature. Its headquarters are in Chicago; its director is the Very Reverend Monsignor Thomas Fitzgerald. Its main purpose is to make it impossible for anybody to buy books and other publications which it does not like. Among them are the works of some of the most distinguished authors now alive—for example, winners of the Nobel Prize, the Pulitzer Prize, and the National Book Award.

Its chief method is to put pressure on news dealers, drug stores, and booksellers, to force them to remove from their stocks every item on the NODL blacklist. Included on this list are reprint editions of books by Ernest Hemingway, William Faulkner, John Dos Passos, George Orwell, John O'Hara, Paul Hyde Bonner, Emile Zola, Arthur Koestler, and Joyce Cary. In some places—notably Detroit, Peoria, and the suburbs of Boston—the organization has enlisted the local police to threaten booksellers who are slow to "co-operate."

This campaign of intimidation has no legal basis. The books so listed have not been banned from the mails, and in the overwhelming majority of cases no legal charges have ever been brought against them. Indeed, it seems that the National Organization for Decent Literature deliberately prefers to ignore the established legal channels for proceedings against books which it thinks improper. Its chosen weapons are boycott and literary lynching.

For example, early last year committees of laymen from Catholic churches in the four northern counties of New Jersey—Union, Hudson, Essex, and Bergen—began to call on local merchants. These teams were armed with the NODL lists. They offered "certificates," to be renewed each month, to those storekeepers who would agree to remove from sale all of the listed publications. To enforce their demands, they warned the merchants that their parishioners would be advised to patronize only those stores displaying a certificate.

Contact, a bulletin published by the Sacred Heart Parish Societies of Orange, New Jersey, listed fourteen merchants in its March 1955 issue. "The following stores," it said, "have agreed to co-operate with the Parish Decency Committee in not displaying or selling literature disapproved by the National Organization for Decent Literature. . . . Please patronize these stores only. They may be identified by the certificate which is for one month only."

Similar tactics have been followed in scores of other communities. Even in Nevada—a state not noted for Puritanical temper—the Council of Catholic Men has asked booksellers to purge from their shelves a list of books which included such widely read novels as *Mr. Roberts* and *From Here to Eternity.* When an Associated Press reporter pointed out that millions of people already were familiar with these works, in print and on film, the state chairman of the campaign, Paul Laxalt of Carson City, replied:

"We've got to stand by the list. If we make one exception the list would be chopped up."

Such tactics are highly effective. Most news dealers, druggists, and similar merchants carry paper-bound books only as a minor side line. Moreover, they receive from the wholesalers more books than they have space for; if they remove one title from their racks, there are plenty of others to take its place. They don't want trouble. It is never good business to argue with a customer—so most of them readily comply with this form of private censorship. After all, their other customers, who might want to read a book by Faulkner or Hemingway or Zola, will never know that it has been suppressed, and when they don't find it on the shelves they probably will buy something else.

For these reasons it was possible for the Archdiocesan Council of Catholic Men in St. Louis to report recently that it had "obtained the consent of about one-third of the store owners approached in a campaign to ask merchants to submit to voluntary screening. . . ."

Something—but not much—can be said in defense of the National Organization for Decent Literature and its local campaigners. A good many tawdry and disreputable magazines, paper-bound reprints, and comic books have been offered for sale on a lot of newsstands. A few publishers unquestionably have tried to base their sales appeal on sex and violence; the pictures and text on the covers of their publications often hint that the contents are far more salacious than they are in fact. (Such misrepresentation, however, is less common now than it was a few years ago, and both the contents and the covers of most pocket-size books seem to be growing less lurid.)

It can be argued, too, that law enforcement agencies in some cities have not been vigorous in enforcing the statutes against obscene publications. Finally, the "decent literature" campaigners apparently feel that their main mission is to protect young people, whose judgment is unformed and who might be attracted to sleazy reading matter by a provocative newsstand display; they seem to take far less interest in the hard-bound editions of the same books available in libraries or regular book stores. The Detroit NODL, for example, states that its list is "not intended as a restrictive list for adults" —though it does not explain how adults could purchase the books if merchants have been persuaded not to stock them.

But the motives of these zealous people are not the issue. The real issue is whether any private group—however well-meaning—has a right to dictate what other people may read.

Clearly any church, or any sub-group within a church, has a right to advise its own members about their reading matter.

Clearly, too, anybody has a right to try to *persuade* other people to read or to refrain from reading anything he sees fit.

The National Organization for Decent Literature, however, goes much further. Its campaign is not aimed at Catholics alone, and it is not attempting to *persuade* readers to follow its views. It is *compelling* readers, of all faiths, to bow to its dislikes, by denying them a free choice in what they buy.[1]

This principle is of course unacceptable to Catholics—as it is to all Americans—if they take the trouble to think about it for a moment. How would Catholics react if, say, a group of Jewish laymen were to threaten merchants with boycott unless they banned from their shops all publications which referred to the divinity of Christ? Some religious denominations believe that gambling is immoral; most Catholics do not, and many of their parishes raise considerable sums by means of bingo games and raffles. What if some Protestant sect were to try to clean out of the stores all publications which spoke tolerantly of gambling, and to boycott every merchant who bought a raffle ticket?

The principle at stake was set forth with admirable clarity by Father John Courtney Murray, S.J., professor of moral theology at Woodstock College, Maryland, in a recent address on "Literature and Censorship." He listed

[1] No doubt unconsciously, the Catholic War Veterans, Our Lady of Sorrows Post No. 1046, underlined the similarity between these tactics and those of the Communists. In a February 25, 1956, mailing to book dealers in Hartford, Connecticut, it enclosed the NODL list of "objectionable" publications—and it quoted the Chinese Communists who have been conducting a campaign of their own against "objectionable" literature:

" 'These books and pictures seriously harm those workers who by constantly looking at them can easily become degenerate in their thinking,' cautions the *Peking Worker's Daily* as quoted by *Newsweek* magazine, January 23, 1956. We have to hand it to the Communists . . . who have launched a nationwide campaign against pornographic trash. . . . Should not this example provoke a similar literary clean-up in our land where the morality of our actions is gauged by service to God and not to an atheistic state?"

four rules, which ought to command the enthusiastic support of all Americans regardless of religious belief:

(1) "Each minority group has the right to censor for its own members, if it so chooses, the contents of the various media of communication, and to protect them, by means of its own choosing, from materials considered harmful according to its standards." (He also pointed out that in the United States "all religious groups . . . are minority groups.")

(2) "No minority group has the right to demand that government should impose a general censorship" on material "judged to be harmful according to the special standards held within one group."

(3) "Any minority group has the right to work toward the elevation of standards of public morality . . . through the use of the methods of persuasion and pacific argument."

(4) "No minority group has the right to impose its own religious or moral views on other groups, through the use of methods of force, coercion, or violence."

And Father Murray went on to warn that methods of coercion are especially imprudent for Catholic associations.

"The chief danger," he said, "is lest the Church itself be identified in the public mind as a power-association. The identification is injurious; it turns into hatred of the faith. And it has the disastrous effect of obscuring from the public view the true visage of the Church as God's kingdom of truth and freedom, justice and love."

He quoted from Jacques Leclercq "of the Catholic University of Louvain, who is no slight authority" the dictum that "no government has ever succeeded in finding a balanced policy of combating unhealthy sexual propaganda without injuring legitimate freedom or provoking other equally grave or worse disorders."

Finally, Father Murray emphasized that "censorship in the civil order must be a judicial process," carried out under the statutes and according to the due processes of law.

The conclusions which flow from Father Murray's teachings seem plain enough:

(1) *For the National Organization for Decent Literature.* It should stop immediately its campaign of threats, blacklisting, and boycott. It should then pursue its aims by the legitimate methods of persuasion, propaganda, and action through the courts. Most states have adequate laws against the publication and sale of indecent literature. In cases where the law seems inadequate, the legislature can be persuaded to amend it, by the normal means of lobbying and petition. In cases where the law is not enforced, public officials should certainly be reminded of their duty—and opposed at the polls, in the democratic way, if they fall down on their jobs.

Above all, the NODL ought to consider the possibility of guiding young readers by positive rather than negative techniques. Youngsters are not likely to read trash whenever they have good books readily available. If they are brought up in homes where good literature is a constant part of their environment—where parents read to them from infancy, and encourage them to build up their own libraries—then there is scant chance that they will be attracted by comics or two-bit horrors.

What has the NODL done to urge parents to give their children such basic moral training? Has it done all it can to foster topnotch libraries—public, school, church, and family? In how many communities has it sponsored campaigns to stimulate good reading?

(2) *For news dealers, booksellers, and other merchants.* They should muster the courage to defy any group of private citizens which tries to impose its own brand of censorship on the publications they offer for sale. And, with equal courage, they should set their own house in order; they should refuse to sell any publication which—in their own untrammeled judgment—falls below their own standards as responsible business men.

(3) *For the patriotic citizen.* He should protest against the lynching of books just as vigorously as against the lynching of people. He should go out of his way to support the merchants who resist such coercion. He should point out to the members of the National Organization for Decent Literature (and to any other self-appointed censors in his community) the immeasurable damage they are doing to the American way of life, to the very foundations of democratic government.

For the gravest harm done here is not to the Catholic Church—though as Father Murray noted, that is dangerous enough—or to the individual who is denied the right to choose his own books. The great peril is to the fabric of orderly government. It is always injured when any group takes the law into its own hands. And whenever such a band of vigilantes succeeds in imposing its will by force, some other—and perhaps more sinister—group is encouraged to try the same thing.

Dean Joseph O'Meara of the Notre Dame Law School recently put it like this:

> Unfortunately many sincere people do not comprehend the genius of our democracy . . . such people would deny free speech to those with whom they are in fundamental disagreement. . . . They would establish a party line in America—*their* party line, of course. This is an alien concept, a totalitarian concept; it is not consonant with the American tradition; it is anti-democratic; it is, in short, subversive and it should be recognized for what it is.

Still another eminent Catholic—John F. Kennedy of Massachusetts—summed up the case in even more prophetic terms.

"The lock on the door of the legislature, the parliament, or the assembly hall," he said, "by order of the King, the Commissar, or the Führer—has historically been followed or preceded by a lock on the door of the printer's, the publisher's, or the bookseller's."

JOHN C. MURRAY, S.J.

The Bad Arguments Intelligent Men Make

This article appeared in *America* for November 3, 1956, and was reprinted in Harold C. Gardiner, S.J., *Catholic Viewpoint on Censorship* (Garden City, N.Y.: Hanover House, 1958).

Father Murray has been professor of theology, Woodstock College, Maryland, since 1937.

From his "Editor's Easy Chair" John Fischer looks out and sees "immeasurable damage" being done "to the American way of life and to the very foundations of democratic government." This has become a familiar vision; many of us share it. But we frequently differ on the question, who or what is doing the damage?

In Mr. Fischer's view the damage is being done by "a little band of Catholics" who are "conducting a shocking attack on the rights of their fellow citizens" through the medium of an organization called the National Organization for Decent Literature, which undertakes to "censor" certain publications.

I take a rather broader view. I see a large band of people, of all faiths, who are conducting a shocking attack on the reason of their fellow citizens through the medium of passionately irrational argument about important public issues. I believe that nothing is more damaging to democracy than lack of rationality in public argument. The foundations of our society are indeed laid in an identifiable consensus. But they are more importantly laid in a reasonable disposition to argue our many disagreements in intelligent and temperate fashion, using restrained language, avoiding misstatements, overstatements or simplifications, and endeavoring to define issues with precision in the light of all the relevant principles and facts. I believe that whatever corrupts rational public arguments corrupts democracy.

It has seemed to me that censorship is one of the public issues that are being deformed by bad argument, emanating from all sides. Hence on May 4, 1956, in a talk given before the Thomas More Association in Chicago and printed in the organ of the Thomas More Book Shop, *Books on Trial,* I made an attempt at a contribution to good public argument on this difficult subject. Part of my argument consisted in stating four practical rules that should govern the action of minority groups in a pluralist society, in their legitimate efforts to improve public morality. These rules were not original. I had seen them stated in substance in a news release of a paper given at Marquette University on March 23, 1956 by Prof. Vernon J. Bourke of St. Louis University.[1]

Mr. Fischer quotes my statement of these four procedural rules in support of certain conclusions of his own with regard to the activities of the National Organization for Decent Literature. Perhaps Mr. Bourke will undertake to say whether, and how far, Mr. Fischer's conclusions follow from the four norms of action for whose formulation, in language somewhat different from my own, he should be given the credit. My own major concern is with a broader question—the quality of public argument. My question is whether Mr. Fischer has made a contribution to rational public argument on the issue of censorship. I am afraid my answer must be No.

Consider the preliminary question of language. In his opening paragraph Mr. Fischer asserts that a "little band of Catholics" is "engaged in an un-American activity which is as flagrant as anything the Communist party ever attempted—and which is in fact very similar to Communist tactics." Does one open a rational public argument by two such attacks on the reason of the reader? That tired old cuss-word, "un-American activity"—has it not gone the way of all cuss-words, into meaninglessness? And the tactics of slapping the label "Communist" on your adversary's position—have we not agreed that this is a tactic of unreason? As for the later argument by epithet (the NODL is "lynching" books), one hardly expects to find it in *Harper's*, however much it may be used on the hustings.

The more substantive question is this: has Mr. Fischer done justice to the NODL's own understanding of its purposes and methods, as these are stated in its explanatory literature?

The literature is easily obtainable from the central office (31 East Congress St., Chicago 5, Ill.). On reading it, one would come, I think, to the following conclusions. The NODL is simply a "service organization," not an "action group." Its major service consists in offering to "responsible individuals and organizations an evaluation of current comic books, magazines and pocket-size books." This is the famous "NODL list." The evaluation of these types of publications (only these) is done singly from the standpoint of what is objectionable as juvenile reading. The standards of evaluation are nine in number. All of them are common-sense norms; none of them are special tenets of any type of "group morality." Methods of review vary for each type of publication. Five reviewers vote on each item. The purpose is to "encourage the publishing and distribution of good literature," as well as to discover what is unfit for adolescents.

NODL also distributes information about ways of organizing decent-

[1] In *Problems of Communication in a Pluralistic Society* (Milwaukee, Wis.: Marquette University Press, 1956).

literature campaigns on the community or parish levels. It is clearly stated that the list is merely an expression of a publication's nonconformity with the NODL code and that "the list is not to be used for purposes of boycott or coercion." The recommended procedures seem to rest on the suppositions that the ordinary merchant is a responsible man; that he would welcome some assistance in ridding his shop of stuff that responsible parents fairly judge to be unfit for their children; that if he accepts the assistance, he is to be commended; that if he rejects it, he is to be left alone. (NODL says: "Instruct your committee workers to leave silently if the owner, manager or clerk refuses cooperation.")

The general conclusion, on the basis of its own statements about itself, would be that the NODL looks to voluntary reform, through cooperation between parent-citizens and merchants, in an area where a special problem of public morality exists. That problem arises out of the ready accessibility to boys and girls of a rather immense amount of cheap literature that is objectionable on common-sense grounds of morality and taste.

Consider now Mr. Fischer's description of the NODL. "Its main purpose is to make it impossible for anybody to buy books and other publications which it does not like." "Its chief method is to put pressure on newsdealers, drug stores and booksellers to force them to remove from their stocks every item on the NODL blacklist." It "deliberately prefers to ignore the established legal channels for proceedings against books which it thinks improper. Its chosen weapons are boycott and literary lynching." It is embarked upon a "campaign of intimidation."

Something is wrong here. When Mr. Fischer describes the NODL he is obviously not describing the same thing that NODL describes when it describes itself. Thus you have reproduced the perfect pattern—the perfectly wretched pattern—of so much American public argument at the moment. There is really no argument at all—at least not yet. The two sides are not talking about the same thing. Hence the exchange proceeds to the customarily futile end. On the basis of his own description Mr. Fischer asserts that NODL "is *compelling* [emphasis his] readers, of all faiths, to bow to its dislikes, by denying them a free choice in what they buy." Hence he defines the issue thus: "The real issue is whether any private group—however well-meaning—has a right to dictate what other people may read."

To Mr. Fischer's charges the NODL would, I expect, reply to this effect: "But we are not compelling anybody to do or not do anything. We are not doing any such arbitrary thing as making our own 'dislikes' the coercive standard for the reading of the general public. We are not trying to do any 'dictating.' And as for denying to readers of all faiths a free choice in what they buy—that is not the real issue at all."

Thus the argument fulfils the customary American pattern. The next step is for the contestants to retire from the field, either in sorrow or in anger or in both. Thereafter their partisans move in. Epithets are bandied; labels are exchanged; non-sequitur's proliferate. Until finally, both sides mutter disgustedly, "So's your old man." And there is, for a time, a sullen silence.

Maybe the argument could be rescued from this dismal end, to which most arguments in America seem to be condemned. Mr. Fischer could have rescued it, but he didn't. The NODL could have obviated the need for rescue, but it hasn't. The point where rescue begins is, of course, a fact. Mr. Fischer notes the fact, but he abuses it to advance his own purposes. The NODL must surely recognize the fact, but it has not acted on the recognition, to the detriment of its own purposes. The fact is that in half-a-dozen or more cities and towns the police have made use of the NODL list in order to threaten, coerce or punish dealers in reading matter.

Unquestionably, officers of the law have full right to use the weapons of law, which are coercive. The point in question, however, is their use of the NODL list. This puts NODL in an ambiguous position. It cannot expect to have the thing both ways. It cannot, on the one hand, protest that "the list is not to be used for purposes of boycott or coercion," and, on the other hand, fail to protest against the use of the list by the police. It has to choose its cooperators—either the merchant or the police. It cannot choose both; for the choice is really between opposed methods of cooperation—the method of voluntary cooperation as between equal citizens, or the method of coercion as used by the police.

If NODL consents to the use of its list by the police, it creates an ambiguity that its critics rightly seize upon, as Mr. Fischer did; what is worse, it obscures from public view its own "idea," the altogether valid idea of voluntary reform. On the other hand, if NODL does not consent to the use of its list by the police, it should say so—publicly, and on every necessary occasion. Surely part of its service must be the supervision, conducted on its own principles, of the uses to which its list is put.

There is another inappropriateness here. Officers of the law must operate under statutes which in this matter are, or ought to be, narrowly drawn. On the other hand, voluntary reform, precisely because it is voluntary, may be based on the somewhat broader categories of common-sense judgment. The latter are employed by the NODL, rightly enough. But for this very reason it is not right for the police to use NODL's judgments in enforcing the law. The law must have its own standards, minimal enough to sustain the challenge of due process.

In this connection another fact must be noted. The fact is that on NODL lists there appear some twenty-odd works that either have received literary honors or at least have been acclaimed by serious critics. Doubtless high-school teachers could not, without absurdity, make them required reading for their students. But the police cannot, without equal absurdity, make them prohibited reading. Such stultification of the law is itself immoral.

There is a third fact of some consequence. The history of censorship has been a history of excess. The NODL has the problem of the local zealot, operating far from the central office in Chicago, and way outside the four pages of sensible procedures sent out from it. He or she "has the zeal of God indeed, but not according to understanding" (Romans 10:2). Such zealots are righteous, usually indignant, people. They have a good cause. They want results. What they lack is St. Paul's "understanding," which bears, he said, on "the *way* of justification."

I shall not labor the analogy. The point of it, in our case, is that the zealot at times fails to see how his zeal for results may betray him into the use of methods that will in turn betray his cause. Mr. Fischer, for example, in his zeal for his own cause, which is a good one, fell into a bad method of argument. Among other faults, he fails to distinguish between the "idea" of the NODL, which is the substantive issue, and the applications of the idea, which raise issues of procedure. In good "liberal" fashion he assigns the primacy to the procedural over the substantive. Contrariwise, in good "Catholic" fashion, the local zealot for the NODL cause assigns the primacy to the substantive over the procedural. He, or she, wants the newsstands "cleaned up"; and he, or she, in some instances doesn't greatly care how.

At that, Mr. Fischer is more nearly right. In this sensitive area the question of procedure is all-important. Part of the service of NODL to its own cause should be what I can only call a service of fraternal correction. It should somehow find a way of rebuking, or at least disavowing, the local zealot who violates, or goes beyond, the cooperative procedures, none of them coercive, which it officially stands for. (As for Mr. Fischer, maybe I have myself done him some service of intellectual charity?)

At this point, with all the ambiguities at least sorted out, if not cleared up, we could begin the rational public argument. The starting-point would be a fact—the existence of a "real national problem" (Mr. Fischer's words). Then the questions arise. For instance, does Mr. Fischer adequately measure the dimensions of the problem? He says:

> A good many tawdry and disreputable magazines, paperbound reprints and comic books have been offered for sale on a lot of newsstands. A few publishers unquestionably have tried to base their sales appeal on sex and violence; the pictures and text on the covers of their publications often hint that the contents are far more salacious than they are in fact.

He adds that "law-enforcement agencies in some cities have not been vigorous in enforcing the statutes against obscene publications." And that's it.

Or is it? Others would maintain that this is an astonishing understatement of the real national problem. They see the problem much more ominously large. A major issue in public morality has arisen; the morals of youth are particularly involved in it; the problem is growing. They further see a causal line between bad magazines, etc., and immorality. And they feel it imperative to "do something" about the bad literature.

When these last statements are made, they start up the current argument between sociology and common sense. The sociologist expresses professional doubt about the causal line between bad reading and immorality; he finds insufficient evidence for it. The common-sense view asserts that the causal line is sufficiently established by the nature, content, tendency, etc., of the literature itself. At least a strong presumption is thus created; and it furnishes reason for action, until—and maybe after—all the Ph.D. theses, pro and con, have been written.

The word "action" disturbs the jealous advocate of civil rights. He therefore comes up with his own causal line—between any attempt at suppressing any kind of literature and the subversion of the foundations of the Republic. The common-sense view expresses doubt about this causal line. There is, it says, insufficient evidence that any such alarming consequences will follow, if the action taken is rational and prudent.

Here the real issue begins to appear: what kinds of action, as taken by whom, are rational and prudent in the circumstances? And what promise of effectiveness do they offer?

Mr. Fischer has his own program of action, which deserves consideration. He recommends two positive courses. The first is self-regulation by newsdealers, booksellers and other merchants. They should, he says, "set their own house in order; they should refuse to sell any publication which—in their own untrammeled judgment—falls below their own standards as responsible businessmen."

A question of fact occurs here: how effective so far has the principle of self-regulation been in the solution of our real national problem? The evidence suggests a discouraging answer. Some efforts in this direction have been made, always under the pressure of public opinion; but their slim success bases little hope for the future. Second, the principle itself may be, and has been, called in question. For instance, in a report entitled *The Freedom to Read,* written for the National Book Committee, Richard McKeon, Walter Gellhorn and Robert K. Merton say this:

> The dangers of police censorship are obvious; but we are convinced that the dangers of a code of self-censorship are even greater. It provides the means by which all kinds of restrictions can be put on freedom of expression, and it places the freedom to read in the hands of a group which does not even have the accountability to the public which a chief of police has (p. 70).

I don't necessarily endorse this judgment; but it may suggest that Mr. Fischer is on shaky ground.

There are other questions too. What, I might ask, is the right of a newsdealer to "untrammeled judgment"? Is his judgment, as a matter of fact, untrammeled? And whether it is or not, why should one trust it as a means of solution for our real national problem? Is he a better critic of literature, a better judge of morality, than the average parent? How is one even to know what his "standards as a responsible businessman" are? And if they could be known, is there to be no possibility of public judgment on them? On what title is this Olympian immunity claimed? One would like to know.

The second positive course is the action of law—legislative and court action. I am inclined to think that Mr. Fischer's confidence in the efficacy of legal action as a corrective in this difficult field of printed media will be astonishing to students of the law. If I mistake not, it is pretty generally admitted that the present legal picture is a muddle. It is further admitted that the difficulties encountered in trying to straighten it out are immense. There are the two sacred legal doctrines that must be protected—prior restraint and due process. Furthermore, there are certain adverse high-court decisions that seem to have reduced the law to a state of practical impotence, not least in the two crucial areas of obscenity and violence.

What is even more decisive, even if the law could be lifted to the full height of its legitimate potency, it would still be largely impotent to cope with the new problem of mass media, whose crude subtleties seem to defeat the subtle crudities of the law. The grounds for accepting the relative ineffectiveness of law in this special field, where the moral issue is not justice, are both theoretical and practical—to be found both in the art of jurisprudence and in the lessons of history.

Mr. Fischer suggests two manners of action—one private, the other public—whose possibilities ought by all means be explored and exploited. But in the course of rational public argument it would, I think, appear that his program of positive action is inadequate to the real national problem that confronts us. His negative demand is more acceptable. He wants organizations of private right to stop campaigns of coercion. So do I. Mr. Fischer's reasons are, I think, doctrinaire; further argument would have to illuminate the fact, if it is a fact. Whereas, I, as a Catholic, am not a doctrinaire.

In my Chicago lecture I said that ". . . it is not possible to prove the position, taken by some, that an action like the boycott of a moving picture is somehow 'unrightful,' or 'undemocratic' or 'unconstitutional.' No one can show that such an action lies beyond the limits of a primeval American right to protest and object. The action may indeed be strenuous; but the American right to protest and object is permitted to run to some pretty strenuous extremes. This said against the doctrinaire, it remains true that methods of action which verge upon the coercive exhibit some incongruity when used by citizen-groups in the interests of morality in literature or on the screen. Even if they raise no issue of abstract right, they do raise the concrete issue of prudence, which, equally with justice, is one of the cardinal virtues."

I hold to this position now, against Mr. Fischer (I think), and also (I think) against the NODL in its present ambiguous situation—certainly in its representation by local zealots and by the secular arm of the police.

I further hold to my previous position that private agencies such as the NODL can perform an indispensable public function in the promotion of public morality—provided they understand what their function is. It is not to supplant the coercive function of the agencies of public law. It is to represent, soberly and honestly, the principle of voluntary reform, to be accomplished on the basis of social cooperation—that sincere cooperation which in America is always ready to be stimulated but often needs stimulation.

This principle of reform is altogether valid in itself. Its applications call for prudence—concretely, as I have previously said, for "men and women of prudence, who understand the art of procedure, and understand too that we are morally bound, by the virtue of prudence, to a concrete rightness of method in the pursuit of moral aims." For the rest, the rationality of this method of social reform will be understood, and its pitfalls will be avoided, if we can all somehow hold to high standards of public discussion. In this respect the editor of *Harper's* has failed. But his failure is less reprehensible than that of Catholics who miss their present opportunity—and duty—to perform the instant task, which is to inject the Catholic tradition of rationality into a mass democracy that is rapidly slipping its moorings in reason.

Critical Note on Fischer and Murray

Most readers come away from the two preceding articles with strong partisan sympathies for either Mr. Fischer or Father Murray. This fervent reaction is especially significant in view of Murray's emphasis on responsible, temperate discussion. Few would quarrel with his belief that such discussion offers the best means of solving social problems wisely and efficiently. It is well worth while, therefore, to assess the rhetoric of these articles as objectively as possible.

Both writers are intelligent, informed, and deeply concerned. Why are they more successful in raising temperatures and confirming opposing views than in achieving understanding and united effort? The strengths and weaknesses of this exchange are typical of much public discussion.

Fischer adopts the pose of a publicist. His plan is the same a speaker might utilize in a similar situation: attract attention; state the problem; propose a solution. But his audience is far from captive. His first paragraph must compete with an advertisement on the facing page of *Harper's* and a slight movement of the right thumb (or left, if you prefer starting at the back of magazines) which will carry the reader along to another article. To arrest the reader's thumb, Fischer employs a shock opening, and this involves slanted language and the questionable analogy which Murray finds objectionable. "Communist" is a dirty word in the public language of our country. It usually effects a strongly emotional response and short-circuits the rational consideration of issues. Therefore, when Fischer accuses his opponents of "Communist tactics," he is bound to provoke an intemperate response in his readers.

The second half of Fischer's discourse is calmer. His reliance on Catholic authorities makes it difficult for Murray to attack his proposals directly and, in fact, forces Murray into a confusing "third party" defense. Since he did use the ideas quoted by Fischer, it would be more appropriate for Murray to discuss their applicability to the question at hand than belatedly acknowledge his source and expect Mr. Bourke "to undertake to say whether, and how far, Mr. Fischer's conclusions follow from the four norms of action. . . ."

Murray's position in his rejoinder is that Fischer is right in condemning censorship by force, but wrong in overestimating the danger of such censorship and underestimating the danger of pornographic material. This is a clear point of view, but Murray's practice of censuring Fischer's methods of argument in the deprecating tone with which one might reprimand a naughty child does not encourage restrained discussion.

Murray takes pains to lay down his premises and then draw his conclusions from them. His procedure is to discuss subordinate ideas first and then state a general conclusion. However, this procedure is not as effective in Murray's hands as it could be. The reason for this limited effectiveness is Murray's refusal to offer the reader any preview of his conclusions. For example, his support of the principle of voluntary reform in the next-to-last paragraph of the article is the first clear declaration of this position. The uncommitted reader will be reluctant to accept each link in Murray's chain of reasoning unless the reader knows where he is being lead. The vagueness of Murray's position until the very end of his discourse encourages readers to prepare their defenses against a possible argumentative trap. They are not encouraged to concentrate on the carefully reasoned argument.

Fischer's eye, then, is too much on his readers; Murray is too little concerned with them. Communication is more effective when speakers and writers seek attention without sensationalism; it is more effective when they accommodate their ideas to their audiences.

Questions

Does Millett argue that censorship in the field of literature and the other arts is usually stupid and always unintelligent in every way, or only that it is *aesthetically* stupid and unintelligent? If the "guardians of the Motion

Picture Code" are not competent to pass judgment on the morality of a play, in what respect is "the judicious Mr. Crowther" so qualified? Is Millett inconsistent when he decries moral evaluation of artistic creations but twice quotes a literary critic's evaluation of the morality of such works?

Do you believe "the censorship of literature is almost invariably self-defeating"? Find out if there have been any important changes in standards of speech, dress, or conduct in the movies since 1920 or in television since 1950. Is there a way better than censorship to maintain accepted standards of morality on public communications media? If you read the last question without blinking, what do you mean by "accepted standards of morality"? If there are any, should they be maintained? Can they be "maintained"?

If we agree that "freedom means effective choice," we seem also to agree that some choices are not permissible. We do not permit people to choose whether they will or will not make off with our money, whether they will or will not use narcotics, whether they will or will not enter an unsafe building no matter how aesthetically pleasing it may be. If a set of principles underlies these limitations, does it have any relevance to the censorship of literature?

Why should Colby College find it appropriate to honor Elijah Parish Lovejoy each year? Do you agree that good fortune has been the chief reason the United States has not succumbed to a dictator? Are Americans a "super race"? More concretely, ask yourself and your friends whether Americans are better poets, or baseball players, or farmers, or architects, or steelworkers than the Russians, or Japanese, or Mexicans, or people of any other nation. Don't settle for glib answers; probe a little to see what you and others really believe, and then try to examine with some objectivity the evidence on both sides of the question. Does it make any difference whether we believe we are a super race or not?

What is the machinery for security classification by the Pentagon? Who classifies? What do they classify? How do they decide? Is there any review after an appropriate period of time? What information is "your government" obligated to give you? Is this really "a great issue of freedom in our time" or merely a newspaperman's griping about the vicissitudes of his way of earning a living?

What do you do when you learn of official misconduct or government policies with which you disagree? What can you do? Is your congressman responsive to the opinions of his constituents? Did you ever take the trouble to find out what Congressmen have said about letters from the people they represent?

Do you see any need for censorship in local bookstores, at the movies, or on television? Is it in the public interest to protect immature minds from exposure to immoral ideas? How would you define "immature"? "Immoral"? To what extent should access to political and social ideas be limited?

Should socialist or communist political theory be taught in colleges? In high schools? What do you think of such laws as that in Connecticut which prohibits distribution of information concerning birth control? Can children achieve a satisfactory understanding of the world if they are fed a steady diet of half-truths and distortions? Should we censor comic strips that utilize racial and national stereotypes, e.g., the Negro servant, the Italian gangster, the Jewish financier, or the Irish drunkard? Does the characterization of Shylock make *The Merchant of Venice* unsuitable for high schools?

Is censorship by any method feasible without opening the door to abuses? More broadly, to what extent can we safely grant individuals (parents, teachers, athletic coaches, religious leaders, civil or military leaders, employers) or institutions (governments, churches, schools, fraternities, corporations, labor unions, social and business clubs) the power to control or command our behavior? Under what circumstances, if any, do an individual's obligations to self outweigh his obligations to his parents? To the other individuals and institutions mentioned above?

Suggestions for Further Reading

Berelson, Bernard, and Patricia J. Salter. "Majority and Minority Americans," *Public Opinion Quarterly,* 10, 1946, p. 168.

Chafee, Zechariah, Jr. *Free Speech in the United States.* 3rd ed. Cambridge, Mass.: Harvard University Press, 1941.

Ernst, Morris L., and Alexander Lindey. *The Censor Marches On.* New York: Doubleday, 1940.

Kerr, Walter. *Criticism and Censorship.* Milwaukee, Wis.: Bruce, 1956.

Kronhausen, Eberhard, and Phyllis Kronhausen. *Pornography and the Law.* New York: Ballantine, 1960.

Lockhart, William R., and Robert C. McClure. "Literature, the Law of Obscenity and the Constitution," *Minnesota Law Review,* 38, 1954, p. 295.

McKeon, Richard, Robert K. Merton, and Walter Gellhorn. *The Freedom to Read.* New York: Bowker, 1957.

Meiklejohn, Alexander. *Free Speech and Its Relation to Self-Government.* New York: Harper, 1948.

Morris, James. "Reflections on the Chatterly Case," New York *Times Magazine,* Dec. 4, 1960, p. 24.

Swezey, Robert D. "Give the Television Code a Chance," *Quarterly of Film, Radio and Television,* 7, 1952, p. 15.

Twomey, John. "New Forms of Social Control over Mass Media Content," *Studies in Public Communications,* 1, 1957, p. 42.

United States Senate Committee on the Judiciary. *Right to Travel and United States Passport Policies.* (85th Congress, 2nd Session, Document 126.) Washington, D.C.: Government Printing Office, 1958.

United States Senate Subcommittee to Investigate Juvenile Delinquency. *Comic Books and Juvenile Delinquency.* (84th Congress, 1st Session.) Washington, D.C.: Government Printing Office, 1955.

———. *Television Programs* and *Motion Pictures and Delinquency.* (84th Congress, 2nd Session.) Washington, D.C.: Government Printing Office, 1956.

Wertham, Frederic. "It's Still Murder," *Saturday Review,* April 9, 1955, p. 46.

Winick, Charles. *Taste and the Censor in Television.* Fund for the Republic pamphlet, 1959.

6. Communications Media

Introduction

There are no more conspicuous institutions in American society than the mass media of communication. There may be more influential forces than television, radio, and newspapers, but there are certainly none that receive so much public attention. This attention is, of course, solicited by the media themselves, which constantly seek to enlarge the size and submissiveness of their audiences.

As these media extend their scope and intensify their potency, their peculiar economic status becomes increasingly apparent. Television and radio are under a clear legal obligation to "serve the public interest." The press has traditionally accepted this same end as a moral obligation. Yet all of these media must depend on advertising for revenue, and all are organized as private businesses which must make profits. The contrary demands of obligation on one side and money-making on the other pose serious dilemmas to the men and women who control the mass media.

Among the speeches and essays which follow are some attempts to give new directions to the mass media and to explore ways by which they may better serve the public interest. Probably no subject is more fervently or skillfully discussed than the mass media, and yet probably no subject encounters more massive public apathy. Whatever the future course of this discussion, it is sure to have decisive effects on the character of our society.

EDWARD R. MURROW

A Broadcaster Talks to His Colleagues

This speech was delivered before the Radio and Television News Directors' Association, and subsequently published in the November 13, 1958, issue of **The Reporter.**

Murrow, one of the most prominent and creative television personalities of our time, has served as European news director and a vice president of the Columbia Broadcasting System. Some of the documentary programs for which he has been responsible, notably one on the late Senator Joseph R. McCarthy, have been influential in American political affairs. Murrow is now serving as director of the United States Information Agency.

This just might do nobody any good. At the end of this discourse a few people may accuse this reporter of fouling his own comfortable nest; and your organization may be accused of having given hospitality to heretical and even dangerous thoughts.

But the elaborate structure of networks, advertising agencies, and sponsors will not be shaken or altered. It is my desire, if not my duty, to try to talk to you journeymen with some candor about what is happening to radio and television in this generous and capacious land.

I have no technical advice or counsel to offer those of you who labor in this vineyard that produces words and pictures. You will forgive me for not telling you that the instruments with which you work are miraculous; that your responsibility is unprecedented; or that your aspirations are frequently frustrated. It is not necessary to remind you—the fact that your voice is amplified to the degree where it reaches from one end of the country to the other does not confer upon you greater wisdom or understanding than you possessed when your voice reached only from one end of the bar to the other. All of these things you know.

You should also know at the outset that, in the manner of witnesses before Congressional committees, I appear here voluntarily—by invitation—that I am an employee of the Columbia Broadcasting System, that I am neither an officer nor a director of that corporation, and that these remarks are of a "do-it-yourself" nature. If what I have to say is responsible, then I alone am responsible for the saying of it. Seeking neither approbation from my employers, nor new sponsors, nor acclaim from the critics of radio and television, I cannot well be disappointed. Believing that potentially the commercial system of broadcasting as practiced in this country is the best and freest yet devised, I have decided to express my concern about what I believe to be happening to radio and television. These instruments have been good to me beyond my due. There exist in my mind no reasonable grounds for personal complaint. I have no feud, either with my employers, any sponsors, or with the professional critics of radio and television. But I am seized with an abiding fear regarding what these two instruments are doing to our society, our culture, and our heritage.

Our history will be what we make it. And if there are any historians about fifty or a hundred years from now, and there should be preserved the kinescopes for one week of all three networks, they will there find recorded in black-and-white, or color, evidence of decadence, escapism, and insulation from the realities of the world in which we live. I invite your attention to the television schedules of all networks between the hours of eight and eleven P.M. Eastern Time. Here you will find only fleeting and spasmodic reference to the fact that this nation is in mortal danger. There are, it is true, occasional informative programs presented in that intellectual ghetto on Sunday afternoons. But during the daily peak viewing periods, television in the main insulates us from the realities of the world in which we live. If this state of affairs continues, we may alter an advertising slogan to read: "Look Now, Pay Later." For surely we shall pay for using this most powerful instrument of communication to insulate the citizenry from the hard and demanding realities which must be faced if we are to survive. I mean the word—"survive"—literally. If there were to be a competition in indifference, or perhaps in insulation from reality, then Nero and his fiddle, Chamberlain and his umbrella, could not find a place on an early afternoon sustaining show. If Hollywood were to run out of Indians, the program schedules would be mangled beyond all recognition. Then some courageous soul with a small budget might be able to do a documentary telling what, in fact, we have done—and are still doing—to the Indians in this country. But that would be unpleasant. And we must at all costs shield the sensitive citizens from anything that is unpleasant.

I am entirely persuaded that the American public is more reasonable, restrained, and more mature than most of our industry's program planners believe. Their fear of controversy is not warranted by the evidence. I have reason to know, as do many of you, that when the evidence on a controversial subject is fairly and calmly presented, the public recognizes it for what it is—an effort to illuminate rather than to agitate.

Several years ago, when we undertook to do a program on Egypt and Israel, well-meaning, experienced, and intelligent friends shook their heads and said: "This you cannot do—you will be handed your head—it is an emotion-packed controversy, and there is no room for reason in it." We did the program. Zionists, anti-Zionists, the Friends of the Middle East, Egyptian and Israeli officials said, with a faint note of surprise: "It was a fair count. The information was there. We have no complaints."

Our experience was similar with two half-hour programs dealing with cigarette smoking and lung cancer. Both the medical profession and the tobacco industry cooperated in a rather wary fashion. But at the end of the day they were both reasonably content. The subject of radioactive fallout and the banning of nuclear tests was and is highly controversial. But according to what little evidence there is, viewers were prepared to listen to both sides with reason and restraint. This is not said to claim any special or unusual competence in the presentation of controversial subjects, but rather to indicate that timidity in these areas is not warranted—by the evidence.

Recently, network spokesmen have been disposed to complain that the professional critics of television have been "rather beastly." There have been hints that somehow competition for the advertising dollar has caused the critics of print to gang up on television and radio. This reporter has no desire to defend the critics. They have space in which to do that on their own behalf. But it remains a fact that the newspapers and magazines are the only instruments of mass communication which remain free from sustained and regular critical comment. If the network spokesmen are so anguished about what appears in print, let them come forth and engage in a little sustained regular comment regarding newspapers and magazines. It is an ancient and sad fact that most people in network television and radio have an exaggerated regard for what appears in print. And there have been cases where executives have refused to make even private comment on a program for which they were responsible until they had read the reviews in print. This is hardly an exhibition of confidence.

The oldest excuse of the networks for their timidity is their youth. Their spokesmen say: "We are young; we have not developed the traditions nor acquired the experience of the older media." If they but knew it, they are building those traditions, creating those precedents every day. Each time they yield to a voice from Washington or any political pressure, each time they eliminate something that might offend some section of the community, they are creating their own body of precedent and tradition. They are, in fact, not content to be "half safe."

Nowhere is this better illustrated than by the fact that the chairman of the Federal Communications Commission publicly prods broadcasters to engage in their legal right to editorialize. Of course, to undertake an editorial policy, overt and clearly labeled, and obviously unsponsored, requires a station or a network to be responsible. Most stations today probably do not have the manpower to assume this responsibility, but the manpower could be recruited. Editorials would not be profitable; if they had a cutting edge they might even offend. It is much easier, much less troublesome, to use the money-making machine of television and radio merely as a conduit through which to channel anything that is not libelous, obscene, or defamatory. In that way one has the illusion of power without responsibility.

So far as radio—that most satisfying and rewarding instrument—is concerned, the diagnosis of its difficulties is rather easy. And obviously I speak only of news and information. In order to progress it need only go backward —to the time when singing commercials were not allowed on news reports, when there was no middle commercial in a fifteen-minute news report; when radio was rather proud, alert, and fast. I recently asked a network official, "Why this great rash of five-minute news reports (including three commercials) on week ends?" He replied: "Because that seems to be the only thing we can sell."

In this kind of complex and confusing world, you can't tell very much about the *why* of the news in broadcasts where only three minutes is available for news. The only man who could do that was Elmer Davis, and his kind aren't about any more. If radio news is to be regarded as a commodity, only acceptable when salable, and only when packaged to fit the advertising appropriation of a sponsor, then I don't care what you call it—I say it isn't news.

My memory also goes back to the time when the fear of a slight reduction in business did not result in an immediate cutback in bodies in the News and Public Affairs Department, at a time when network profits had just reached an all-time high. We would all agree, I think, that whether on a station or a network, the stapling machine is a poor substitute for a newsroom typewriter.

One of the minor tragedies of television news and information is that the networks will not even defend their vital interests. When my employer, CBS, through a combination of enterprise and good luck, did an interview with Nikita Khrushchev, the President uttered a few ill-chosen, uninformed words on the subject, and the network practically apologized. This produced a rarity. Many newspapers defended the CBS right to produce the program and commended it for initiative. But the other networks remained silent.

Likewise when John Foster Dulles, by personal decree, banned American journalists from going to Communist China and subsequently offered contradictory explanations. For his fiat the networks entered only a mild protest. Then they apparently forgot the unpleasantness. Can it be that this national industry is content to serve the public interest only with the trickle of news that comes out of Hong Kong? To leave its viewers in ignorance of the cataclysmic changes that are occurring in a nation of six hundred million people? I have no illusions about the difficulties of reporting from a dictatorship; but our British and French allies have been better served—in their public interest—with some very useful information from their reporters in Communist China.

One of the basic troubles with radio and television news is that both instruments have grown up as an incompatible combination of show business, advertising, and news. Each of the three is a rather bizarre and demanding profession. And when you get all three under one roof, the dust never settles. The top management of the networks, with a few notable exceptions, has been trained in advertising, research, sales, or show business. But by the nature of the corporate structure, they also make the final and crucial decisions having to do with news and public affairs. Frequently they have neither the time nor the competence to do this. It is not easy for the same small group of men to decide whether to buy a new station for millions of dollars, build a new building, alter the rate card, buy a new Western, sell a soap opera, decide what defensive line to take in connection with the latest Congressional inquiry, how much money to spend on promoting a new program, what additions or deletions should be made in the existing covey or clutch of vice-presidents, and at the same time—frequently on the same long day—to give mature, thoughtful consideration to the manifold problems that confront those who are charged with the responsibility for news and public affairs.

Sometimes there is a clash between the public interest and the corporate interest. A telephone call or a letter from the proper quarter in Washington is treated rather more seriously than a communication from an irate but not politically potent viewer. It is tempting enough to give away a little air time for frequently irresponsible and unwarranted utterances in an effort to temper the wind of criticism.

Upon occasion, economics and editorial judgment are in conflict. And there is no law which says that dollars will be defeated by duty. Not so long ago the President of the United States delivered a television address to the nation. He was discoursing on the possibility or probability of war between this nation and the Soviet Union and Communist China—a reasonably compelling subject. Two networks—CBS and NBC—delayed that broadcast for an hour and fifteen minutes. If this decision was dictated by anything other than financial reasons, the networks didn't deign to explain those reasons. That hour-and-fifteen-minute delay, by the way, is about twice the time required for an ICBM to travel from the Soviet Union to major targets in the United States. It is difficult to believe that this decision was made by men who love, respect, and understand news.

So far I have been dealing largely with the deficit side of the ledger, and the items could be expanded. But I have said, and I believe, that potentially we have in this country a free-enterprise system of radio and television which is superior to any other. But to achieve its promise, it must be both free and enterprising. There is no suggestion here that networks or individual stations should operate as philanthropies. But I can find nothing in the Bill of Rights or the Communications Act which says that they must increase their net profits each year, lest the Republic collapse. I do not suggest that news and information should be subsidized by foundations or private subscriptions. I am aware that the networks have expended and are expending very considerable sums of money on public affairs programs from which they cannot hope to receive any financial reward. I have had the privilege at CBS of presiding over a considerable number of such programs. I testify and am able to stand here and say that I have never had a program turned down by my superiors because of the money it would cost.

But we all know that you cannot reach the potential maximum audience in marginal time with a sustaining program. This is so because so many stations on the network—any network—will decline to carry it. Every licensee who applies for a grant to operate in the public interest, convenience, and necessity makes certain promises as to what he will do in terms of program content. Many recipients of licenses have, in blunt language, welshed on those promises. The money-making machine somehow blunts their memories. The only remedy for this is closer inspection and punitive action by the FCC. But in the view of many this would come perilously close to supervision of program content by a Federal agency.

So it seems that we cannot rely on philanthropic support or foundation subsidies, we cannot follow the "sustaining route," the networks cannot pay all the freight, and the FCC cannot or will not discipline those who abuse the facilities that belong to the public.

What then is the answer? Do we merely stay in our comfortable nests, concluding that the obligation of these instruments has been discharged when we work at the job of informing the public for a minimum of time? Or do we believe that the preservation of the Republic is a seven-day-a-week job, demanding more awareness, better skills, and more perseverance than we have yet contemplated?

I am frightened by the imbalance, the constant striving to reach the largest possible audience for everything; by the absence of a sustained study of the state of the nation. Heywood Broun once said, "No body politic is healthy until it begins to itch." I would like television to produce some itching pills rather than this endless outpouring of tranquilizers. It can be done. Maybe it won't be, but it could. Let us not shoot the wrong piano player. Do not be deluded into believing that the titular heads of the networks control what appears on their networks. They all have better taste. All are responsible to stockholders, and in my experience all are honorable men. But they must schedule what they can sell in the public market. And this brings us to the nub of the question.

In one sense it rather revolves around the phrase heard frequently along Madison Avenue: "The Corporate Image." I am not precisely sure what this phrase means, but I would imagine that it reflects a desire on the part of the corporations who pay the advertising bills to have the public imagine, or believe, that they are not merely bodies with no souls, panting in pursuit of elusive dollars. They would like us to believe that they can distinguish between the public good and the private or corporate gain. So the question is this: Are the big corporations who pay the freight for radio and television programs wise to use that time *exclusively* for the sale of goods and services? Is it in their own interest and that of the stockholders so to do? The sponsor of an hour's television program is not buying merely the six minutes devoted to his commercial message. He is determining, within broad limits, the sum total of the impact of the entire hour. If he always, invariably, reaches for the largest possible audience, then this process of insulation, of escape from reality, will continue to be massively financed, and its apologists will continue to make winsome speeches about giving the public what it wants, or "letting the public decide."

I refuse to believe that the presidents and chairmen of the boards of these big corporations want their "corporate image" to consist exclusively of a solemn voice in an echo chamber, or a pretty girl opening the door of a refrigerator, or a horse that talks. They want something better, and on occasion some of them have demonstrated it. But most of the men whose legal and moral responsibility it is to spend the stockholders' money for advertising are removed from the realities of the mass media by five, six, or a dozen contraceptive layers of vice-presidents, public-relations counsel, and advertising agencies. Their business is to sell goods, and the competition is pretty tough.

But this nation is now in competition with malignant forces of evil who are using every instrument at their command to empty the minds of their subjects, and fill those minds with slogans, determination, and faith in the future. If we go on as we are, we are protecting the mind of the American public from any real contact with the menacing world that squeezes in upon us. We are engaged in a great experiment to discover whether a free public opinion can devise and direct methods of managing the affairs of the nation. We may fail. But we are handicapping ourselves needlessly.

Let us have a little competition. Not only in selling soap, cigarettes, and automobiles, but in informing a troubled, apprehensive, but receptive public. Why should not each of the twenty or thirty big corporations which dominate radio and television decide that they will give up one or two of their regularly scheduled programs each year, turn the time over to the networks, and say in effect: "This is a tiny tithe, just a little bit of our profits. On this particular night we aren't going to try to sell cigarettes or automobiles; this is merely a gesture to indicate our belief in the importance of ideas." The networks should, and I think would, pay for the cost of producing the program. The advertiser, the sponsor, would get name credit, but would have nothing to do with the content of the program. Would this blemish the corporate image? Would the stockholders object? I think not. For if the premise upon which our pluralistic society rests—which as I understand it is that if the people are given sufficient undiluted information, they will then somehow, even after long, sober second thoughts, reach the right decision—if that premise is wrong, then not only the corporate image but the corporations are done for.

There used to be an old phrase in this country employed when someone talked too much. It was "Go hire a hall." Under this proposal the sponsor would have hired the hall; he has bought the time; the local station operator, no matter how indifferent, is going to carry the program—he has to. Then it's up to the networks to fill the hall. I am not here talking about editorializing, but about straightaway exposition as direct, unadorned, and impartial as fallible human beings can make it. Just once in a while let us exalt the importance of ideas and information. Let us dream to the extent of saying that on a given Sunday night the time normally occupied by Ed Sullivan is given over to a clinical survey of the state of American education, and a week or two later the time normally used by Steve Allen is devoted to a thoroughgoing study of American policy in the Middle East. Would the corporate image of their respective sponsors be damaged? Would the stockholders rise up in their wrath and complain? Would anything happen other than that a few million people would have received a little illumination on subjects that may well determine the future of this country, and therefore the future of the corporations? This method would also provide real competition between the networks as to which could outdo the others in the palatable presentation of information. It would provide an outlet for the young men of skill—and there are some even of dedication—who would like to do something other than devise methods of insulating while selling.

There may be other and simpler methods of utilizing these instruments of radio and television in the interests of a free society. But I know of none that could be so easily accomplished inside the framework of the existing commercial system. I don't know how you would measure the success or failure of a given program. And it would be hard to prove the magnitude of the benefit accruing to the corporation which gave up one night of a variety or quiz show in order that the network might marshal its skills to do a thoroughgoing job on the present status of NATO or plans for controlling nuclear tests. But I would reckon that the president, and indeed the majority of shareholders of the corporation who sponsored such a venture, would feel just a little bit better about the corporation and the country.

It may be that the present system, with no modifications and no experiments, can survive. Perhaps the money-making machine has some kind of built-in perpetual motion, but I do not think so. To a very considerable extent the media of mass communications in a given country reflect the political, economic, and social climate in which they flourish. That is the reason ours differ from the British and French, or the Russian and Chinese. We are currently wealthy, fat, comfortable, and complacent. We have currently a built-in allergy to unpleasant or disturbing information. Our mass media reflect this. But unless we get up off our fat surpluses and recognize that television in the main is being used to distract, delude, amuse, and insulate us, then television and those who finance it, those who look at it and those who work at it, may see a totally different picture too late.

I do not advocate that we turn television into a twenty-seven-inch wailing wall, where longhairs constantly moan about the state of our culture and our defense. But I would just like to see it reflect occasionally the hard, unyielding realities of the world in which we live. I would like to see it done inside the existing framework, and I would like to see the doing of it redound to the credit of those who finance and program it. Measure the results by Neilsen, Trendex, or Silex—it doesn't matter, the main thing is to try. The responsibility can be easily placed, in spite of all the mouthings about giving the public what it wants. It rests on big business, and on big television, and it rests at the top. Responsibility is not something that can be assigned or delegated. And it promises its own reward: good business and good television.

Perhaps no one will do anything about it. I have ventured to outline it against a background of criticism that may have been too harsh, only because I could think of nothing better.

Someone once said—I think it was Max Eastman—that "That publisher serves his advertiser best who best serves his readers." I cannot believe that radio and television, or the corporations that finance the programs, are serving well or truly their viewers or listeners, or themselves.

I began by saying that our history will be what we make it. If we go on as we are, then history will take its revenge, and retribution will not limp in catching up with us.

We are to a large extent an imitative society. If one or two or three corporations would undertake to devote just a small fraction of their advertising appropriation along the lines that I have suggested, the procedure would grow by contagion, the economic burden would be bearable, and there might ensue a most exciting adventure—exposure to ideas, and the bringing of reality into the homes of the nation.

To those who say, "People wouldn't look, they wouldn't be interested, they're too complacent, indifferent, and insulated," I can only reply: "There is, in one reporter's opinion, considerable evidence against that contention." But even if they are right, what have they got to lose? Because if they are right, and this instrument is good for nothing but to entertain, amuse, and insulate, then the tube is flickering now and we will soon see that the whole struggle is lost.

This instrument can teach, it can illuminate; yes, and it can even inspire. But it can do so only to the extent that humans are determined to use it to those ends. Otherwise it is merely wires and lights in a box. There is a great and perhaps decisive battle to be fought against ignorance, intolerance, and indifference. This weapon of television could be useful.

Stonewall Jackson, who knew something about the use of weapons, is reported to have said: "When war comes, you must draw the sword and throw away the scabbard." The trouble with television is that it is rusting in the scabbard during a battle for survival.

JOHN FISCHER

Television and Its Critics

John Fischer, who conducts "The Easy Chair" column in Harper's, published this essay in the July 1959 issue. The essay elicited more than 700 letters from readers, many asking what they could do to help improve the quality of television programs. This is an extraordinary response and can be taken to indicate either that Fischer's essay was quite provocative to his audience, or that Fischer was writing on a subject in which many of his readers were intensely interested.

In the hurt tones of a misunderstood man, Robert W. Sarnoff recently complained that television is getting a raw deal. Its critics, he said, are calling it bad names—"mediocre" . . . "unworthy" . . . "time-wasting."

This, he intimated, is both unfair and damaging to the industry. TV is giving the public what it wants, and the public loves it. Its critics are either misinformed, or they have a selfish interest in discrediting TV; or they are intolerant intellectuals who despise the mass taste and want to impose their own arcane standards on a reluctant America.

If this keeps up, he warned, TV will face two hideous dangers. Its audience and advertisers may drift away, because they are constantly being told that watching their favorite programs is "a shameful act." Worse yet, the government might start meddling with TV programing.

So Mr. Sarnoff urged his industry to launch "a massive communications effort" to answer its critics. It should explain that "a principal function" is to serve up light entertainment—to "meet the need of most active Americans for relaxation." (Well, all right, maybe it ought to provide something for "minority tastes" as well—but that is secondary.) And the industry ought to make clear that it finds no conflict between serving the public and serving advertisers; what is good for the sponsor is good for the United States.

Since Mr. Sarnoff is boss of NBC and since he was talking to the broadcasters' trade association, he got action. Committees were set up, money was raised, and the industry is now planning a heavy-caliber campaign to defend itself.

Mr. Sarnoff has a point. Four points, to be precise.

Much criticism of TV *has* been misinformed. Some of it has come from professional intellectuals whose main stock in trade is lament over the malodorous decay of American culture. (A classic example is Gunther Anders' essay in *Mass Culture: The Popular Arts in America,*[1] in which he deplores TV for 4,500 words without once touching on anything so vulgar as a fact. One of his conslusions is that "because the world is brought into our homes, we do not have to explore it . . . modern man travels only as a last resort." To preserve his intellectual purity, Dr. Anders evidently avoids not only TV, but also highways, airports, trains, and docks.)

Perhaps it is also true—though hard to prove—that some of the newspaper and magazine criticism of TV has been snide and hostile, because TV is a strong competitor for audience and advertising.

Surely, Mr. Sarnoff is right in fearing that government domination would be a bad thing. The Federal Communications Commission has made sorry use of what power over broadcasting it now has; and foreign experience—notably in England—suggests that government-operated TV has about as many (though different) failings as the American system. Then, too, it is always dangerous to let politicians or bureaucrats get their fingers on *any*

[1] Edited by Bernard Rosenberg and David Manning White; published in 1957 by the Free Press, Glencoe, Illinois.

channel of communication. The temptation to use it for propaganda is too great a strain to put on any conscience.

Finally, for whatever one man's opinion is worth, it seems to me that TV is better than many of its critics are willing to admit. In a slow and spotty way, it may actually be improving. At least in the New York area, where the network programs usually originate, anybody willing to hunt a little can now find one or two worthwhile programs almost every day—ranging from history lectures to Eugene O'Neill, from first-rate jazz to Leonard Bernstein. (True enough, local stations in the hinterland often refuse to carry the best of the network offerings; they can make more money by running ancient movies.) In the household I know best, TV has caused none of the disasters predicted by the gloomier sociologists. My children haven't turned into videots, or even neglected their homework much. And if my own brain is softening, I can't honestly blame it on my watching an occasional prize-fight, baseball game, or Phil Silvers comedy.

But if we grant all this, the fact remains that Mr. Sarnoff and many of his fellow broadcasters don't seem to understand what their responsible critics are really saying. These critics too have some valid points—and they cannot be answered by any "communications effort," however massive. The only possible answer would be a basic change in the organization of the industry.

The true indictment against TV is not that it is all bad, but rather that it is not nearly as good as it could be—nor as good as the public has a right to expect. The public is now paying a high price for something it has been promised, and is not getting. With the best will in the world, the industry *in its present form* evidently is powerless to deliver what it has promised—solemnly and legally—that it would deliver.

Some specifications of this charge were set forth most vigorously, not by a cloistered intellectual, but by one of the most respected and successful executives in broadcasting, Edward R. Murrow. Last October he scandalized the industry by saying, right out loud, that its performance is timid, trivial, and escapist. He pointed out that in the all-important prime time period—the hours between 8:00 and 11:00 P.M., which are the only ones when most people are free to use their sets—the air is full of froth. Normally all three networks and all local stations offer much the same fare: frivolous entertainment, consisting of Westerns, vaudeville, quiz shows, and an occasional detective story.

In practice, then, during the prime hours you and I do not have that "freedom of choice" which Mr. Sarnoff speaks of so reverently. Candy is dandy, as Ogden Nash has observed—but what if you want beef steak for a change? You won't get it. The sponsors in their infinite wisdom have decided that most people want candy between 8:00 and 11:00 P.M.—and you will, by God, take it or go hungry.

The result is that the best brains in television, its best hours, and its best dollar are dedicated to making the American people fat, dumb, and happy. Or, as Mr. Murrow put it, to "decadence, escapism, and insulation from the world in which we live."

Is this good enough? Can we afford to use our best resources in this way, at a moment when the Soviets are straining all their resources to make *their* people lean, smart, and tough? Even if most of the customers (and sponsors) do eat it up, does it really make sense? Isn't it like feeding candy to a diabetic—without warning him that sugar may kill him? For, as Mr. Murrow pointed out, prime hour TV makes "only fleeting and spasmodic reference to the fact that this nation is in mortal danger.[1]

Many people in television are aware of these questions, and uneasy about them. One is Mr. Sarnoff. Shortly after his speech about the critics, I talked to him at some length, and have no doubt that he is a conscientious and intelligent man, eager to do what he can to improve his industry. So too with the responsible executives at CBS—notably its president, Dr. Frank Stanton, a former professor who is at least as thoughtful as any of his intellectual critics; and its TV chief, Louis Cowan, a former aide of Adlai Stevenson.

The trouble is they can't do much.

As the industry is now organized, *nobody*—neither networks, nor local stations, nor sponsors—has much leeway to attempt anything more than marginal improvements.

Some such modest improvements already are in prospect. Mr. Sarnoff recently announced that NBC is planning seven hour-long informational programs, plus some operas and original plays, to be presented at peak viewing periods. Dr. Stanton has said that next year CBS will schedule "regular hour-long informational broadcasts once a month in prime evening time," and that later he hopes to offer such programs twice a month and eventually every week.

These are remarkably courageous steps. Even if the network chiefs get away with them, however, that will still mean that only about one twenty-eighth of the prime hours will be salvaged from the froth. And to judge from past experience, many of the networks' affiliated stations will refuse to carry such programs.

[1] On rare occasions the networks do venture to slip a morsel of protein into the evening menu—a documentary, a prestige show, an interview with Robert Frost. But ordinarily, as we all know, if you want to get your teeth into something, you have to search for it at unearthly hours—such as 6:30 A.M., midnight, or Sunday afternoon.

Even then we don't have much freedom of choice. On Sundays, for example, the sponsors assume that all right-thinking consumers are outdoors playing golf or inhaling exhaust fumes. Consequently these relatively worthless hours can be used as sops for the intellectual—and all the sops are tossed on his plate at once. On May 10, for instance, if you had wanted to listen to Senator Javits and Bergen Evans and Tom Mboya and the *New York Times* Youth Forum and a panel of scientists, you couldn't do it. All were scheduled on different channels at the same hour.

The reason why such improvements are so daring and difficult is, in a word: Money. Those prime hours are enormously valuable. Their sale to advertisers brings in most of the network's income. From this profit it pays for unsponsored programs, for its costly news service, and for those cultural items which appear at dawn and on Sunday afternoon. From this same profit it must pay its dividends. If the networks give away too many of these golden hours for "informational broadcasts," the stockholders will soon want to know why. They may even want a new president. After all, TV is not a philanthropic enterprise.

Each local station is under similar pressure. When it carries an unsponsored network public-service program it is actually out of pocket; but if it rejects that program and sells the time to half a dozen local sponsors, it makes a tempting profit. What would you do if you were the station manager?

Why, then, don't some of the big corporations sponsor an occasional program dealing with "ideas and information," as Mr. Murrow suggested? Again, because they feel they can't afford to. It costs a sizable fortune to put an evening program on a national network. The sponsor will get his money back only if he draws the largest possible audience. If horse opera sells more autos than Ed Murrow—as it does—then the advertiser has to go for horse opera. The fact that he, personally, may prefer Murrow makes no difference. If he should yield to such a whim, his harder-headed competitors will soon run him out of the market.

Actually the sponsor doesn't even have the freedom to take that chance. Once in a long while some advertiser may be rich enough—or stubborn enough—to put on a program which strikes his fancy, even though it does not fetch a whopping audience. One such was Firestone. Until recently it presented a program of semi-serious music—not great art, but certainly a high cut above the quality of most evening shows. Although its audience was relatively small, Firestone was content.

The ABC network was not. It was afraid to carry a low-rating show at 9:00 P.M., because millions of viewers might switch to a competing channel —and stay there for the rest of the evening. So ABC told Firestone that it would have to shift to a less strategic hour or get off the air. No other network could find a place for "The Voice of Firestone" in prime time either—and at this writing the program apparently is doomed.

Everybody feels awfully sorry about this—and everybody is helpless. Them, as Jimmy Durante used to say, is the conditions which prevail.

Our system of broadcasting was not meant to work that way. When it got started, a generation ago, everybody recognized that radio (and later TV) could serve as an immensely powerful instrument of public education and enlightenment. In theory, every station is supposed to put that purpose first. It is licensed to broadcast, under the Federal Communications Act, in order to serve "the public convenience and necessity."

Such a license is a gold mine. It gives the lucky applicant a monopoly on the use of a particular piece of public property—a radio wave-length or TV channel. It costs him nothing, though it may earn him a fortune. Some licenses have been sold, shortly after they were granted by the FCC, for as much as $8 million.

In return for this magnificent gift of public property, the station owner is supposed to devote a considerable part of his air time to public service programs. Naturally the competition is keen for every one of the available channels, and each of the competing applicants makes impressive promises about the public service he will provide. (Sometimes, as the Harris Committee discovered, he also tries to bribe an FCC commissioner.)

These promises are seldom, if ever, kept. The Federal Communications Commission has made no serious effort to enforce them. No station's license has ever been revoked, or refused renewal, because the operator broke his pledge. In practice, therefore, most stations simply ignore this obligation, and sell every hour they can for as much money as they can get. Much of their programing consists of showing old movies in fifteen-minute slices—with as many as six consecutive commercials sandwiched in between all the segments. (Watching one of these mutilated dramas is enough to make a man wonder about Mr. Sarnoff's conviction that "broadcasting's responsibility to the public is harmonious with its responsibility to advertisers.")

If some undesirable time remains unsold, then the station may use it as a cheap gesture toward the public service—often by running a sermon by some local minister.

The upshot is that we are all paying dearly for something we don't get. We are letting the broadcasters use valuable public property, for free—and they are not delivering in return the public service which they promised.

Can anything be done to stop this scandal?

Well, of course, the FCC might try to enforce its own rules—but that seems most unlikely with the caliber of men now on the commission and the political atmosphere in which it operates.

There is, however, another possible solution. It would, I think, meet most of the points raised by the responsible critics of broadcasting. It would give the public real freedom of choice in programs. It would avoid the dangers of government control. Finally, it would remove the economic pressures which now bear down so painfully on people like Sarnoff, Stanton, Murrow, and others who would like to improve TV and radio, but can do so only with great difficulty and risk.

In bare outline, it might work something like this:

(1) Instead of giving away its air channels, from now on the government

would rent them. Each local TV and radio station would pay a modest percentage of its annual earnings—say 10 or 15 per cent. This would be no great hardship, since most broadcasters are now making very comfortable profits. For example, CBS earned $7 million in the first quarter of the year, a gain of nearly 8 per cent over the same period in 1958. Radio Corporation of America, the parent company of NBC, reported first quarter earnings of nearly $13 million, for a 44 per cent gain; but some of this came from the sale of TV sets and other equipment, rather than from broadcasting.

The earnings of all the hundreds of local stations are hard to discover, so I have no idea how much money such rentals might bring in. Certainly it would be substantial. For the sake of illustration, let's assume that they might total $50 million a year.

(2) This money would be turned over to a National Broadcasting Authority—a public body chartered by Congress but carefully insulated from politics. Its directors would be five men who already hold responsible positions in the fields of education, culture, and information. They must not be governmental appointees; they must be free from economic and political pressures; they must not represent any competing media; they should represent a broad spectrum of the public interest; and they must command respect.

Such a board might include the president of Harvard, the heads of the Carnegie and Rockefeller foundations, the director of the Metropolitan Museum, and the chief of the National Radio and Television Center at Ann Arbor. (Again, this list is merely illustrative; no doubt it could be improved upon.) The essential point is that the men who hold such jobs at any given moment would *ex officio* become directors of the National Broadcasting Authority. They should be well paid for their part-time services. I can think of no better method to select a board of assured competence, and above suspicion of any interest except the public welfare.

(3) The board would hire a Program Manager, and would give him general policy directives—much as a corporation board of directors deals with the company's president. This manager would, of course, be an experienced broadcasting executive. Mr. Murrow, for example.

(4) The main job of the Authority and its manager would be to produce public-service programs—news-in-depth, top-quality music and theater, documentaries dealing with science, the arts, and public affairs, plus any kind of experimental features they might want to try. In the beginning, they might attempt three hour-long programs each week for TV and an equal number for radio.

(5) Each program would have to be carried by one of the major networks and all of its affiliated stations, in prime evening time. Monday's program, for example, might be assigned to NBC, Wednesday's to CBS, and Friday's

to ABC. This hour would be an additional rental-in-kind, demanded of the broadcasters in part-payment for the privilege of using the public's air waves. (Unaffiliated stations might be required to devote an equal amount of time to showing the Authority's kinescopes.)

Thus the viewer would have genuine freedom of choice. If he is not interested in the Authority's report on the Berlin crisis, scheduled for 9:00 P.M. Monday on NBC, then he can turn to a western on CBS or a song-and-dance act on ABC. And *vice versa.* (He would even get a chance to see an occasional program uninterrupted by commercials, since the Authority would have no need for advertising.) Such an arrangement would, moreover, expose the Authority's program producers to the bracing effects of competition for their audience.

(6) This system would cost the broadcasters far less than you might think. For the networks and the few conscientious local stations would be relieved of the painful and expensive duty of producing public-service programs. And those stations which now evade this duty would be forced to bear their fair share of the Authority's cost.

All broadcasters could then go merrily about their primary business of selling advertising—undistracted by the present conflict between their duty to their stockholders and their duty to the public service. Nagging consciences would be stilled, snarling critics would be silenced—or, at least, largely diverted to watching the Authority's programs—and ulcers might no longer be the TV man's occupational disease.

(7) The Authority would open up a stimulating new opportunity for broadcasting talent. I personally know a dozen top-flight producers, writers, and actors who would jump at the chance to work for such an outfit, even if it meant a cut in salary—simply because they are tired, as one of them put it, of "producing garbage."

(8) The plan would not cost the taxpayer a penny; it could be put into effect with a simple piece of legislation; and it would require no governmental machinery to operate it.

Do you think such a plan might be worth a trial?

If so—or if it strikes you as a bad idea—I hope you will drop me a postcard or a note. Better yet, let me know how you think it might be improved; as sketched here, it probably has a lot of flaws I have not been able to see.

I am eager to know how many other people feel, as I do, that our broadcasting system might be made to serve us better. Any comment that readers of this column may care to send me will get careful attention—and later they will be turned over to a member of Congress who is interested in the possibility of doing something about it.

ROBERT W. SARNOFF

Television and Its Critics: A Reply

Robert Sarnoff, chairman of the board of the National Broadcasting Company, published the following response to Fischer's essay in the September 1959, issue of Harper's.

To the Editors:

I am much intrigued by John Fischer's proposal for a National Broadcasting Authority, which would be supported by an ingenious double levy of time and money on American broadcasters and, as a *quid pro quo,* would relieve these same broadcasters of "the painful and expensive duty of producing public-service programs."

That I, as a broadcaster, might disagree with some aspects of the proposal does not lessen my appreciation of Mr. Fischer's very earnest and sincere effort to solve a problem that has bothered us for many years. We are still groping for solutions, and his thoughtful attempt to provide them should be cause for gratitude, not irate reproach.

My principal quarrel with Mr. Fischer's idea relates to its area of application and to the fact that he nowhere suggests that it be pre-tested. The very name National Broadcasting Authority has a ring of granitic permanence; and before anything so radically and challengingly different is imposed on the infant, sprawling, enormously complex television industry, I would like to see a trial run in a more mature, more stable branch of the mass communications family.

I suggest magazines for the test, and I believe the data developed through a National Magazine Authority would be enormously useful in fashioning any future NBA—far more, in fact, than might at first blush be apparent.

It is hardly necessary, in proposing this to *Harper's* readers, to elaborate on the imbalance of mass-appeal magazines. In 1958, for example, nearly one-third of all weekly magazine serials (as well as mass-market paperbound fiction) consisted of Westerns—a ratio several times greater than the ratio of Westerns to other programs on the NBC Television Network.

Why should the great mass of American magazine readers—those who read *Look, Playboy,* the *Saturday Evening Post,* to say nothing of such chastised brethren as *Confidential*—never be exposed to Alfred Kazin's analysis of the fiction of the 'fifties [published in October 1959 in *Harper's*] or a piece by the Bolshoi Ballet's Galina Ulanova on how she created the role of Juliet [July 1959]? Why not give readers of *Time, Life,* and *Fortune* a crack at articles with such titles as "The Hidden Affair Between Big Business and Big Labor" [July 1959]?

As with television, there are two valid reasons to promote greater cultural, educational, and "public-service" content in our mass magazines. One is that it would help to raise public taste and broaden public interests. The other affects readers who already count themselves among the cultural elite. Why should a member of this elite who happens to find some amusement in *Reader's Digest* be saddled with the expense and trouble of finding more specialized fare in smaller publications, any more than the *avant-garde* television viewer should undergo the inconvenience of tuning to his special preferences at hours or on days when he may want to be doing something else?

Mr. Fischer has pointed the way to the remedy. In proposing that television and radio stations and networks be taxed twice (once in funds and again in segments of choice time) to underwrite an NBA, he noted that the broadcasters are commercial beneficiaries of the free public air, obliged by law to operate in the public interest, convenience, and necessity.

Magazines too are on the receiving end of substantial public bounty, although a more old-fashioned type: money. In 1958, the U.S. Post Office put the subsidy represented by second-class mailing privileges at $272,096,464.[1] The largest group beneficiary was magazines, with the most popular, mass-appeal magazines naturally benefiting to the greatest extent. Moreover, Congress clearly intended this privilege to encourage the spread of public enlightenment; the law grants it expressly "for the dissemination of information of a public character, or devoted to literature, the sciences, arts, or some special industry."

Nothing could be more in keeping with the spirit of this clause, and with the thrust of Mr. Fischer's idea, than to tax the recipients of this public largesse to implement the very ends it was intended to serve. A nominal levy on the profits of each magazine, even less than the "modest percentage" of 10 per cent or 15 per cent that Mr. Fischer would impose on broadcasters, could underwrite the costs of a National Magazine Authority, a public body chartered by Congress but carefully insulated from politics.

The five directors of this Authority should meet all the exacting criteria that Mr. Fischer has prescribed for the NBA. They should be men of impeccable professional competence, high intellectual stature, and detachment. Under their general policy directives, exemplary articles, fiction, reviews, and verse would be solicited and conceived, assigned and written, and generously paid for. These efforts would be placed regularly, on a staggered basis, in the commandeered pages of national magazines of vast circulation.

Thus, for example, every other issue of the *Ladies' Home Journal* would be required to devote, say, six pages in the front of the magazine to the kind of worthwhile prose and poetry that ripens almost unnoticed in such esoteric periodicals as *Hudson Review, Sewanee Review,* and *Commentary.*

[1] *As Mr. Sarnoff states, these are Post Office figures; in fact they are highly controversial interpretations of cost accounting.*—The Editors of *Harper's*

Or if J. D. Salinger wants to undertake another extraordinary effort such as the 34,000-word story "Seymour," which appeared in a single issue of the *New Yorker* last June, the NMA could place it for him in a magazine of far greater circulation, say the *Reader's Digest*.

Just consider what a refreshing and uplifting change of pace, what a stimulus to further creativity, this procedure promises for those literary figures who now scorn the mass magazines because they dislike being forced to write "garbage."

My NMA plan would cost magazines far less than they might fear. Conscientious editors and publishers would be largely relieved of the painful and expensive duty of ferreting out, encouraging, and publishing obscure works of genuine distinction. All that would be taken care of for them by the NMA, and they could concentrate instead on income-producing Western and private-eye serials for the millions. And those magazines which totally evade their moral obligations under the second-class mail privilege—for example, the semi-pornographic magazines that dominate so many newsstands —would be forced to bear their fair share of the Authority's cost.

For the NMA to serve as an adequate test of Mr. Fischer's basic idea, at least two years might be needed, and I do not think it ought to be rushed just to get at television. Indeed, he has my assurance that the one-hour weekly quota of prime-time, prime-quality programs assigned under his plan to the NBC Television Network will in fact be fulfilled two to three times over in the forthcoming season, and without the help of any Authority. Among these programs, during peak evening viewing hours, will be original dramas by such playwrights as Archibald MacLeish and James Costigan; news-in-depth specials on such subjects as the rise of African nationalism; adaptations of outstanding works, *e.g.*, Maugham's "The Moon and Sixpence," starring Sir Laurence Olivier, "What Makes Sammy Run" by Budd Schulberg, and Shakespeare's "The Tempest"; historical dramas filmed on the actual scenes of the events, *e.g.*, Jefferson at Monticello, and numerous music specials with artists of the caliber of Renata Tebaldi, Harry Belafonte, Isaac Stern, Eileen Farrell, and the New York City Center Ballet.

Since these projects and many others like them involve lengthy contractual commitments by NBC, it seems only fair that we have the opportunity to fulfill our contracts before we are relieved of the painful and expensive duty of presenting any further programs of this kind.

LOUIS HAUSMAN

Legislators, Broadcasters and the Public Interest

This speech was delivered at a dinner meeting attended by members of the New York State Association of Broadcasters and members of the State Legislature of New York in Albany, the state capital, March 1, 1960.

Hausman is director of the Television Information Office, a public relations organization which receives its financial support from television stations. It is a wing of the National Association of Broadcasters.

There is a striking parallel between the two groups gathered here this evening. Each is mandated to serve the public interest. Each does its job only with the consent of the majority. And the performance of each is judged by the electorate which regularly votes its approval or disapproval.

But the parallel goes further.

It starts with a threshold requirement that is common to both legislators and broadcasters. This requirement is to engage the loyalty and approval of the majority. For it is clear enough that if legislators don't get elected, if broadcasters—particularly those in television—fail to engage the attention of most people, neither has an opportunity to serve.

Only if this majority acceptance is secured can a basic function of legislator and broadcaster be performed: to promote the general welfare and to serve the public interest. It seems to me that few other groups in a democracy share this opportunity and responsibility as fully as the two groups in this room.

And this responsibility is to *all* the people who make up the community. Merely to satisfy the majority is too narrow a goal for an advancing democracy. No responsible broadcaster or legislator ever settles for so little.

After he has won the approval of the majority—not always an easy vote to get—the legislator or broadcaster comes up against a key question. Simply stated, it is "How do you serve the interests of the special groups in the community without losing the confidence and attention of the majority?" And to push the question further, "How do you serve the majority and not disregard the legitimate needs of the minorities?"

To do this successfully calls for a very special kind of understanding and wisdom. It requires you to be responsive without being servile. It requires you to evaluate and act on the numerous countervailing pressures that minorities bring to bear upon you, and at the same time, not damage the interests of the majority.

Every Senator and Assemblyman recognizes this problem when he tries to put together a legislative program. Every *broadcaster* is familiar with it when he plans a program schedule. However, each may not be aware that the other often comes up against the same kind of problems.

This mutual lack of awareness can reduce the capacity of both legislator and broadcaster to perform his most effective public service.

Before suggesting what each of you might do to strengthen your mutual effectiveness, I would like to discuss very briefly the role of a popular medium in our mid-century democracy. I would like to specify some of the problems in the field of broadcasting, and particularly in television. In doing this, those of you in government may be able to identify certain parallels with your own activities.

It is evident that today virtually every special group—educational, civic, governmental—quite properly regards television as the greatest potential force for bringing information and cultural awareness to the total American public. The medium's capacity to perform this service is based on the attention paid it by some 87 per cent of all U.S. families who spend more than five hours a day looking at its programs.

It is equally evident that our people made their $16 billion investment in television sets primarily for entertainment. Diminish this universality and concentration of attention—created in the first place by entertainment programs—and you diminish the medium's potential to inform the public at large and to enrich its cultural life.

It seems to me that impractical demands for an overweighting of special-interest programs can threaten this potential.

Thoughtless yielding to such demands would inevitably reduce the overwhelming attention paid to the medium, and television would cease to represent the single widest avenue to the American public. If television's purpose is to serve the many instead of the few, entertainment must continue to be the single largest element of the television schedule.

It is interesting to note that Gilbert Seldes, who calls himself the inventor of egghead criticism, and is now Director of the Annenberg School of Communications at the University of Pennsylvania, made this very point almost 23 years ago. He was trying to foresee some of the problems of television in the light of radio's experience. He had this to say in an article in the *Atlantic Monthly* of May, 1937:

> The high-minded do not like to face the actual situation in radio, which is that all of its desirable effects are based on the habit of listening which was created largely by programmes trivial and banal in themselves. In countries with highly centralized authority it is possible that people listen to the radio because what they hear is important; and the extreme form is obligatory listening as it is practiced in Germany. In a democratic country the emphasis is on the other side: radio is important because people listen to it, even when it is trivial; the audience which listened to the radio debate on the Supreme Court was created in the first place by Ed Wynn, Rudy Vallee, Amos 'n' Andy, and Kate Smith.

Mr. Seldes then continued: ". . . I have a feeling that the most important thing for television is to make sure of its own popularity. Like the moving pictures and the radio, television would act against its own nature if it did not try to be virtually a universal entertainment."

I think today many outspoken critics are inclined to underrate the importance of the entertainment factor in television. Most of them have available other forms of professional entertainment—music, theatre, nightclubs and sports. They are inclined to look to television for what they don't get elsewhere: its coverage of international events, its interviews and conversations with world figures, its excursions into the experimental arts. They wish there were more of that. But to millions of their fellow citizens, television is the principal, if not the only professional entertainment available—the one major relief from job, housework, or school.

Now, there are critics who accept the fact that television should primarily furnish entertainment. But *their* complaint is "Why does so much of this entertainment have to be so second-rate?"

The direct answer is that television, along with the press, movies, theatre and publishing, suffers from limitations in the abilities of its creative talent. No craftsman, however, gifted comes up with a winner every time—whether his name is Shakespeare or Chayevsky, Lippmann or Murrow.

Clearly, television does not invariably produce programs which please every individual group or viewer—or even, every broadcaster. But neither does any other medium—class or mass.

Since the work of legislators and broadcasters has to take into account people's tastes, I would like to digress a moment and report on these tastes as reflected in the kind of books that people buy.

This is reported in the book *Sixty Years of Best Sellers, 1895-1955,* by Alice Payne Hackett. In the introduction to this book, "best sellers" was defined as "A term . . . to describe what were not necessarily the best books but the books that people liked best . . . It is important to note," the introduction continued, "not only what people could have read, or should have read, but what they did read. The record of what books a great many people have bought and read is part of the social history of those people."

Well, here is the record: during these sixty years the fifteen best sellers in this country included nine novels, three inspirational books, two cookbooks and one baby book. Of the nine novels that made the best seller list, seven were by Mickey Spillane! And this selection took place under conditions of complete free choice among the several thousand books published each year.

Facts such as these remind us that, while television can and does provide many of the rewards of concert and lecture hall, it must do this only within the context of its primary function, which is to maintain its position as a popular medium.

In our democratic society, we long ago chose the *general* welfare as against the education and the enlightenment of the privileged few. As a nation, we have been criticized for this. But we stubbornly cling to our conviction that the American assignment is to see that everybody gets at least a chance to better himself.

I think that television at its best expresses this same democratic point of view. It may well be more valuable to expose millions of people to "Hamlet" or "The Tempest" than it would be to conduct a six-month television seminar on the origins of the Elizabethan theater for the highly limited number who are legitimately interested in this subject.

In working toward the goal of improving the conditions of all the electorate, broadcasters, no less than legislators, have been accused of lack of intelligence, lack of responsibility and of disregard for the interests of the people.

Each is subject to vocal and powerful pressures by special-interest groups. Clearly, the needs of these groups must be recognized. But special pleadings cannot be allowed to determine finally the decisions of either broadcaster or legislator.

Progress is made by taking one step at a time—in programing as in legislation. You cannot legislate taste or morality. Unless we are willing to settle for a totalitarian approach, we cannot force people to watch or listen to what they don't want or to obey laws for which there is no broad public acceptance.

Both legislator and broadcaster are subject to contradictory and self-defeating pressures.

Legislators are constantly asked to legislate more services and lower taxes; more patronage and less waste; fewer laws and greater safeguards.

Broadcasters are urged to program more realistic adult dramas and at the same time make then appropriate for children; to produce programs on more controversial issues and no material which might be offensive to minority groups; to schedule informational programs during peak viewing times and to avoid conflict with popular, wide-appeal shows.

These is no easy answer to such conflicting demands. But it seems to me, in striving for balance, broadcaster and legislator alike must avoid two extremes. One extreme says, "If the public likes it, it's good"; the other extreme says, "If the public *doesn't* like it, it's good." The first is the refuge of the huckster and the demagogue, while the super-egghead and the impractical do-gooder hide behind the other viewpoint.

Polls and ratings and surveys describing what people like or want or will accept are guide posts, not anchor points. Responsible and imaginative leadership must view such findings in perspective. Only if this is done can the goals of our society be met.

How can legislator and broadcaster help each other to attain these goals?

I would suggest a two-part answer to this question. Part one concerns itself with responsible restraint; part two involves a greater understanding.

Neither broadcasters nor legislators can afford, it seems to me, to engage in activities which diminish the public's respect for the work of the other.

This does not imply that either government or broadcasting should be free from criticism. This does not suggest that immoral or irresponsible acts on the part of individuals in either field should not be brought to the attention of the public, fully aired, and steps taken to prevent their recurrence.

All of us here tonight are uncomfortably aware of the damage which inheres in irresponsible investigation and over-anxious reporting. Recent events underscore this painfully. A useful guide for both legislator and broadcaster is suggested in the old journalistic aphorism, "It is more important to get the facts *straight* than to get them first."

Thoughtful broadcasters avoid adding to the stereotype of the irresponsible legislator: the cartoon caricature of the backroom politician, which is easier to draw than to justify. It is more dramatic to play up an occasional transgression on the part of an individual than it is to describe the activities of the hundreds and thousands of hard-working and dedicated officials. But conscientious broadcasters avoid the easy lure of sensational journalism.

Broadcasters can and should seek out ways to add to the prestige of responsible legislators.

They do this positively in a number of ways.

They make available to the public through various programs information on the workings of our government and the work of elected officials. They do this in cooperation with the legislator himself—enabling him to report on a regular basis to his constituents. There is a continuing need for this because government, itself, is a continuing process—not an every two- or four-year event. Broadcasters help the cause of good government by making it understood through work with organizations such as the League of Women Voters. They do it by furnishing broadcast time to opposing points of view so that the public can understand not only the issues but the implications of the issues.

The legislator has a role directly parallel to that of the broadcaster. By what he says on the floor of the legislature; by the scope and tenor of the hearings he conducts; by his response to his constituents he has the power to influence the public's image of broadcasting. If he does this with awareness of the facts, even though what he says is critical, he can be helpful.

It has long been apparent that the two letters "T" and "V" in conjunction represent the surest way to get space and attention. It is somewhat less clear why all the lapses in advertising should be laid at the door of broadcasting.

It is also somewhat less than accurate to blame television for all the faults of our civilization. If Nick Carter and William S. Hart didn't cause the downfall of this country, then it is not likely that "Hawaiian Eye" and "Wagon Train" will.

In this year of national elections radio and television will be heavily relied upon to expose campaign issues to the voters. Broadcasting's huge circulation—created primarily by entertainment programs—is a major reason for its usefulness.

But circulation, in itself, is not enough. It is important not to impair the demonstrated public confidence in broadcasting by uninformed and irresponsible criticism. To do so would be to blunt one of the most useful tools in the functioning of our democracy.

It would seem unreasonable for critics to characterize broadcasting as irresponsible, culture-destroying, youth-corrupting and in the next breath expect it to be effective in clarifying important local and national issues. On the other hand, the medium's potential can be increased through thoughtful criticism based on understanding.

There are many mechanisms available for creating such understanding. The Television Information Office is one of them; a gathering such as this is clearly another. Whether or not there should be formalized machinery set up to speed this flow of mutual understanding, I leave to your judgment. Certainly, there is enough information available and the easiest way to get it is to want to get it.

At a minimum, I would urge each of you to meet regularly with his legislative or broadcast counterpart in the community. In this way you will be able to bring into the open matters of mutual concern. Sometimes, I suspect, there may be no satisfactory answers but, at least, you will be aware that there are questions.

Broadcasters and legislators play a very special role in this country. Perhaps, more than any other groups they are charged with the duty of advancing the cause of all the electorate while safeguarding the interests of minorities.

This is not an easy role to fill in a democracy. It is always harder to make a free choice than it is to follow a dictated command. But none of us would willingly give up the freedom to make a choice.

ROBERT M. HUTCHINS

The Responsibility of the Press

Delivered at the annual meeting of the American Society of Newspaper Editors in Washington, D.C., April 21, 1955.

Hutchins is a distinguished educator and trenchant commentator on national and world affairs. He served as dean of the Yale University Law School while still in his twenties, and in 1929, at the age of thirty, he became president of the University of Chicago. During the next twenty-one years, as president and chancellor, he instituted sweeping changes in administration and curriculum, abolished intercollegiate football, started the Great Books program, and launched the atomic research program under the direction of Enrico Fermi. Hutchins was associate director of the Ford Foundation from 1951 to 1954, and since 1954 he has been president of the Fund for the Republic.

Not surprisingly, the American Society of Newspaper Editors did not react favorably to this speech. Editors and publishers interviewed after Hutchins spoke rejected as unnecessary his proposed agency to appraise the performance of the

press. They challenged his assertions concerning the monopoly newspaper, claiming that the rapidity of modern transportation encourages direct competition between newspapers published in widely separated cities.

Twenty-five years ago, almost to the day, I last had the honor of addressing this society. The quarter of a century between has been the longest in history. That was a different world, before the depression, before the New Deal, before the Newspaper Guild, before the suburbs, before they charged for newsprint, before the atom, before television. It was a world in which you were powerful and numerous. You are powerful still; but some 800 papers that were alive then are gone now. Twenty-five years hence, when I am 81, where will you be?

When I was here last, I said, "the greatest aggregation of educational foundations is the press itself. . . . If the American press does not need or cannot get the leadership of some endowed newspapers, we must fall back on the long process of education through educational institutions, hoping that in the long run we may produce a generation that will demand better things of you. This process will be tedious and difficult, because of the power of the press itself over the minds and habits of those whom the educational institutions produce."

You paid no attention. Well, I would merely remind you that a great many men who paid no attention then are not here now.

I joined in another effort in your behalf in 1947, when the report of the Commission on the Freedom of the Press appeared. The commission felt a little sad. It said, "the outstanding fact about the communications industry today is that the number of its units has declined." It expressed a high opinion of your role in life, for it said, "Freedom of speech and freedom of the press are moral rights which the state must not infringe." And again, "We must recognize that the agencies of mass communication are an educational instrument, perhaps the most powerful there is."

You were furious. Your President issued a statement in six paragraphs, in three of which he said that the members of the commission were "leftwing," and in all of which he stated his conviction that, since most of the members of the commission were professors without experience in the newspaper business, nothing they said could be of any importance, although it might be dangerous. At the meeting of this society in 1947, to which I had been invited to receive your congratulations, the only thing that saved me from condemnation was the expressed unwillingness of your committee to "dignify" me by such action.

All over the country you attacked the report. I hope that you will read it sometime. But for fear you won't, I shall quote a passage from it that will give you the main idea: "If modern society requires great agencies of mass communication, if these concentrations become so powerful that they are a threat to democracy, if democracy cannot solve the problem simply by breaking them up—then those agencies must control themselves or be controlled by government. If they are controlled by government, we lose our chief safeguard against totalitarianism—and at the same time take a long step toward it."

A kind of neurotic sensitivity is characteristic of the press throughout the English-speaking world. The British papers were outraged by the report of the Royal Commission on the Press, which was almost as mild as ours. I don't know what makes you feel this way. After all, in this country you have a special amendment to the Constitution, and the first one at that, protecting you. Perhaps it is this special dignity that sometimes leads you to confuse your private interests with those of the public. . . . About once a week you break out in exasperation against anybody who tries to keep anything from you, for reasons of state or for any reason at all. You are the only uncriticized institution in the country. You will not criticize one another, and any suggestion that anybody else might do so sets you to muttering about the First Amendment.

I know that lately life has been hard for you. And it may get even worse; for it may turn out that reading is an anachronism. When I was a boy, reading was the only established and available path to knowledge, information, or even entertainment. But the other day in Hollywood I met a man who was putting the great books on records. Everything else has already been put on records or films. One glance at the school children making for the television set on their return from school is enough to show that this is a different world. The habit of reading, which my generation fell into, may have too much competition.

The competition may win. Gresham's law of culture is that easy stuff drives out hard. It is harder to read, even after Dr. Flesch has finished with the printed page, than it is to look and listen. I do not believe that newspapers can do what comic books, picture magazines, motion pictures, and television can do in glorious technicolor. Since they can do this kind of thing better, why should you do it at all?

You may say it is the only way to survive. John Cowles suggests it may be a way to die. In his Sigma Delta Chi speech he said newspapers have realized that complete and fair coverage builds circulation. With few exceptions, he said, those newspapers which "have had the heaviest circulation losses are not papers that regard full and fair news presentation as their primary function and reason for existence." If so good a business man as Mr. Cowles can think there is any chance that sensationalism and entertainment are not good for business, a layman may perhaps be forgiven for being impressed.

Emboldened by his example, I will say that newspapers should do as well as they can the things that they can do best, and they should leave to others the responsibility of entertaining the public. If you are worried about who is going to discharge that responsibility, read the March 21 issue of *Newsweek,* which says that television is abandoning "Johns Hopkins Science Review," "Princeton '55," and "The Search." These programs have won many honors and audiences that look large to people who do not work in advertising agencies.

A couple of years ago Henry Luce was discussing the monopoly newspaper. He said the argument against it was that it deprived the community of differing presentations of news and opinions. He went on, "like so many high-brow discussions about newspapers (I notice that journalists invariably use the word "high-brow" when referring to criticisms of the press, even when, as in this case, the truth of the criticism is self-evident to the merest moron) this one is fine, except that it ignores the actual nature of a newspaper. Does any one feel strongly that a city ought to have several newspapers in order to offer the community a greater variety of comic strips, breakfast menus, and cheesecake?" If this is the actual nature of a newspaper, the fewer papers the better. Certainly the special constitutional protection thrown about them seems no more warranted than such protection would be for acrobats, chefs, beauty parlor operators, and astrologers.

What the framers of the First Amendment had in mind was debate, a great continuing debate, with the people hearing all sides and getting all the facts. If government could be kept from interfering with this debate, nothing could interfere with it; for a man who differed with the existing papers could start one of his own. The Founding Fathers did not foresee that 94 per cent of American cities and eighteen American states would be without competing papers. In the overwhelming majority of communities there can now be no debate among rival editors. The editor in a one-paper town has the only voice there is and the only one there is likely to be. The debate has become a soliloquy.

Talk about the virtue of monopoly is the flimsiest rationalization, as is shown by the poor quality of the papers in many monopoly towns. Monopoly cannot be a good thing. At its best it can be like a benevolent despotism, good while the benevolence lasts, but an accident in any case. Monopoly may in the present state of affairs be a necessary evil, but let us not pretend that it is not an evil.

Rising costs have put the publisher in the driver's seat, where he has no business to be. The First Amendment was not instituted to give a preferred position to people who were making money out of papers as against those who were making money out of other articles of commerce. The amendment was to protect the content of the press, not the cash return from it. The reason the publisher is in the driver's seat is that it costs so much money to own and operate a newspaper, and more all the time. . . .

In the absence of some new technological revolution, the number of papers per community in this country seems unlikely to increase. Nothing suggests that cost will fall. Television and suburbanization are driving ahead as fast as they can go. As monopoly continues to spread, the ancient check of competition can, of course, no longer be relied on.

This should lead to the burial of that consoling reference to Jefferson's second inaugural, an ever-present refuge in time of criticism, which made its last formal appearance here in the report of the committee reporting on the report of the Commission on the Freedom of the Press. Jefferson said, in effect, that the people would make their views of a newpaper felt by refusing to read, believe, or buy it. The theory that the daily test of the market-place is an expression of public criticism, and all that is needed, is reduced to absurdity when the public has no option, when it has to buy the newspaper that is offered or go without. . . .

The purpose of a newspaper, and the justification for the privilege of the press, is the enlightenment of the people about their current affairs. No other medium of communication can compete with the newspaper in the performance of this task. A newspaper that is doing this job well is a good newspaper, no matter how deficient it may be in astrology, menus, comics, cheesecake, crime and Republican propaganda. A newspaper that is doing this job deserves protection against government, and it will certainly need it.

A newspaper that is doing this job will have to bring before its readers points of view with which it disagrees and facts that it deplores. Otherwise in monopoly towns the people cannot expect to be enlightened; for television and radio are unlikely to be in the same class with a well-run newspaper in telling what is happening and what it means. Television and radio are, moreover, controlled by a governmental agency, and one that does not inspire much confidence today.

A good many newspapers take seriously their responsibility to enlighten the people about current affairs. It is generally agreed that the best American papers are as good as any in the world and that the average is high. Our question is how to maintain the good newspapers in the faith and how to convert the others.

I think you should reconsider your opposition to the principal recommendation of the Commission on the Freedom of the Press. That was that a new agency be established to appraise and report annually upon the performance of the press. The commission said, "It seems to us clear that some agency which reflects the ambitions of the American people for its press should exist for the purpose of comparing the accomplishments of the press with aspirations which the people have for it. Such an agency would also educate the people as to the aspirations which they ought to have for the press." The commission suggested that this agency be independent of government and of the press; that it be created by gifts, and that it be given a ten-year trial, at the end of which an audit of its achievement could determine anew the institutional form best adapted to its purposes. The fact that the British commission independently reached an identical recommendation seems to me highly significant.

Such an agency should contain representatives of the press; it should also contain laymen. My guess is that the weakness of the Press Council in Sweden results from the fact that it is composed entirely of representatives of the newspapers. I believe that the British Council will go the same way because the press rejected the recommendation of the Royal Commission that the Council should have lay members and a lay chairman. If its first report is suggestive of the future, this group is likely to manifest its fearless and high-principled character by speaking sternly to newspapers on trivial subjects.

The *Nieman Reports,* the Press Institute statements, A. J. Liebling's "Wayward Press," Bob Lasch in *The Progressive,* occasional studies by schools of journalism, these are all we have in this country. They are too casual and limited, and, since most of them are directed at the press, they do not perform one function that the Commission on the Freedom of the Press regarded as essential: they do not "educate the people as to the aspirations which they ought to have for the press."

Your own efforts to act as a critical agency have come to nothing. You appointed a committee in 1949 "to examine the desirability of sponsoring an appraisal of the self-improvement possibilities of American newspapers." The committee reported in 1950 as follows: "Our committee recognizes and reiterates that the American Society of Newspaper Editors is, itself, and must be, a continuing committee of the whole on self-examination and self-government. But, in addition, we urge the society to call upon its board of directors to take whatever action may be necessary from time to time to clarify understanding of American newspapers by the public, and to keep editors alert to their responsibilities in fulfilling the public's right to an adequate, independent newspaper press."

This sounds as though it was written by a public relations man. In these sonorous sentences we hear the cadence of the Psalms.

The great issues of our times are peace and freedom. A new critical agency might appraise the performance of the newspapers in correcting, or contributing to, our vast confusion on these subjects. We know that the peoples of the earth are now equipped to turn one another into radioactive cinders. Can you say that you have given Americans the material they need to reach a conclusion on the course they should follow, on the choice between seeking peace through purchase and intimidation and seeking it through total, enforceable disarmament, the choice between competing nationalisms and world law? . . .

You are educators, whether you like it or not. You make the views that people have of public affairs. No competition can shake you from that position. You will lose it only if you neglect or abandon it. As the number of papers per community declines, the responsibility of each one that remains increases. This is a responsibility that is discharged by being a *newspaper,* by giving the news. The editorial function is to make sure that it is given in such a way that it can be understood. The people must see the alternatives before them; otherwise they cannot be enlightened.

Enlightenment means telling the people where they are in time and space. It means engaging in systematic criticism. The criticism of current affairs has to be made in the light of some standard. This must be something more than a set of partisan slogans. The standard by which the American press must judge current events is derived from an understanding of, and sympathy with, the deepest aspirations of the American people, those for peace and freedom. A press that serves its country in this way need have no concern about the future.

CLARE BOOTHE LUCE

What's Wrong with the American Press?

This speech was given at the Women's National Press Club Dinner in honor of the American Society of Newspaper Editors in Washington, D.C., April 21, 1960.

Mrs. Luce, a successful playwright and former member of Congress, was ambassador to Italy under the Eisenhower administration. She is known for the ardor of her convictions and the sharpness of her wit.

I am happy and flattered to be a guest of honor on this always exciting and challenging occasion. But looking over this audience tonight I am less happy than you might think and more challenged than you could know. I stand here at this rostrum invited to throw rocks at you. You have asked *me* to tell *you* what's wrong with *you*—the American press. The subject not only is of great national significance but also has, one should say, infinite possibilities —and infinite perils to the rock thrower.

For the banquet speaker who criticizes the weaknesses and pretensions, or exposes the follies and sins of his listeners—even at their invitation—does not generally evoke an enthusiastic—no less a friendly—response. The delicate art of giving an audience hell is always one best left to the Billy Grahams and the Bishop Sheens.

But you are an audience of journalists. There is no audience anywhere who should be more bored—indeed, more revolted—by a speaker who tried to fawn on it, butter it up, exaggerate its virtues, play down its faults, and who would more quickly see through any attempt to do so. I ask you only to remember that I am not a volunteer for this subject tonight. You asked for it!

For what is good journalism all about? On a working, finite level it is the effort to achieve illuminating candor in print and to strip away cant. It is the effort to do this not only in matters of state, diplomacy and politics but also in every smaller aspect of life that touches the public interest or engages proper public curiosity. It is the effort to explain everything from a summit conference to why the moon looks larger coming over the horizon than it does when it has fully risen in the heavens. It is the effort too to describe the lives of men—and women—big and small, close at hand or thousands of miles away, familiar in their behavior or unfamiliar in their idiosyncrasies. It is—to use the big word—the pursuit of and the effort to state the truth.

No audience knows better than an audience of journalists that the pursuit of the truth, and the articulation of it, is the most delicate, hazardous, exacting and *inexact* of tasks. Consequently, no audience is more forgiving (I hope) to the speaker who fails or stumbles in his own pursuit of it. The only failure this audience could never excuse in any speaker would be the failure to try to tell the truth, as he sees it, about his subject.

In my perilous but earnest effort to do so here tonight, I must begin by saying that if there is much that is wrong with the American press, there is also much that is right with it.

I know then, that you will bear with me, much as it may go against your professional grain, if I ask you to accept some of the *good* with the bad—even though it may not make such good copy for your newspapers.

For the plain fact is that the U.S. daily press today is not inspiringly good; it is just far and away the best press in the world.

To begin with, its news gathering, news printing, news dissemination techniques and capacities are without rivals on the globe.

The deserving American journalist himself enjoys a far more elevated status than his foreign counterpart anywhere. And this, not only because Americans passionately believe that a free press is vital to the preservation of our form of democracy, but because the average American journalist has, on the record, shown himself to be less venal, less corrupt, and more responsible than the average journalist of many foreign lands.

No capital under the sun has a press corps that is better equipped, and more eager to get the news, the news behind the news, and the news ahead of the news, the inside—outside—topside—bottom-side news, than the Washington press corps.

I must add only half-jokingly that if the nation's dailies are overwhelmingly pro-Republican in their editorial policy, then the Washington press corps is a large corrective for this political imbalance. Not because Washington reporters are *all* Democrats. Rather because they place on the administration in power their white-hot spotlight of curiosity and exposure. So that no one—Republican or Democrat—can sit complacently in office in this capital unobserved by the men and women of the press who provide the news and information that can make or break an elected or appointed officeholder.

Certainly no press corps contains more journalists of competence and distinction, zeal and dedication. What minds regularly tap more "reliable sources" in government, politics, diplomacy? What breasts guard and unguard more "high level" confidences more jealously? What hearts struggle more conscientiously and painfully to determine to what extent truth-telling, or shall we say "leaking," will serve or unserve the public interest? What typewriters send out more facts, figures, statistics, views, and opinions about great public questions and great public figures?

And in what other country of the world are there so many great newspapers? Who could seriously challenge the pre-eminence among the big-city quality press of *The New York Times*? Where in the world is there a "provincial" newspaper (I use the term only in its technical sense) greater than, to take only one outstanding example, the *Milwaukee Journal*? Even the biggest and splashiest of the foreign English-language press, the *London Daily Mirror,* cannot touch in popular journalism the *New York Daily News.* (And since we are talking in superlatives—good and bad—is there a worse paper in England, Japan, France or India than the New York Sunday *Enquirer*?)

While the range between the best and the worst is very wide, America's some 1800 newspapers nevertheless average out a higher quality, variety and volume of information than any other press in the world.

Certainly no other press has greater freedom, more freely granted by the people, to find the news and to print it as it finds it. The American press need not be caught in the subtle toils of subsidies by groups or interests. It does not have to fight government newsprint allocations—that overt or covert censorship exercised in many so-called "free countries." Except as the American press is guided by the profit motive, which is in turn guided by the public demand for its papers, it is an unguided press.

All this is what is right with the American press. And the result of this situation is that our people have more ways to be well informed about issues and events near and far than any people in the world. And they are, by and large, better informed.

But now let us come to the question of the evening: "What is wrong with the American press?" We cannot answer this question unless we will voluntarily abandon our relative measurement of it against the press of *other* countries. We must measure it, in absolute terms, against its own highest ideal of freedom, responsibility—and let us not forget, success.

It is easy to point to many instances in which the American press—especially its individual members—tend to abuse their freedom and shirk their responsibility.

For example, one could note that nowadays the banner of press freedom is more often raised in matters of printing crime, sex and scandal stories, than it is in matters of printing the truth about great national figures, policies and issues. Or that too many members of the working press uncritically pass on—even if they do not personally swallow—too much high level government and political cant, tripe, and public relations; or that there are too many journalists who seem willing to sell their birthright of candor and truth in order to become White House pets, party pets, corporation pets, Pentagon or State Department or trade union or Governor's Mansion pets; who wistfully yearn after Grey Eminency, or blatantly strive for publicity for themselves, on lecture platforms or political rostrums.

While agreeing with most journalists that people are not as much interested in the issues as they should be, one could at the same time note that neither are many journalists. One could mention that such journalists seem to have forgotten that *men, not names* alone, make news, and that men are made by the clarity with which they state issues, and the resolution with which they face them. One could express the hope that more journalists would encourage rather than avoid controversy and argument, remembering that controversy and argument are not the enemies of democracy, but its friends. One could wish for fewer journalist prodigies of the well written factual story, and more gifted talents for drawing explanations from the facts, or that working pressmen would be more creative in reporting the news, or that they would reflect less in themselves of what in this decade they have so rounding condemned in American leadership: apathy, cynicism, luke-warmness, and acceptance of the *status quo* about everything, from juvenile delinquency to nuclear destruction. One could pray, above all, for journalists who cared less about ideologies, and more about ideas.

But such criticisms and complaints—important as they may be—cover only one area of the American press. It is, alas, a relatively small area. A large, unmeasurable percentage of the total editorial space in American newspapers is concerned not with public affairs or matters of stately importance. It is devoted instead to entertainment, titillation, amusement, voyeurism and tripe.

The average American newspaper reader wants news but he wants lots of things from his newspaper besides news: he wants the sports page, the comics, fashion, home-making, advice-to-the-lovelorn, do-it-yourself psychiatry, gossip columns, medical, cooking and decorating features, TV, movie and theater coverage, Hollywood personality stories, Broadway and society prattle, church columns, comics, bridge columns, cross-word puzzles, big-money contests. Above all, he wants news that concerns not a bit the public weal but that people just find "interesting" reading.

I confess to enjoying much of this myself. And I do not mean to suggest that every newspaper must read like the *London Times.* But the plain fact is that we are witnessing in America what Professor William Ernest Hocking and others have called the debasement of popular taste.

Is it necessary? An editor of my acquaintance was asked recently whether the new circulation rise of his increasingly wild-eyed newspaper was being achieved at the expense of good journalism. He replied: "But you don't understand; our first journalistic need is to survive." I submit that a survival achieved by horribly debasing the journalistic coin is short lived. The newspaper that engages in mindless, untalented sensationalism gets caught up in the headlong momentum it creates in its readers' appetites. It cannot continue satisfying the voracious appetites it is building. Such journalism may suddenly burn brightly with success; but it will surely burn briefly.

We have the familiar example of television closely at hand. The American press has rightly deplored the drivel, duplicity and demeaning programing that has marked much of television's commercial thrust. A critic, of course, need not necessarily always have clean hands. The press is right to flail what is wrong in television just as it is obliged to recognize the great service television has provided in areas where its public affairs, news and good programs have succeeded in adding something new and enriching to American life.

But if the press criticizes what is wrong in television without recognizing the moral for itself, it will have missed a valuable and highly visible opportunity for self-improvement.

The double charge against the American press may thus be stated: its failure to inform the public better than it does is the evasion of its responsibility; its failure to educate and elevate the public taste rather than following that taste like a blind, wallowing dinosaur, is an abuse of its freedom.

In view of the river of information which flows daily from the typewriters of American correspondents at home and abroad, why are the American people not better informed? Whose fault is it? At first glance it would seem to be the fault of the publishers and especially editors. But the publisher or editor who does not give his readers plenty of what they want is going to lose circulation to a competitor who does. Or if he has a news monopoly in his city, and feels too free to short change them on these things, he is going to lose circulation as his reader-slack is taken up by the radio, the TV, and the magazines.

Add that even the news the reader wants in most cities, especially the smaller cities throughout the United States, is primarily local news. He remains, even as you and I, more interested in the news of his neighbors, his community, and his city, than he is in the news out of Washington, Paris or Rome.

Can we quarrel with this? We cannot. The Declaration of Independence itself set the pattern of the American way, and with it American reading habits. Life, liberty and the pursuit of *happiness* were to be man's prime and legitimate goals.

Perhaps the history of our country would have been better—and happier—if "the pursuit of truth, information and enlightenment" had been his third great goal. But that was not the way our Founding Fathers saw things. And that is not the way the American public sees them now.

The fact is that while "man" is a rational animal, *all* men and *all* women are not pre-eminently rational, logical and thoughtful in their approach to life. They do not thirst, above all, for knowledge and information about the great domestic and international issues, even though these issues may profoundly affect not only their pocket-books, but their very lives.

Today, as yesterday, people are primarily moved in their choice of reading by their daily emotions, their personal, immediate, existential prejudices, biases, ambitions, desires, and—as we know too well in the Freudian age—by many sub-conscious yearnings and desires, and irrational hates and fears.

Very well then: let us accept the fact.

Should the American press bow to it? Accept it? Cater to it? Foster it?

What else (the cynical and sophisticated will ask) is there to do?

The American press, no less than the TV and radio, is Big Business. It is now, as never before, a mass medium. As Big Business it faces daily vast problems of costliness and competition. As a mass medium it cannot handle these problems without seeking to satisfy the public's feelings, desires and wants. It publishes in the noisiest and most distracted age in our history. It seems doomed to satisfy endlessly the tastes of the nation—pluralistic, pragmatic, emotional, sensuous, and predominately irrational. By its Big Business mass media nature it seems compelled to seek ever more and more to saturate the mass markets, to soak the common denominator reader-sponge with what it wants.

Certainly we must face this fact: if the American press, as a mass medium, has formed the minds of America, the mass has also formed the medium. There is action, re-action, and inter-action going on ceaselessly between the newspaper-buying public and the editors. What is wrong with the American press is what is in part wrong with American society.

Is this then to exonerate the American press for its failures to give the American people more tasteful and more illuminating reading matter? Can the American press seek to be excused from responsibility for public lack of information as TV and radio often do, on the grounds that after all, "We have to give the people what they want or we will go out of business?"

No. Not without abdicating its own American birthright, it cannot. The responsibility *is* fixed on the American press. Falling directly and clearly on publisher and editor, this responsibility is inbuilt into the freedom of the press itself. The freedom guaranteed by the Constitution under the First Amendment, carries this responsibility with it.

"Freedom," as Clemenceau said, "is nothing in the world but the opportunity for self-discipline"; that is to say voluntarily to assume responsibility.

There are many valiant publishers, editors and journalists in America who have made and are making courageous attempts to give readers a little more of what they *should* have, and a little less of what they want—or, as is more often true, what they only *think* they want, because they have no real knowledge of what is available to them. America owes these publishers and editors and journalists an incomparable debt of gratitude.

What is really wrong with the American press is that there are not enough *such publishers and editors.* There is hardly an editor in this room who could not—if he passionately would—give every day, every year, a little more honest, creative effort to his readers on the great issues which face us—the issues which, in the years to come, must spell peace or disaster for our democracy. A beginning would be to try courageously, which is to say *consistently,* to keep such news (however brief) on the front page playing it in some proportion to its real importance. For a newspaper which relegates to the back pages news which is vital to the citizenry as a whole, in favor of sensational "circulation-building" headlines about ephemeral stories of crime, lust, sex and scandal, is *actively* participating in the debasement of public taste and intelligence. Such a newspaper, more especially its editor, is not only breaking faith with the highest of democratic journalism, he is betraying his nation. And, you may be surprised to hear me say, he may even be courting commercial failure.

For there is enough in American life in these exciting sixties to keep interested and absorbed many of the readers who have been written off as impossible to reach except through cheap sensationalism. The commercial challenge is not to achieve success by reaching backward into cliché-ridden ideas, stories and situations. It is rather to recognize that uniquely now in this country there is a natural and self-propelled drive toward a better life, more sustaining and relevant interests. There is, in sum, an infinity of new subjects that make exciting, inviting and important exploration for the American press.

There can be no doubt that honorable and patriotic publishers and devoted and dedicated editors can increase little by little, in season and out, the public's appetite for better information. There can also be no doubt that they can also decrease, little by little, in the rest of their papers the type of stories which appeals to the worst in human nature by catering to the lowest common denominator taste in morals and ethics.

Teddy Roosevelt once said that a good journalist should be part St. Paul and part St. Vitus.

A good editor today must be part Santa Claus, part St. Valentine, part St. Thomas (the doubter), part St. Paul, and certainly he must be part St. Jude. St. Jude, as you know, is the patron saint of those who ask for the impossible.

It is not impossible to ask that the American press begin to reverse its present trend, which Dean Ed Barrett of the Columbia School of Journalism calls "giving the public too much froth because too few want substance." If this trend is not reversed (which it can be only by your determined effort) the American press will increasingly become the creature, rather than the creator of man's tastes. It will become a passive, yielding and, curiously, an effeminate press. And twixt the ads for the newest gas range, and the firmest girdle, the cheapest vacuum cleaner, and the best buy in Easter bonnets; twixt the sports page, the fashion page, the teen-age columns, the children's comics; twixt the goo, glop and glamour hand-outs on Elvis Presley and Elizabeth Taylor, and above all twixt the headlines on the sexiest murders, and the type of political editorializing which sees the great presidential issues of the day as being between the case of the "boyish forelock" versus the "tricky ski-jump nose," the press will lose its masculine prerogative which is to educate, inform, engage the interest of and guide the minds of free men and women in a great democracy.

As I know that the American Society of Newspaper Editors holds hard to the belief in masculine superiority in the realm of the intellect, and could only view with horror the picture of the Fourth Estate as the "kept man" of the emotional masses, I—for one—am certain this will not happen.

Let us watch then, with hope, for the signs of a new, vigorous, masculine leadership in the American press. For if you fail, must not America also fail in its great and unique mission, which is also yours: to lead the world towards life, liberty, and the pursuit of enlightenment—so that it may achieve happiness? It is that goal which the American press must seize afresh—creatively, purposefully, energetically, and with a zeal that holds a double promise: The promise of success and the promise of enlightenment.

Critical Note on Luce

It is evident from the introductory section of this speech that Mrs. Luce was given her subject, "What's Wrong with the American Press?" by the organization which invited her to speak. There is—or could be—some awkwardness in being invited to "throw rocks" at the audience, but Mrs. Luce turns this potential awkwardness to good account through her sparkling introductory comments.

We should not exaggerate the dangers inherent in her speaking assignment. It is true, she must discourse upon the weaknesses and failures of an institution (the press) whose representatives constitute her audience. However, the members of the Women's National Press Club, which consists mainly of working reporters, would hardly feel responsible for the character of any such formidable institution as "the American press." It is not unusual for a working journalist to be highly critical of his newspaper and still be powerless to affect its character or policies. The ladies of the Women's National Press Club may well have anticipated with some relish a candid examination of the press's flaws.

Members of the American Society of Newspaper Editors, who were guests at this dinner, would be more sensitive to criticism. Editors and publishers, with their vested and proprietary interests in newspapers, would be likely to interpret criticisms of the press as criticisms of themselves. However, Mrs. Luce has a nonrhetorical advantage, even here. It was well known to this audience that Mrs. Luce's husband, Henry Luce, is one of the most successful publishers in the country (*Time, Life, Fortune, Sports Illustrated, Architectural Forum*). The editors and publishers would hardly regard the wife of Henry Luce as their persecutor. Consequently, the possibility that this audience will be hostile to Mrs. Luce's speech is not as great as it might, at first, appear.

The initially friendly disposition of the audience notwithstanding, Mrs. Luce has designed her speech on the assumption that her listeners will be skeptical of or hostile to criticisms of the American press. The result of this assumption is an introduction of considerable grace and interest. The speaker's celebrated wit is displayed in the playful exaggeration of her rhetorical predicament. She credits her audience with honesty and candor and thus both compliments them and associates herself with these virtues. As a final preliminary to discussing what is wrong with the press, she duly notes what is right with it. What is right with the press is, largely, the high quality and integrity of journalists: again, a compliment to this audience.

It is instructive to compare this introduction to the introduction of Robert Hutchins's speech before the American Society of Newspaper Editors, published elsewhere in this section. Unlike Mrs. Luce, Hutchins takes no time to establish friendly relations with his audience. From his first sentence Hutchins is swinging away, fully expecting a hostile response from his audience, and getting it. Mrs. Luce appears in the role of friendly critic; Hutchins is the gadfly. Mrs. Luce argues; Hutchins excoriates. Obviously, the editors and publishers in the audience are much more likely to be persuaded by Mrs. Luce's speech than by Hutchins's.

We must note, in justice to Hutchins, that the aggressiveness of his speech is not the product merely of tactlessness. The very nature of his proposals indicate that Hutchins despairs of editors and publishers reforming themselves. He wants an independent agency of reform. Mrs. Luce, by contrast, has faith in the ability and inclination of editors and publishers to improve their own products. Her proposals are much less drastic than Hutchins's; hence, it is easier for her to design a cordial and tactful approach to her audience.

Finally, we must note an interesting technique which Mrs. Luce employs in the final three paragraphs of her speech. In this concluding section, she equates responsible journalism with "masculinity"; irresponsible journalism becomes "effeminate." Considering that the sponsor of this meeting is an organization consisting entirely of women, and that the guests—the editors and publishers—are almost all men, the audience as a whole is probably more than usually conscious of the sexual differential. Men in the presence of women are notoriously conscious of their own masculinity. Mrs. Luce's association of her proposals with masculinity, and of their opposites with effeminacy, is a subtle and, no doubt, an effective touch.

Questions

When criticisms are leveled against radio and television, the station executives blame the networks, the networks blame the advertising agencies, the agencies blame the sponsors, and the sponsors blame either their stockholders or the public taste. Who *is* responsible for the quality of radio and television programs? Is the public taste lower than we might reasonably expect it to be? Is the quality of American communications media a cause or symptom of the public taste? How large a segment of the listening and viewing audience objects when a program of political or social importance displaces a popular entertainment show? How large a segment approves?

Since Murrow's pathbreaking critique in 1958, editorials, longer newscasts, and a greater number of documentary and public service programs have appeared on radio and television. What forces are responsible for the change? Can we depend on continued change in this direction or on a maintenance of the status quo? Does self-regulation, government regulation, or prompting by a group of private citizens constitute a feasible means of improving radio and television? Is it possible to bring effective pressure to bear without infringing on the right of free speech?

Clearly it is a minority, as Hausman argues, which presses for more educational and cultural programing. Are they right in attempting to force their will on the majority? Is this what they're trying to do? Are the recent changes in radio and television programing an improvement over the situation which existed in 1958? In what ways do radio and television continue to fall short of the full contribution they might make to American society? Would Fischer's proposal do more than guarantee three high-quality hours a week? Might it have adverse effects? Has Sarnoff's proposal, ironically made, any real merit? Could Hausman be interpreted as conveying a not-so-thinly-veiled threat to the legislators in his audience? Could the threat be carried out?

Newspapers are private property. Do they have public as well as private responsibilities? How well do American newspapers serve the public? Do they discharge their responsibilities? Absolute objectivity in reporting the news is impossible, of course, as long as human beings must write the stories. But some newspapers strive to report news clearly and concisely with no criticism or interpretation, while others tell their readers when an accurate quotation is also an inaccurate statement of the truth or when a government release represents a trial balloon rather than a firm intention. Which method do you prefer? What dangers are inherent in each? What can be done to make national and international stories more interesting and comprehensible for the average reader?

You may find it enlightening to compare the coverage in your favorite newspaper of some story which interests you with the coverage in news magazines and other papers. Does rapid modern transportation really make it possible for newspapers printed in different cities to compete with one another? Can radio and television stations provide effective news competition for monopoly newspapers? Do newspapers which must compete with one another tend to be better than those which enjoy a monopoly?

Suggestions for Further Reading

Chenery, William L. *Freedom of the Press.* New York: Harcourt, Brace, 1955.

Ernst, Morris L. *The First Freedom.* New York: Macmillan, 1946.

Head, Sidney W. "Content Analysis of Television Drama Programs," *Quarterly of Film, Radio, and Television,* 9, 1954, p. 175.

"Here, We Would Suggest, Is A Program for the F.C.C.," *Consumer Reports,* February 1960, p. 93.

Jones, Dorothy B. "Quantitative Analysis of Motion Picture Content," *Public Opinion Quarterly,* 6, 1942, p. 411.

Lippmann, Walter. *The Public Philosophy.* Boston: Little, Brown, 1955.

McConnell, James V., Richard L. Cutler, and Elton B. McNeil. "Subliminal Stimulation: An Overview," *American Psychologist,* 13, 1958, p. 231.

Mitgang, Herbert. *Freedom to See: The Khrushchev Broadcast and Its Meaning for Television.* Fund for the Republic pamphlet, 1958.

The Press and the People. Fund for the Republic pamphlets, 1958-59. Fourteen discussions of problems involved in securing and transmitting news.

"Recommendations of the Subcommittee on Broadcasting Practices, United States Senate Committee on Legislative Oversight," New York *Times,* Feb. 7, 1960, p. 62.

"Where, May We Ask, Was the F.C.C.?" *Consumer Reports,* January 1960, p. 9.

Wiebe, Gerhart D. "Mass Communications," in Eugene L. and Ruth E. Hartley, *Fundamentals of Social Psychology.* New York: Knopf, 1952, p. 159.